FOR THE WORLD'S PROFIT

FOR THE WORLD'S PROFIT

How Business Can Support Sustainable Development

HOMI KHARAS, KOJI MAKINO,
JOHN W. McARTHUR,
AND JANE NELSON

EDITORS

Published by Brookings Institution Press®
1775 Massachusetts Avenue, NW
Washington, DC 20036
www.brookings.edu/bipress

Co-published by Bloomsbury Academic
Bloomsbury Publishing Inc, 1385 Broadway, New York, NY 10018, USA
Bloomsbury Publishing Plc, 50 Bedford Square, London, WC1B 3DP, UK
Bloomsbury Publishing Ireland, 29 Earlsfort Terrace, Dublin 2, D02 AY28, Ireland
https://www.bloomsbury.com/us/

Copyright © 2025 by Brookings Institution Press®

Typeset in Janson Text
Composition by Circle Graphics
Printed and bound in the United States of America

All rights reserved. No part of this publication may be: i) reproduced or transmitted in any form, electronic or mechanical, including photocopying, recording or by means of any information storage or retrieval system without prior permission in writing from the publishers; or ii) used or reproduced in any way for the training, development or operation of artificial intelligence (AI) technologies, including generative AI technologies. The rights holders expressly reserve this publication from the text and data mining exception as per Article 4(3) of the Digital Single Market Directive (EU) 2019/790.

The Brookings Institution is a nonprofit organization devoted to research, education, and publication on important issues of domestic and foreign policy. Its principal purpose is to bring the highest quality independent research and analysis to bear on current and emerging policy problems. Brookings' publications represent the sole views of their author(s).

Library of Congress Control Number: 2025936155

ISBN: 978-0-8157-4101-5 (hbk. : alk. paper)
ISBN: 978-0-8157-4102-2 (pbk. : alk. paper)
ISBN: 978-0-8157-4104-6 (ebook)
ISBN: 978-0-8157-4103-9 (ePDF)

For product safety related questions contact productsafety@bloomsbury.com.

Contents

Acknowledgments   vii

The Sustainable Development Goals   ix

1 For the World's Profit: Overview   1
HOMI KHARAS, KOJI MAKINO, JOHN W. McARTHUR, AND JANE NELSON

PART I
Business Actors

2 What Next for Sustainable Development?
Business, Courage, and the Need to Accelerate   35
PAUL POLMAN

3 Strengthening Small Businesses to Support
Sustainable Development   51
NDIDI OKONKWO NWUNELI

4 Key Actions for Corporate Boards in Accelerating
Sustainable Development   69
EMILY FARNWORTH AND ELDRID HERRINGTON

5 Industry and Multisector Alliances to Achieve
System-Level Impact 91
JANE NELSON

PART II
Financial Actors

6 Scaling Sustainable Finance: The Role of Asset Owners 121
SASJA BESLIK

7 Aligning International Banking Regulation
with the SDGs 139
LILIANA ROJAS-SUAREZ

8 Stewarding a Resilient Future: Why Insurance Matters 155
EKHOSUEHI IYAHEN

PART III
Policymakers and Regulators

9 Global Sustainability Reporting Standards:
On the Threshold of a New Era of Internationally
Coherent Regulation? 173
RICHARD SAMANS

10 Assurance and Its Contribution to Sustainable Development 199
TOM SEIDENSTEIN AND WARREN MAROUN

11 The Institutionalization of Corporate Contributions
to the SDGs in India 215
KATSUO MATSUMOTO

12 The "Lobbying Gap" in the SDG Agenda:
Aligning Corporate Political Engagement with Global
Sustainable Development 227
ALBERTO ALEMANNO

13 How the Japanese Business Community Has Embraced
Sustainability 247
ICHIRO SATO AND KEI ENDO

Contributors 267

Index 269

Acknowledgments

The success of a book of this type hinges on the chapter authors. We, the editors, are deeply grateful to all the authors—Alberto Alemanno, Sasja Beslik, Kei Endo, Emily Farnworth, Eldrid Herrington, Ekhosuehi Iyahen, Warren Maroun, Katsuo Matsumoto, Ndidi Okonkwo Nwuneli, Paul Polman, Liliana Rojas-Suarez, Rick Samans, Ichiro Sato, and Tom Seidenstein—for their generous contribution of time and expertise.

Behind the authors, however, an enormous effort is needed to bring a book to life. We are so grateful to Clea McElwain, Odera Onyechi, and Charlotte Rivard in the Brookings Center for Sustainable Development for tremendous assistance with logistics, fact-checking, and organization. We further thank Marjorie Pannell for copy editing; Shavanthi Mendis for visual design; Yelba Quinn for her steadfast support at Brookings Institution Press; Jon Sisk at Rowman & Littlefield and Haaris Naqvi at Bloomsbury for their help in facilitating the publication process; Caren Grown for editorial guidance; Zena Creed and Carsten Stendevad for thoughtful inputs at various stages of drafting, including during an authors' workshop; Robin Brooks for helpful review of a draft "Overview" chapter; and Sanjay Patnaik for careful peer review of the overview and feedback on various draft chapters. Brahima Coulibaly, Elisabeth Donahue, Jessica Harris, Shannon

Meraw, Esther Rosen, Jared Schott, and Valerie Wirtschafter all provided important institutional support across Brookings throughout various stages of the project.

Brookings gratefully acknowledges project support provided by the JICA-Ogata Sadako Research Institute for Peace and Development, and we thank Erin Clements, Sara Coffey, Chiaki Lee, and Yukari Saito for making the collaboration between our two institutions so smooth.

Brookings recognizes that the value it provides is in its commitment to quality, independence, and impact. Activities supported by its donors reflect this commitment.

The Sustainable Development Goals

1 NO POVERTY

2 ZERO HUNGER

3 GOOD HEALTH AND WELL-BEING

4 QUALITY EDUCATION

5 GENDER EQUALITY

6 CLEAN WATER AND SANITATION

7 AFFORDABLE AND CLEAN ENERGY

8 DECENT WORK AND ECONOMIC GROWTH

9 INDUSTRY, INNOVATION AND INFRASTRUCTURE

10 REDUCED INEQUALITIES

11 SUSTAINABLE CITIES AND COMMUNITIES

12 RESPONSIBLE CONSUMPTION AND PRODUCTION

13 CLIMATE ACTION

14 LIFE BELOW WATER

15 LIFE ON LAND

16 PEACE, JUSTICE AND STRONG INSTITUTIONS

17 PARTNERSHIPS FOR THE GOALS

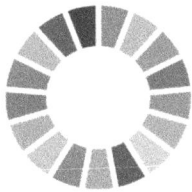

ONE

For the World's Profit: Overview

HOMI KHARAS, KOJI MAKINO, JOHN W. McARTHUR, AND JANE NELSON

We are at a pivotal historical moment for the intersection of capitalism and sustainable development. For centuries, private enterprise has been a powerful force in reducing human deprivation, promoting prosperity, and solving societal challenges around the world. The profit-driven activities of capital allocation, risk-taking, competition, innovation, and production have created countless goods and services that improve human well-being. At the same time, market forces have failed to adequately address—indeed, have often created or exacerbated—many of humanity's deepest challenges and the planet's greatest stresses.

As one indicator of how the world is doing, most of the 17 Sustainable Development Goals (SDGs)—the economic, social, and environmental targets established by all countries in 2015—are well off-track from being achieved by the deadline of 2030.[1] So too is the 2015 Paris Agreement ambition to limit average global temperature rise to 1.5 degrees Celsius above preindustrial-era levels. Meanwhile, biodiversity experts warn of ongoing

---

1. Kharas, McArthur, and Onyechi (2024).

species loss and the risk of mass extinctions. On some issues there may be catastrophic tipping points beyond which it will be difficult to recover.[2]

When the SDGs were designed and approved, there was a general understanding that business would be crucial to their successful implementation. There was little understanding, however, of how to involve business in practical terms, let alone how to do so on a large scale across diverse industry sectors, jurisdictions, and different goals. One could say that the goals were set first and then the question of what business should and could do came second.

Over the subsequent years, considerable public dialogue and commitments have raised awareness of the importance of business leadership on global issues. This has included a particular focus on climate change but has also extended to a strong interest among a vanguard of business leaders to be a constructive force in working with governments and civil society organizations to address other complex societal issues. These initial efforts have mainstreamed the idea that business should do more, despite significant pushback from certain industries and jurisdictions. Nevertheless, there is now momentum among business leaders, financial actors, and regulators to alter the ecosystem of how capital is allocated and used, and a growing consensus on mechanisms for holding business and the financial sector accountable for their impact.

Amid profound shortfalls in progress, the world is at an important juncture to consider how business, financial, and policy constituencies can better align to support sustainable development. Fast-changing market, policy, and regulatory frontiers mean little time remains to clarify how business can support better global outcomes by 2030. Moreover, only a narrow, near-term window exists to identify how post-2030 goals could better leverage the forces of market innovation out to 2045 or 2050.

Many of the issues boil down to considering—and returning to the origins of—the word *profit*, defined not only in financial returns but also as broader gains accruing to everyone involved in the market economy. The Latin root word *proficere* focuses on the concept of progress. This term evolved, along with the Old French word *profiter*, into the Middle English word *profit*, meaning advantage or benefit. In this spirit, no less a scribe than Shakespeare used the term around the turn of the seventeenth century, including in *Hamlet*: "Expend your time with us awhile / For the supply and profit of our hope."[3]

---

2. Ibid.
3. *Hamlet*, act II, scene ii, spoken by Queen Gertrude.

This edited volume does not aim to mirror the poetic brilliance of literary monuments. But it does argue that the world is at a key juncture for considering how the targeted pursuit of business profits can better add up to the world's profit, broadly defined. The book brings together a remarkable array of distinguished corporate, investor, government, academic, and nonprofit perspectives to reflect on the world's profit. The authors tackle such questions as how businesses can work more effectively with governments, financial institutions, and civil society to mitigate their own enterprise risk alongside risks to people and planet; how private resources, innovation, and networks can be mobilized to create value in solving major social and environmental challenges; and what types of accountability structures are needed to set boundaries, provide oversight, and create positive incentives for business performance. Their perspectives offer insights into how sustainability can be introduced into business practices, finance, and policymaking in a way that expands market opportunities and accelerates progress toward the SDGs.

Old Questions, New Contexts

Considerations around the role of business in society are not new. Adam Smith, often dubbed the parent of modern capitalism, discussed this in his 1759 *Theory of Moral Sentiments*. In that book, he wrote of "the virtues of justice and beneficence—of which the one restrains us from hurting, the other prompts us to promote that happiness." Smith cared deeply about the social agenda, particularly about the distribution of income between capital and labor. He felt that sustained high profits reflected cartels, monopolies, and a lack of competition, rather than good business. He similarly asserted, in his 1776 *The Wealth of Nations*, that good governance and proper taxation could only be enacted by parliamentarians suspicious of employers who "say nothing concerning the bad effects of high profits."[4] One could argue that the essence of Smithian capitalism is that individuals and businesses should be free to pursue their own interest, but only by acting in the right way.

Smith's normative emphasis on justice, beneficence, and good governance has informed many commercial, political, and legal debates over the ensuing centuries. Although most of today's social and environmental externalities were not significant when Smith was writing, it is conceivable

---

4. Smith (1776).

that he might have argued for such externalities to be mitigated and that any damage to others or to the environment should be compensated by the perpetrator. This concern is now firmly entrenched in tort law in many jurisdictions.

In contemporary business terms, Smith's arguments can be mapped to evolving views around risk management, value creation, and accountability, respectively. Each of these dimensions continues to engender debates over how to delineate boundaries between the responsibilities of a firm and those of governments or other actors. The search for coherent approaches for all three dimensions across the global economy lies at the heart of the world's sustainable development challenges.

Managing sources of operational and financial risk, for example, has long been at the heart of ensuring an enterprise's long-term viability. But broader sources of social, environmental, and reputational risks have become tangible business risks to a wide range of companies. A 2023 global investor survey, for example, found that more than a third of respondents considered climate change to pose a near-term risk to their portfolios over a one-year horizon.[5] Considerations of risk have also given rise to the evolving concept of "double materiality," according to which companies should explicitly assess and manage the effects of their actions on society and the environment, in addition to effects on the financial performance of the business.[6]

Issues of double materiality intersect with debates over value creation. Commercial entities have always had to create value for their customers in order to prosper. In the 1970s and 1980s, such academics as Klaus Schwab and R. Edward Freeman argued that, over the long term, companies would be more successful if they created value for all their stakeholders and thereby expanded the total economic pie.[7] This perspective stood in contrast to the shareholder primacy work of Milton Friedman, also in the 1970s, which has dominated business discourse and incentives for much of the following decades.[8] In recent years, concepts of stakeholder capitalism and shared value have regained attention, with many companies facing increasing pressure to identify and enhance the shared value or impact they are creating for all their stakeholders, not just shareholders, even as

---

5. Chalmers and Picard (2023).
6. European Commission (2022).
7. See Schwab (1973) and Freeman (1984).
8. See Friedman (1970) for the original argument as presented in the *New York Times*.

dissenting voices worry about excessive burdens on firms or resource misallocations among market players.[9]

These debates in turn affect outlooks on corporate accountability. Friedmanite schools of thought argue that companies' fiduciary responsibilities should be targeted to mandatory accountability structures related to issues affecting financial profit and losses and balance sheets, with further nonfinancial reporting undertaken on a voluntary basis and at the discretion of the company itself. Meanwhile, stakeholder capitalism stresses the need for companies to also identify and mitigate negative environmental and social externalities and enhance societal impacts, with growing calls for mandatory reporting and public accountability on these issues in addition to mandatory financial reporting. But there remain insufficient market incentives or regulatory requirements for the majority of companies to take on the additional costs of embedding all stakeholder considerations into their core business activities. This gap is consequential if the benefits of improved market operation occur only when a critical mass of companies is subject to the same rules.[10]

Evolving Actors and Trends

The perspectives offered in this book build on several decades of relevant initiatives and debates spanning academia, business, civil society, and the public sector. The Sullivan principles were established in 1977, for example, to drive voluntary corporate responsibility standards for U.S. companies that remained invested in apartheid-era South Africa.[11] Subsequent initiatives, such as the Fair Labor Association, various fair trade alliances, the Extractive Industries Transparency Initiative, and the Carbon Disclosure Project, are all examples of international efforts aiming to improve market alignment with key ingredients of sustainable development.[12] Regulators from diverse regional, national, and subnational jurisdictions have taken pioneering steps in this regard.

The United Nations has also played an important role in advancing normative, values-based principles and standards for business behavior.

---

9. See, e.g., Porter and Kramer (2011) on "creating shared value"; the Business Roundtable (2019) statement on redefining the purpose of a corporation; and Schwab (2019), presenting the 2020 Davos Manifesto on the "universal purpose of a company."
10. Fuhrmann (2024).
11. See, e.g., Boston University Trustees (n.d.).
12. One of the authors, Jane Nelson, has served as an adviser to or has served on boards related to industry alliances mentioned in this chapter, including EITI, ICMM, and the WBCSD Vision 2050 initiative.

In 1990, for example, what became the World Business Council for Sustainable Development (WBCSD) was established at the invitation of Maurice Strong, secretary-general of the UN Conference on Environment and Development, to promote sustainable development among global business leaders in preparation for the 1992 "Earth Summit" in Rio de Janeiro, Brazil.[13] In 1997, the United Nations Environment Programme supported the establishment of the Global Reporting Initiative, which initially focused on environmental issues, then broadened its mandate to include social, economic, and governance issues.[14]

In 2000, UN Secretary-General Kofi Annan launched the Global Compact, aimed at promoting "a set of core values in the areas of human rights, labour standards, and environmental practices" for companies around the world.[15] Four years later, in 2004, the Global Compact released a seminal report, *Who Cares Wins*, which presented financial industry recommendations "to better integrate environmental, social and governance issues"—thereby inaugurating the "ESG" shorthand.[16] ESG issues then provided a cornerstone of the six UN Principles for Responsible Investment (UN PRI), launched in 2006 and directed toward institutional asset owners and asset managers.[17]

Since then, the terms "ESG" and "sustainability" have evolved and often blurred to become loose catch-all phrases for responsible business practice, while still distinct from the more explicitly outcome-oriented frameworks of "shared value" and "impact investing," which accelerated through a formal global network founded in 2009.[18] The ESG label itself became associated with both corporate and financial institutions' risk management and enlightened business approaches. Many investment products and rating and ranking systems also made use of the term, often charging a premium in management fees.[19]

Meanwhile, the sustainable finance market has grown quickly. To take one component of sustainable finance as an example, sustainable bond

---

13. See WBCSD, "Our History" (https://www.wbcsd.org/who-we-are/our-history/).
14. Global Reporting Initiative (2022).
15. See United Nations (1999, 2000).
16. Global Compact (2004).
17. Global Compact (2004); United Nations Principles for Responsible Investment, "About the PRI" (https://www.unpri.org/about-us/about-the-pri). The 2011 UN Guiding Principles on Business and Human Rights have also been highly influential.
18. See Porter and Kramer (2011) and the web page of Global Impact Investing Network, "About the GIIN" (https://thegiin.org/about/).
19. Baker, Egan, and Sarkar (2022).

issuances grew from less than $100 billion of issuances in 2015 to more than $1 trillion in 2021.[20] Nonetheless, the issuances remain geographically concentrated in advanced economies and only a small share is going to emerging and developing economies outside China, which face private financing gaps for sustainable investments on the order of $500 billion per year.[21]

Diversity of metrics and measurement methods has also made it difficult to credibly assess and compare investor or company performance against ESG or sustainability ambitions, even within specific industries or with respect to specific topics. Among other challenges, this situation has led to "aggregate confusion," with leading rating agencies often generating different assessments of corporate ESG performance.[22] Perhaps not surprisingly, in light of the range of indicators used by different analysts, there is mixed evidence regarding the extent to which ESG- or sustainability-focused strategies drive either better market or better societal outcomes.

In the early 2020s, a growing chorus calling for enlightened private sector leadership in tackling societal challenges began running into new resistance, especially in the United States, which is still the world's largest capital market and hence carries an outsized influence in global business debates. Some critics decried the mixing of politics with business as forsaking principles of shareholder value, including for all-important public pension systems. Others expressed concern over potential "greenwashing" in the form of businesses making empty long-term pledges as virtue signaling, especially in the climate domain, with little substance to back up these pledges.[23] In many cases, a generalized murkiness around what counts as sustainable or ESG-consistent business operations rendered branded initiatives increasingly vulnerable to attack.

America's culture wars have intersected with the debates, with many Democratic voices arguing for increased private sector responsibilities and many Republicans pushing back with "antiwoke" efforts. Partisan debates over climate policies mean that recent reporting guidance from, for example, the U.S. Securities and Exchange Commission faces an unclear future.[24] State-level legislation has played an important role, too. California, for

---

20. Bloomberg Professional Services (2024); Cochelin, Popoola, and Sugrue (2023).
21. Independent Expert Group (2023).
22. Berg, Kölbel, and Rigobon (2022).
23. See, e.g., United Nations High-Level Expert Group on the Net Zero Emissions Commitments of Non-State Entities (2022).
24. See U.S. Securities and Exchange Commission (2024).

instance, passed a series of laws in 2023 requiring, among other things, climate-related disclosures from large public and private companies operating in the state.[25] That same year, Florida passed explicitly anti-ESG legislation requiring the state's pension managers and local governments to make investment decisions based only on "pecuniary factors" and prohibiting the consideration of any "social, political, or ideological interests."[26]

The political debates may be locale-specific, but the consequences can be far-reaching. California would be the world's fifth largest economy if it were a country, so international companies with an existing or aspirational footprint in the state face strong incentives to align with local reporting requirements.[27] Meanwhile, a fund manager on another continent may choose to avoid public references to ESG or sustainability in order to court investments from U.S. state pension funds operating under anti-ESG legislation. The term "greenhushing" has emerged to describe executives' avoidance of speaking publicly about their ESG initiatives.[28] The upshot is a risk that high-level political conflicts may upend many years of analytical and operational progress.[29]

Momentum has also been mixed in other major economies and jurisdictions. In the EU, progress toward encouraging corporate responsibility and sustainability has accelerated over the past five years in the form of mandatory social and environmental reporting and due diligence requirements and through such initiatives as the European Green Deal and the Carbon Border Adjustment Mechanism, but these efforts face increased political and business opposition too.[30] Countries such as Brazil, China, India, and Indonesia have also become increasingly influential in the debate over the role of business in sustainable development, especially with respect to evolving expectations of corporate accountability and the role of small and medium-size enterprises (SMEs).[31]

Nevertheless, a longer view of history underscores that a profound shift is underway in the movement toward requiring coherent norms and reporting standards across nonfinancial aspects of business activities (box 1.1). Considerable differences still exist in approaches and scope across jurisdictions, but the increasingly integrated worldwide conversation that has emerged through

---

25. California bills SB 253, SB 261, and AB 1305 were all signed into law in October 2023.
26. Florida bill HB 3 was signed into law in May 2023.
27. Governor of California (2024).
28. Eccles (2024).
29. Berg, Jay, Kölbel, and Rigobon (2023).
30. See, for example, *Financial Times* editorial board (2024).
31. See, for example, Confederation of Indian Industry—B20 India Secretariat (2023).

bodies such as the International Sustainability Standards Board (ISSB) provides considerable opportunity. Jurisdictions representing over half of global GDP, more than 40 percent of global market capitalization, and more than half of global greenhouse gas emissions have taken steps toward operationalizing ISSB standards.[32] Importantly, these jurisdictions include many

---

Box 1.1. The Shift toward Mandatory Reporting

Despite debates around "wokeness" in the United States and other key market geographies, many regulators around the world have begun to introduce a wave of new standards for mandatory disclosure of material, nonfinancial information. Following are some of the evolving reporting requirements in various jurisdictions:

- In the UK, large listed companies must now report against certain sustainability standards, following an amendment of the Companies Act in 2022, and additional disclosure requirements are expected in 2025.

- The EU's Sustainable Finance Disclosure Regulation entered into force in 2021 for the owners of financial services advisers and providers, aiming to improve transparency and reduce greenwashing. The EU's complementary and broader Corporate Sustainability Reporting Directive took effect in 2023, requiring large companies across the region to report on a range of ESG metrics as of 2024. This was followed by approval of the Corporate Sustainability Due Diligence Directive in 2024, which imposes a duty on certain companies to undertake and report on human rights issues and environmental due diligence efforts.

- In March 2023 the Financial Services Authority of Japan implemented new rules mandating all publicly listed companies to disclose sustainability information relating to strategy, governance, metrics and targets, and risk management.

- In July 2023 the International Organization of Securities Commissions (IOSCO) called on its 130 members, whose number includes many developing countries, to incorporate the ISSB's initial requirements for disclosure of sustainability-related financial information (IFRS 1) and climate-related disclosures (IFRS 2) into national regulatory frameworks. As of mid-2024, countries as diverse as Bangladesh, Brazil, Costa Rica, India, Nigeria, the Philippines, Singapore, and Turkey had all announced their intention to phase in varying degrees of mandatory reporting linked to ISSB standards.[33]

(cont.)

---

32. IFRS (2024b).
33. IFRS (2024a); Laidlaw (2024).

- In March 2024 the U.S. SEC finalized a climate disclosure regulation mandating publicly traded companies to provide standardized, quality information on risks, opportunities, and governance related to climate change. This regulation followed major climate- and social equity–focused disclosure laws passed in the State of California in October 2023.

In short, a major change in corporate reporting is taking place throughout the world. It is too early to understand how it will affect markets and companies and whether business practices will change significantly or simply absorb a paper-pushing exercise into existing practices, but there is no doubt that an unprecedented movement is underway toward expanded firm-level reporting responsibilities.

Sources: Deloitte (2024); Samans (see chapter 9); Laidlaw (2024); Lawless, Ushijima, and Hara (2023); O'Donnell (2024); Philippines Securities and Exchange Commission (2023); Sustainable Stock Exchange Initiative (2024).

developing and emerging economies. If relevant policy conversations continue to converge, the outcome may be as transformational for global business and capital markets as the consolidation of generally accepted accounting principles was after the stock market crash of 1929.

Mobilizing Business for the World's Profit: Enter the SDGs

In a contested political, definitional, and methodological space, it is worth pausing to ask some basic questions. In what areas, for example, should business contributions be measured, valued, and promoted? What are the relevant standards for benchmarking societal progress? Where should companies, investors, civil society organizations, and policymakers focus their attention and resources? In this book, we take the SDGs as a starting point, along with the 2015 Paris Agreement on climate change and subsequent core international agreements such as the 2022 Kunming-Montreal Global Biodiversity Framework.[34] For the remainder of this introductory

---

34. Goal 13 of the SDG framework, adopted by all 193 UN member states in September 2015, makes explicit reference to the central role of the UN Framework Convention on Climate Change, which generated the Paris Agreement in December 2015. Meanwhile, SDG 14, "Life Below Water," and SDG 15, "Life on Land," originally drew on targets established through the UN Convention on Biological Diversity (CBD) in Aichi, Japan, in

chapter, we use the term "SDGs" as shorthand for the universal goals of these key international agreements.

Even though the SDG targets were established and agreed on by governments, many of the aspirations embedded in the goals require leadership, resources, and innovation from all sectors—research, civil society, financial institutions, and business. For the private sector, every goal has some relevance from either a risk management or a value creation perspective, although not all businesses are equally relevant for all goals. Simply put, the achievement of the SDGs requires active contributions from private companies and investors around the world.[35]

Despite the engagement of business leaders who have participated in relevant bodies—including business platforms such as the UN Global Compact and the WBCSD, and multistakeholder efforts such as the UN Secretary-General's High Level Panel of Eminent Persons on the Post-2015 Development Agenda—it has been hard for many business leaders to see how, or even if, they should make investments or change their operations or business models to better support the goals.[36]

Several initiatives have sought to inform the debate. In 2016, the high-level Business and Sustainable Development Commission—the members of which came from business, finance, labor, civil society, and international organizations—emphasized the value creation side of the calculus, estimating $12 trillion in market opportunities in four sectors crucial to the SDGs: food and agriculture, cities, energy and materials, and health and well-being. The commission emphasized that business could not afford to be a bystander but had a responsibility to act on the SDGs: "The Global Goals really need business: unless private companies seize the market opportunities they open up and advance progress on the whole Global Goals package, the abundance they offer won't materialise."[37]

By 2020, through a gradual process of diffusion and heightened awareness, a broad array of business-focused enterprises and initiatives had started

---

2011. The CBD targets were subsequently updated in the 2022 Kunming-Montreal Global Biodiversity Framework, which established objectives for 2030 and has been adopted by 196 countries. We recognize the unique situation of the United States vis-à-vis these two environmental agreements, including its leaving and then rejoining the Paris Agreement and never having adopted the Kunming-Montreal framework.

35. For a broad framework on the relevance of the SDGs to business, see the United Nations Global Compact at https://unglobalcompact.org/.

36. United Nations High-Level Panel of Eminent Persons (2013).

37. Business and Sustainable Development Commission (2017).

to engage explicitly with SDG-relevant frameworks. The UN Global Compact and the WBCSD published practical guidance for companies and business leaders to implement the SDGs, and they continue to undertake surveys and share good practices. Some industry platforms followed suit, ranging from the International Council on Mining and Metals (ICMM), which brings together two dozen of the world's largest mining companies and more than thirty-five major national, regional, and global commodity associations, to the Global System for Mobile Communications Association (GSMA), which unites over one thousand mobile operators and businesses in the mobile ecosystem.[38]

Several multistakeholder or business-led platforms have also emerged to develop metrics, benchmarks, and accountability mechanisms to explicitly drive business support for the SDGs. The World Benchmarking Alliance was launched in 2018 with the aim to "develop a range of corporate benchmarks by 2023 to comprehensively assess the progress of 2,000 companies across major areas of transformation required to achieve the SDGs."[39] In 2020, the International Business Council of the World Economic Forum joined with the "Big Four" accounting firms to publish a core set of twenty-one common corporate reporting metrics to align with the SDGs as the overarching "road map."[40]

As of 2023, SDG terminology remained vastly less common than ESG jargon in public companies' earning calls.[41] At the same time, an assessment of the top one hundred companies by revenue in each of fifty-eight countries and territories found that more than two-thirds of those reporting on sustainability or ESG matters included SDG-relevant issues in 2022.[42] Thailand notably marked the largest share, with more than nine out of ten companies

---

38. See the following websites and pages: UN Global Compact, "Global Goals for People and Planet" (https://unglobalcompact.org/sdgs/about); World Business Council for Sustainable Development, "The Building Blocks of Transformation" (https://www.wbcsd.org/); the International Council on Mining and Metals, "Supporting the Sustainable Development Goals" (https://www.icmm.com/en-gb/our-work/supporting-the-sustainable-development-goals), and the GSM Association, "About Us" (https://www.gsma.com/about-us/). (One of the editors of this volume, Jane Nelson, previously served on an advisory council for the ICMM.)

39. World Benchmarking Alliance (2018).

40. Moynihan (2020). The world's four largest accounting firms by revenue are Deloitte, PricewaterhouseCoopers (PwC), Ernst & Young (EY), and Klynveld Peat Marwick Goerdeler (KPMG).

41. United Nations Global Compact and Accenture (2023b), 20.

42. KPMG (2022), 57.

in the sample identifying specific SDGs most relevant to their business.[43] Japan's largest business federation, Keidanren, revised its Charter of Corporate Behavior "with the primary aim of proactively delivering on the SDGs" and established an initiative to help members contribute to the goals.[44]

On the investor side of the market equation, many prominent commercial banks, pension funds, insurance companies, private equity firms, hedge funds, and fixed income managers have launched products or pledged explicit support to some dimension of the SDGs. The Principles for Responsible Investment is one of several financial sector platforms that has issued guidance to investors on implementing the SDGs.[45] In addition, the Global Investors for Sustainable Development Alliance was launched in 2019 and unites a mix of major financial institutions and corporations with UN leadership to scale up private investments in achieving the SDGs. A global group of asset owners launched the Sustainable Development Investments Asset Owners Platform in 2020.[46] In April 2021 the Glasgow Financial Alliance for Net Zero (GFANZ) launched a sector-wide coalition for financial institutions to support an accelerated transition to a net-zero global economy.[47] In November 2023, more than a dozen major financial institutions and related stakeholders launched the Impact Disclosure Taskforce to draft "voluntary guidance for entity-level disclosure and mechanisms to facilitate impact reporting, analysis, and financing in pursuit of [the SDGs]."[48]

Gaps and Obstacles to Scaling Up Business Contributions to the SDGs

Despite growing private sector awareness and efforts relating to the SDGs, the world is still far off-track relative to its 2030 ambitions. Why? From the vantage point of market actors, part of the challenge lies in the diversity of

---

43. Ibid., 58. The results in Thailand are likely related to the Stock Exchange of Thailand requiring sustainability reporting for listed companies beginning in 2022.
44. See Keidanren (2022).
45. United Nations Principles for Responsible Investment, "About Us" (https://www.unpri.org/about-us/about-the-pri).
46. See the SDI Asset Owner Platform web page "An Asset-Owner Led Approach" (https://www.sdi-aop.org/about/).
47. See the GFANZ web page "About Us" (https://www.gfanzero.com/about-announcement/).
48. Center for Global Development (2023).

industries in which people are working and the varying degrees of interface with different SDG priorities. A 2022 KPMG survey of more than 3,200 major companies across fifty-eight countries and territories found that more than 70 percent considered SDG 8, concerning decent work and economic growth, to be relevant to their business, as did more than 60 percent with respect to SDG 13, concerning climate action.[49] But fewer than 10 percent prioritized SDG 15, for life on land, and fewer than 20 percent noted SDG 14, for marine life, as a priority.[50]

As a further layer, the historical diffusion of ESG metrics naturally focused attention on some SDGs more than others. One recent study looked at more than two hundred common ESG metrics and found that seventy-four of these—the largest number of metrics—aligned with SDG 12, for responsible consumption and production, while sixty-nine metrics could map to SDG 16, on peace, justice, and strong institutions, but only four common ESG metrics linked to SDG 2, concerning hunger, six linked to SDG 1, on poverty, and eight linked to SDG 4, on education.[51]

Another aspect of the variation in business perspectives and practices is the extent to which companies focus and report on their positive contributions to SDG-relevant issues without considering negative or net contributions. When KPMG researchers looked at leading companies reporting on ESG or sustainability topics across fifty-eight geographies, only 10 percent were found to include both positive and negative aspects. Among the world's largest 250 companies by revenue, the corresponding figure is only 6 percent.[52]

A wider-lens assessment considered whether the private sector's net impact was positive or negative on individual SDGs and the extent to which companies' net revenue is aligned with each SDG.[53] The headline finding was a positive private sector impact on seven goals, mixed impact on three, and negative impact on another seven, especially in the environmental domain. What's worse is that private sector efforts to maximize revenue were found to be positively linked with achievement of only five goals (SDGs 4, 7, 8, 9, and 17), mixed for three, and negative for the other nine.

---

49. KPMG (2022), 60.
50. Ibid.
51. United Nations Global Compact and Accenture (2023b).
52. KPMG (2022), 60.
53. United Nations Global Compact and Accenture (2023b), 23–27.

This implies that, for most industries and most SDGs, a company's profit is not yet the world's profit. This is not because the two are mutually incompatible. The problem is that individual businesses cannot exploit these opportunities if there are insufficient incentives or regulatory requirements to do so and if other businesses, especially competitors and business partners, do not act in concert. A single business can do only so much to slow deforestation for palm oil production, for example, but if a critical mass of companies in the palm oil value chain commits to better practices, those companies can establish a level playing field for everyone that proscribes the production of palm oil in newly deforested areas.

What are the main obstacles to scaling up business alignment with the SDGs and broader sustainable development needs? Several differing frameworks have been proposed. One of these was developed through an extensive consultation process led by the WBCSD to survey the views of corporate leaders, policymakers, and sustainability experts. This "Vision 2050" exercise identified five broad types of constraints on achieving greater scale and systemic impact:[54]

- Inappropriate norms and values, such as the ongoing dominance of short-termism and shareholder capitalism;
- Poor information flows, including insufficient awareness of the costs of inaction and a lack of universally agreed-on metrics or accounting standards to assess corporate sustainability performance and to hold companies to account;
- Misdirected financial flows, including misaligned incentives, a lack of risk capital, and a lack of appropriate pricing signals for essential public goods and negative externalities;
- Inadequate technology owing to insufficient incentives, investments, and R&D at the nexus of digital, materials, and life sciences; and
- Gaps in policies and regulations, including uncertainty, inconsistency, weak public institutional capacities, corporate capture, and delays in needed reforms.

Some of these obstacles can be addressed by businesses themselves, individually or in coalition with each other. Others require action by

54. WBCSD (2023).

investors. And still others need to be addressed by government policymakers and regulators, with complementary attention from civil society.

Levers for Scaling Up Business Contributions and Impact

What do businesses want to see? Do they actually care about the SDGs, or is it simply too early yet to see larger-scale impact? Remarkably, many business leaders themselves are concerned about how little business is contributing to achieving the SDGs. A 2023 global survey of more than 2,800 business leaders found that fewer than half of them, only 48 percent, agreed that the private sector was "doing enough to contribute to the SDGs."[55]

Business leaders are not opposed to greater clarity and accountability. According to the same survey, business leaders' top ask of policymakers was for consistent sustainability reporting and disclosure mandates. More than three quarters of respondents commented on the need "to help ensure all businesses are held to the same standard both nationally and globally."[56] A close second ask was to adjust national minimum wages to living-wage levels. A majority of respondents also supported requirements for all business to reach net zero emissions by 2050, mandatory reporting on nature-related risks and impact (including water consumption), and mandatory disclosure of gender pay gaps.

It is in this context that many jurisdictions have initiated efforts to support mandatory corporate reporting on nonfinancial performance. While different jurisdictions have developed their own standards, many have also shared their perspectives with each other to promote interoperability and a building block approach that permits a phased implementation over time toward higher levels of reporting standards.

We invited a dozen experts to contribute their thoughts on these questions and on the topic of scaling up business contributions to the SDGs more broadly. Our aim is not to be comprehensive and exhaustive but rather to give voice to those with specific ideas that can move the needle in some way—sometimes broadly, sometimes very narrowly and specifically. Each chapter, therefore, presents its own recommended next steps. As volume editors, we have summarized a key message from each chapter in box 1.2.

---

55. United Nations Global Compact and Accenture (2023b), 17.
56. Ibid., 145.

Box 1.2. A Selection of Key Messages from This Book

At the risk of oversimplification, this box highlights a single leading recommendation from each of the book's twelve ensuing chapters:

Corporate Actors

1. Challenge corporate leaders to embrace a net positive mindset, giving more to the world than they take, and to publicly disclose goals and pathways for achieving this.

2. Incentivize large companies and local organizations to help micro, small, and medium-size enterprises to build capacity to act sustainably.

3. Legally require corporate boards to establish and disclose their governance structures and competencies for governing sustainability strategies, risks, opportunities, and performance.

4. Create precompetitive thematic and sectoral sustainability platforms to shape markets and scale industry-wide standards, resources and advocacy at global and local levels.

Financial Actors

5. Translate sustainability goals and metrics into explicit investment commitments or mandates by asset owners.

6. Adjust Basel III risk weights for lending to small and medium-size enterprises and sustainable infrastructure to reflect the evidence on default risk and loss-given-default in developing countries.*

7. Narrow insurance protection gaps in developing countries through concerted action to integrate risk management into public policy.

Policymakers and Regulators

8. Broaden acceptance of IFRS standards and ISSB disclosure standards and encourage more jurisdictions to tackle political and technical implementation hurdles.

9. Agree on International Standard on Sustainability Assurance (ISSA) 5000 rollout and strengthen the assurance ecosystem.

10. Learn and share lessons from India's experience with implementing mandatory requirements for corporate social responsibility financial contributions.

11. Mandate public disclosure of corporate political activities and advocacy-focused thought leadership led or funded by business.

12. Build broad political support at a national level for business sustainability through multipronged campaigns.

*The industry term "loss-given-default" estimates the amount of loss if a credit default occurs. Multiplying default risk (the likelihood of a default) and loss-given-default gives the expected loss on an investment.

Organization of the Book

The rest of this book is divided into three parts, with each exploring a different set of levers of change. Part I conveys the perspective of corporate executives, boards of directors, entrepreneurs, and business-led coalitions. The chapters in this part discuss how to move from reporting to impact, examining the role of business leadership, linkages between large and small businesses, new models of corporate governance, and large-scale partnerships that can shape markets through collective action. Part II turns to the role of the financial sector in directing capital to "better" corporations and increasing private investment to support achieving the SDGs. Here, better does not just mean more profitable but more aligned with the broad spectrum of societal well-being. The chapters in this part show that capital is not monolithic. Commercial banks, insurers, asset owners, and other financial actors have their own perspectives. Part III considers the role of policymakers and regulators in shaping the type and credibility of sustainability information that is provided by companies and investors and in establishing regulations, laws, international standards, and incentives to drive business contributions toward achieving the SDGs.

Part I: Business Actors

In chapter 2, Paul Polman makes the case that business leaders need to show more courage in mainstreaming sustainability. He acknowledges the major strides made by business in recognizing the importance of sustainability over the past few decades, but, as he puts it, "We're still trying to beat exponential problems with incremental and linear solutions, and it doesn't work." Being less bad is not good enough.

Polman sees some bright lights in the fact that most of the technology needed to incorporate sustainability in a sensible way already exists; in the growing alignment of regulations and public incentives to do the right thing, particularly in the area of decarbonization; and in a financial landscape that is directing capital toward sustainable activities. But he is also clear-eyed in recognizing that for any CEO, prioritizing sustainability is like taking a big bet that others will act in the same way so that collective societal goals are met. His challenge to corporate leaders is that they ask themselves a simple question: Is the world better off because your business is in it? If enough companies can answer yes, systemic change for the better will happen. He describes this as a shift from "less bad" to a net positive mindset. It entails a higher level of ambition with respect to sustainability, more collaboration, and constructive advocacy in place of self-serving lobbying. Ultimately, Polman's message is hugely optimistic about the change that is possible.

Large companies may lead many high-profile efforts in changing corporate behavior, but SMEs account for 90 percent of all businesses and two-thirds of the jobs and value added in most economies, so any pursuit of sustainability needs to speak to these companies' practical challenges too.[57] In chapter 3, Ndidi Okonkwo Nwuneli starts her analysis of SMEs by noting that they face more hurdles in greening their activities because of limited knowledge, talent, and funding. Consequently, only a small fraction of all SMEs have set measurable sustainability targets.

Many large companies and business associations provide support, including digital platforms, that make it easier for SMEs in their value chains or locations of operation to take strategic measures to improve their sustainability. Nwuneli gives examples of some successful initiatives in a number of sectors and suggests that these efforts grow by incentivizing local organizations that can assist SMEs in upgrading their standards. But SMEs are a highly diverse group, so there is a danger that mandating SME behavior or targets in a standardized way, as is done for large companies, could exclude many SMEs that simply lack the resources or capabilities to comply.

In chapter 4, Emily Farnworth and Eldrid Herrington focus on the role boards of directors play in accelerating changes in corporate management. Board members already have the juridical space to consider the long-term value of business activities. But only quite recently have comparative metrics permitted substantive board discussions on sustainability, especially regarding climate action and the preservation and conservation of nature. These metrics have opened up two new spaces for thought and action: (1) a greater role and responsibilities for non-executive directors, who may take upon themselves the task of representing a broader range of stakeholders beyond shareholder groups, and (2) a longer-term perspective to avoid the "tragedy of the horizon," critical during periods of major changes in business practices.[58]

57. Madgavkar et al. (2024).
58. "Tragedy of the horizon": see Carney (2015) for a discussion of how the near-term horizons of business cycles, political cycles, and monetary policy mandates impede necessary action on climate change: "Once climate change becomes a defining issue for financial stability, it may already be too late."

Farnworth and Herrington argue that the biggest hurdle faced by boards is keeping their attention focused on strategy. They regard board members as stewards of good corporate governance whose role is evolving because inevitable policy responses to climate change may well be forceful, abrupt, and disorderly, with large associated risks and opportunities. A process that looks narrowly into the future can degenerate into an operational management tool that considers what is known today rather than engaging in a broader discussion of alternative futures. That said, they also emphasize the need for consequences for not delivering on strategic goals and for clear points of accountability, including for individual board members. Absent more legally binding "have to do" things, the pace of change to embed sustainability into business practices may continue to be too slow.

In chapter 5, Jane Nelson describes ways in which companies can work together to take a systems approach to set industry standards, accelerate innovation and market development, and undertake joint policy advocacy and government engagement. She illustrates how such alliances can change systems within a sector or within a geographic space, such as a country, local area, or city.

However, Nelson also warns that operating large-scale alliances can be costly, especially as benefits only accrue over a long period of sustained engagement, and that companies can become exposed to antitrust enforcement threats or sanctions. Despite these obstacles, she forcefully advocates for multistakeholder alliances as an effective way of driving system change, especially if led by the largest companies in the sector or geography.

Part II: Financial Actors

Two goals for financial actors are to demonstrate how sustainability is being integrated into financial systems and to funnel capital to sustainable investments. In chapter 6, Sasja Beslik discusses the implications for asset owners, who operate under fiduciary obligations to promote the interests of beneficiaries in a prudent fashion. Beslik starts with a sober assessment of the current situation. After recognizing many individual examples of good practice, global initiatives, net zero commitments, and the like, across a broad range of asset owners, from pension funds to insurance companies to high-net-worth individuals, Beslik concludes that "lofty investment beliefs or statements promoting sustainability and ESG principles frequently do not translate into actionable strategies for realizing investment commitments and mandates." He attributes part of this deficit to outmoded ways of thinking about fiduciary responsibilities, part to inadequate models linking investments to impact and returns, and part to the financial system's practice of quarterly or annual assessment of returns, on which they base the compensation provided to investment advisers.

If asset owners are to overcome these obstacles, they must develop a new framework to address the SDGs. Such a framework should start with an ambitious vision of the impact that can be made, continue with practical steps, even if small, and then rapidly scale up and engage policymakers and industry associations to broaden reach. The mantra becomes "Think big, start small, and scale up fast."

In chapter 7, Liliana Rojas-Suarez looks at the unintended consequences of Basel III regulations for the activities of commercial banks with respect to sustainable development. She highlights two areas for analysis: lending to SMEs and lending for sustainable infrastructure.

Rojas-Suarez's starting point is the trade-off between financial stability and financial inclusion in many emerging economies. As she points out, poorer countries tend to overcompensate for perceived risk to the financial system by "gold-plating" the minimum capital requirements for their banks. When such overcompensation is coupled with high risk weights for SMEs, which are apportioned using a standardized approach rather than an evidence-based approach, the result may be a decline in lending to SMEs. Rojas-Suarez recommends the use of data from credit registries to improve the analysis of risk weights. However, she cautions that this approach needs the active support of the Basel Committee, and therefore urges the committee to recognize the large variation in SME repayment records in setting appropriate risk weights.

The second major issue addressed by Rojas-Suarez is the constraint on financing for sustainable infrastructure that emanates from the failure to recognize infrastructure as its own asset class. Empirical evidence suggests that infrastructure projects have lower default rates and higher loan recovery rates than general project finance loans, but this is not recognized in bank accounting standards. One solution would be to adapt the two binding Basel regulations on the net stable funding ratio and the output floor on use of internal risk models. However, Rojas-Suarez is skeptical about the political willingness to take on this adaptation and therefore recommends an alternative approach whereby infrastructure would be recognized as its own asset class and assigned a clear set of risk weights by the Basel Committee.

Chapter 8 draws attention to the particular difficulties faced by developing countries when it comes to insurance markets. Ekhosuehi Iyahen identifies the lack of attention to risk and risk-reducing behaviors as a key impediment to building sustainability. Developing countries in particular are significantly underinsured and have enormous insurance protection gaps for natural catastrophes, health care, and old age. What to do?

Iyahen recommends starting with a better understanding and management of risk. Even though science and analytical advances point to new ways of assessing risk, we are still trapped in a repeating cycle of disaster-response-rebuild instead of a more cost-effective approach of loss prevention and resilience. Nowhere is this more important than for climate-related concerns, where dialogue between and among insurers, regulators, and policymakers is still inadequate, barriers to entry are high, and innovation in products, such as microinsurance, is low.

Risk may not have received adequate attention in the design of the SDGs—appearing in only three of the 169 targets—but Iyahen argues persuasively that achievement of the goals will be impossible without tapping into the risk management expertise of global insurers.

Part III: Policymakers and Regulators

When data and information lack comparability, consistency, and assurance, they cannot be used for risk management in a useful way. In chapter 9, Richard Samans outlines recent major steps made toward the mandatory provision of nonfinancial sustainability information while cautioning that there is still a long way to go and that many obstacles remain. The complexity of the system and the materiality of different pieces of information to different stakeholders have given rise to multiple initiatives in different jurisdictions and a "patchwork quilt" of tools—so much so that some large companies' reports now have annexes reporting sustainability information in multiple different templates.

Thankfully, there is considerable overlap emerging between the standards and templates because of a process of consultation and alignment among voluntary standards-setting organizations. This process helped to enable establishment of the ISSB in 2022 under the leadership of the IFRS Foundation. An authoritative baseline global standard has begun to emerge in the form of the first two disclosure requirements issued by the ISSB that are applicable starting with companies' 2024 disclosure reports. These requirements are focused on sustainability-related and climate-related financial information; however, they are designed to be interoperable with, and can be complemented by, additional national standards, such as the EU's so-called double materiality approach.

What remains to be done requires a combination of political interest in implementation and technical work to deepen coverage and relevance. On the political side, numerous governments and regulators have welcomed the IFRS Foundation's work, but many have also expressed reservations about rapid implementation of the reporting standards owing to the perceived unreadiness of their business community to manage the rigorous standards that have emerged. On the technical front, companies have reported difficulty in complying with some aspects of the standards, such as the application of different climate scenarios. Implementation therefore will inevitably evolve in line with the practical experiences of companies as they apply disclosure rules in different contexts, and unevenness in pace is to be expected.

How reliable is the information being reported? Answering this simple question, crucial to the use of sustainability data for decision-making, is at the heart of chapter 10, by Tom Seidenstein and Warren Maroun. They note that financial accounts are audited by independent experts to reduce the risk of decisions being made on the basis of deliberate or accidental misstatements. The same applies to sustainability reporting. The International Auditing and Assurance Standard Board has therefore developed guidance for reviewing the information presented in the most common forms of sustainability reporting. This guidance, ISSA 5000, was published in November 2024. It focuses on principles and outcomes, under the general ethos of responsible capitalism, rather than on procedures.

Most large companies are already using some form of third-party assurance for sustainability-related disclosures, but the field is in its infancy. Its flexibility and adaptability are strengths, in light of the current flux in sustainability reporting, but that same flexibility means multidisciplinary teams are needed to provide proper judgments. Where skills and data are scarce, assurance may be "limited." Where they are stronger, assurance can reach a "reasonable" standard. Although still in a developmental stage, stronger assurance is in the throes of shifting from a compliance exercise to one that brings confidence to the capital market and to corporate managers and owners making decisions on how to advance sustainability through business practices.

Assurance can help companies understand their impact. In chapter 11, Katsuo Matsumoto documents a novel approach to sustainability used in

India. There, large corporations are mandated to devote 2 percent of net profits to corporate social responsibility (CSR) activities. This experiment, institutionalized in the 2013 Companies Act amendment, is now generating over $3 billion in private money for sustainable development in India, roughly comparable in size to net disbursements to India from a large development agency such as the World Bank.

Matsumoto lays out the limitations of such schemes. The target geography for CSR activities is typically close to a firm's plant or offices. The kind of CSR activities undertaken dovetail with the firm's policy rather than with community needs. And capacity to deliver effective programs can be weak. Nevertheless, there are strengths to the approach. Firms are forced to think about sustainable development in the context of discrete projects. CSR no longer becomes a theoretical reporting or compliance notion but has very practical and measurable outcomes. Through this, the beliefs and habits of mind of corporate leaders with respect to stakeholder capitalism also change. Many CEOs find the alternative of paying a higher tax and leaving sustainable development to the government to be an unattractive proposition.

Matsumoto offers some hope that partnerships with local government and with third-party nonprofit sustainable development providers will boost the effectiveness of a national CSR ecosystem. In measuring the success of this, the SDG framework provides a common language that government, business, external aid agencies, and the nonprofit community can use.

Corporate engagement in politics is the subject of chapter 12, by Alberto Alemanno. He focuses on the impact of extensive corporate political activities (CPAs), from lobbying to the funding of think tanks and research to advocacy by trade associations. Such activities can be powerful drivers of either a positive agenda of progressive legislative change or a negative agenda of resistance by vested interests. Alemanno's key insight is that there is no transparency on corporate influence and that reporting directives do not sufficiently consider this issue.

Alemanno has developed The Good Lobby Tracker to benchmark the different rating standards that have been introduced in an emerging ecosystem that monitors corporate political conduct. His conclusion: "None of the initiatives reviewed appears to contribute to their stated goals of increasing transparency and accountability in CPAs." This leads Alemanno to recommend including mandatory standards for disclosure of corporate political activities in sustainability reporting. The European Union is the first jurisdiction to take this up, but for now, corporate political reporting remains largely on a voluntary basis. It will, however, be challenging to develop a worldwide standard on such a politically fraught issue. How corporate political power is exercised and regulated will be a key issue for the era beyond the 2030 SDG deadline.

Ultimately, business will take on responsibilities for sustainable development only if there is strong social pressure to do so. In chapter 13, Ichiro Sato and Kei Endo provide an account of how Japanese society has become one of the leading forces pushing the business community to integrate sustainable development into their operations. This was not always the case. Just five years ago, awareness of the SDGs among Japanese firms, especially small enterprises, was among the lowest in the world. Three years later the Japanese business community had become world leaders, both in recognition of corporate responsibilities for sustainability and in specific activities aimed at achieving the SDGs.

A multipronged approach that included changes in school curricula, mass media campaigns, government guides and awards, and small financial subsidies at the local level drove this change. Japan's policymakers have been able to extend the coverage of sustainability to many more companies. Large companies that are mandated to abide by the Corporate Governance code account for only 0.2 percent of Japanese companies. Their influence is extended through their supply chain, but Japan's real success in creating good corporate citizens has come at the local level, where SMEs dominate. There, companies with a track record of contributing to the SDGs are given preference in local public procurement. Partnerships with local government on innovations also spur the adoption of new technologies while contributing to the SDGs. The Japanese example provides an important lesson that corporate engagement in sustainability is ultimately a societal project that must enjoy widespread support if it is to be successful and sustained.

Near-Term Implications and Ideas for Post-2030

The coming years out to 2030 offer an important opportunity for learning how better to align market players with improved SDG outcomes and how to reframe any successor goals to be more intuitively tractable and actionable for private sector actors. Learning will need to be highly iterative as new reporting frameworks, measurement techniques, policy shifts, market incentives, and political, social, environmental, and technological changes continue to emerge. New goals to guide the world out to 2045 or 2050 will need to build on the latest insights into what business is already doing, what more it could be doing, and the incremental—or transformational—contributions possible if better policy mandates and incentives are enacted.

One element of this ecosystem depends on corporate leadership: voluntary actions by individual companies to embed sustainability priorities in core business practices and corporate governance. The early tactical win-win solutions of reducing risk and economizing on material inputs to raise profitability are evolving into strategic planning in the most progressive companies whereby goals, targets, and pathways are aligned with a net positive ambition. Core business processes such as corporate governance, strategy, enterprise risk management, planning, within-enterprise capital allocation, operations and value chain management, and stakeholder engagement are all being affected in these instances.

This is easier said than done. As illustrated by the practical difficulties of implementing climate emissions reporting requirements across supply chains, new questions arise constantly. How can CEOs best think about risk management, value creation, and accountability when addressing sustainability issues? How can boards of directors provide appropriate oversight and stewardship in this new context? How can impact be broadened to include the extraordinary diversity of SMEs in the world? How can precompetitive alliances advance industry-wide practical norms and standards?

A second element of the ecosystem is the role being played by financial actors in allocating capital to companies that have superior sustainability risk management, value creation, and accountability approaches and can demonstrate impact. Impact investing, ESG financial products, sustainability bonds and credits, and other financial innovations have expanded rapidly but remain small relative to global capital markets. Moreover, only a small fraction ends up reaching developing economies that need the resources the most, partly because of the current difficulties in comparing sustainability impact in different locations. None of this may be surprising, given the practical difficulties of evaluating nonfinancial information. What is new is the emergence of standardized, mandatory, comprehensive reporting for large companies in jurisdictions representing most of the global economy.

If this information changes capital allocation processes, it will have a dramatic impact on sustainability worldwide, and potentially also on the opportunities for mobilizing sustainable development financing even in lower-income countries. It remains to be seen who will lead the change: asset owners and managers, banks, stock exchanges, insurance companies, or others. What is clear is that capital owners are worrying about risk, value, and accountability in very different ways now. The institutional structures to guide them will need to evolve in tandem.

The third element discussed in the book is public policies and regulation. It is tempting to think of policymakers and regulators as technocrats promoting more efficient markets, but the experience of the past few years shows how pervasive politics has become in the process. There is the politics of understanding the instruments that governments might use: regulation, public procurement, public investment, awareness-raising campaigns, and specific financial incentives. The politics of engaging at both central and local government levels. The politics of ensuring public awareness and support for sustainable development priorities as a basic condition for broader progress. And the politics of vested interests, lobbying, and the dissemination of misinformation by those adversely affected by change. Perhaps a fundamental question is how to build trust in the information that is provided. Are assurance standards adequate? Can more be done without undue cost? How should assurance bodies respond to malfeasance? Each of these questions involves policymakers outside the traditional range of corporate and financial regulators. But broadening the scope of relevant policymaking risks complicating the bureaucracy and stifling innovation—a trade-off that must be delicately handled to seek a balance.

The normalization of multidimensional corporate and investor metrics that extend beyond core financial accounts could mark a profound shift in how market players define longer-term success. Mandatory and comprehensive reporting for large companies might be just the tip of the iceberg of new accountabilities, societal expectations, and opportunities for the private sector. Reporting and governance standards will continue to evolve based on real-life experience. What is the right balance of factors to include in firm-level discussions of risk management, value creation, and accountability? What is the best way to engage SMEs in relevant debates and implementation efforts, in light of their crucial role in so many economies? Will environmental metrics with readily quantifiable and comparable data dominate and detract from other sustainability considerations?

How realistic is it to include suppliers in climate reporting and human rights due diligence reporting, and, if so, on what elements and how widely across complex global supply chains? How should different metrics be weighted? How will capital markets change their allocations when new information becomes available? What changes might occur in company behavior, and how can regulations best support rather than stifle innovation? What might be the unintended consequences of high and complex reporting burdens, especially for smaller companies?

Answers to these questions will continue to inform a great social movement to refine the very nature of capitalism. This movement has already begun to take shape. It goes by many names and is proceeding at different paces in different industries and jurisdictions, but with a widespread understanding that there should be some common features across diverse contexts. Within such a complex endeavor, it can be easy to become paralyzed by the desire for a perfect system, or to be disenchanted when one part of a system feels glaringly inadequate. Our purpose in this book is not to assess all the activities currently underway or to make specific recommendations. Instead, our goal is to help inform and spark debate on the wide range of changes already underway, and on the spectrum of changes needed in the future to align the unique contributions of market-based enterprise with the global needs of sustainable development. Within the next several years, the world can achieve extraordinary success if it charts a course for every private firm's success to be for the world's profit.

REFERENCES

Baker, M., M. L. Egan, and S. K. Sarkar. 2022. "How Do Investors Value ESG?" NBER Working Paper 30708. Cambridge, MA: National Bureau of Economic Research,

Berg, F., J. Jay, J. F. Kölbel, and R. Rigobon. 2023. "The Signal in the Noise." *EconPol Forum* 24:23–27.

Berg, F., J. F. Kölbel, and R. Rigobon. 2022. "Aggregate Confusion: The Divergence of ESG Ratings." *Review of Finance* 26 (6): 1315–44.

Bloomberg Professional Services. 2024. "Green Bonds Reached New Heights in 2023." February 8.

Boston University Trustees. n.d. "The Sullivan Principles." https://www.bu.edu/trustees/boardoftrustees/committees/acsri/principles/ (accessed August 28, 2024).

Business Roundtable. 2019. "Statement on the Purpose of a Corporation." August 19.

Business and Sustainable Development Commission. 2017. *Better Business, Better World*. London.
Carney, M. 2015. "Breaking the Tragedy of the Horizon: Climate Change and Financial Stability." Speech given at Lloyd's of London, September 29.
Center for Global Development. 2023. *Impact Disclosure Taskforce*. Concept note. November 28.
Chalmers, J., and N. Picard. 2023. "PwC's Global Investor Survey 2023." PwC, November 15.
Cochelin, P., B. Popoola, and D. Sugrue. 2023. "Global Sustainable Bonds 2023 Issuance to Exceed $900 Billion." S&P Global, September 14.
Confederation of Indian Industry—B20 India Secretariat. 2023. "Sustainability & Development Imperatives and the Role of Standards." Background paper for B20 India.
Deloitte. 2024. "Central Bank of India Publishes Draft Disclosure Framework for Climate-Related Financial Risks." March 4.
Eccles, R. G. 2024. "Moving beyond ES." *Harvard Business Review*, September.
European Commission. 2022. "Sustainable Finance." July 26.
Financial Times Editorial Board. 2024. "Europe's Green Backlash." June 11.
Freeman, R. E. 1984. *Strategic Management: A Stakeholder Approach*. Boston: Pitman Publishing.
Friedman, M. 1970. "A Friedman Doctrine: The Social Responsibility of Business Is to Increase Its Profits." *New York Times*, September 13.
Fuhrmann, R. 2024. "Stock Exchanges around the World." *Investopedia*, January 31.
The Global Compact. 2004. *Who Cares Wins: Connecting Financial Markets to a Changing World*. United Nations.
Global Reporting Initiative. 2022. *25 Years as the Catalyst for a Sustainable Future: 1997–2022*. Boston.
Governor of California. 2024. "California Remains the World's 5th Largest Economy." Gavin Newsom, Governor. Press release, April 16.
Independent Expert Group. 2023. *The Triple Agenda: Report of the Independent Experts Group. Volume 1*. Report of the Independent Experts Group on Strengthening Multilateral Development Banks, commissioned by the Indian G20 Presidency.
IFRS (International Financial Reporting Standards). 2024a. "Progress towards Adoption of ISSB Standards as Jurisdictions Consult." Press release, April 3.
———. 2024b. "Jurisdictions Representing over Half the Global Economy by GDP Take Steps towards ISSB Standards." Press release, May 28.
Keidanren. 2022. *Charter of Corporate Behavior*. Tokyo: Keidanren (Japan Business Federation), December.
Kharas, H., McArthur, J. W., and Onyechi, O. 2024. "How Is the World Doing on the SDGs? Four Tests and Eight Findings." Brookings Center for Sustainable Development working paper 188. July.

KPMG. 2022. *Big Shifts, Small Steps: Survey of Sustainability Reporting 2022.* KPMG International.

Laidlaw, J. 2024. "Where Does the World Stand on ISSB Adoption?" S&P Global, April 9.

Lawless, K., K. Ushijima, and K. Hara. 2023. "What's Next for Japanese Sustainability Disclosure Standards." EY, October 13.

Madgavkar, A., et al. 2024. *A Microscope on Small Businesses: Spotting Opportunities to Boost Productivity.* McKinsey Global Institute.

Moynihan, B. 2020. "We Can Now Measure the Progress of Stakeholder Capitalism. Here's How." World Economic Forum, October 21.

O'Donnell, J. 2024. "ESG Regulations: What's Coming Next?" *Compliance & Risks*, February 6.

Philippines Securities and Exchange Commission. 2023. "SEC to Issue Revised Sustainability Reporting Guidelines for Publicly Listed Companies." Press release 2023–75, October 5.

Porter, M. E., and M. R. Kramer. 2011. "Creating Shared Value: How to Reinvent Capitalism—and Unleash a Wave of Innovation and Growth." *Harvard Business Review*, January–February.

Schwab, K. 2019. "Davos Manifesto 2020: The Universal Purpose of a Company in the Fourth Industrial Revolution." Cologny, CH: World Economic Forum, December 2.

———. 1973. *Davos Manifesto 1973: A Code of Ethics for Business Leaders.* Cologny, CH: World Economic Forum.

Smith, A. 1776. *The Wealth of Nations.* London: W. Strahan and T. Cadell.

———. 1759. *The Theory of Moral Sentiments.* London: A. Millar; Edinburgh: A. Kincaid and J. Bell.

Sustainable Stock Exchange Initiative. 2024. "SSE Materials Used to Train Bangladesh Regulatory Authority on ISSB Standards." February 28.

United Nations. 2000. "Secretary-General Welcomes International Corporate Leaders to Global Compact Meeting." Press release, July 27.

———. 1999. "Secretary-General Proposes Global Compact on Human Rights, Labor, Environment, in Address to World Economic Forum in Davos." Press release, February 1.

United Nations Global Compact and Accenture. 2023a. *Reimagining the Agenda: Unlocking the Global Pathways to Resilience, Growth, and Sustainability for 2030.* United Nations Publications.

———. 2023b. *SDG Stocktake: Through the Eyes of the Private Sector.* United Nations Publications.

United Nations High-Level Expert Group on the Net Zero Emissions Commitments of Non-State Entities. 2022. *Integrity Matters: Net Zero Commitments by Businesses, Financial Institutions, Cities and Regions.* United Nations Publications.

United Nations High-Level Panel of Eminent Persons. 2013. *The Report of the High-Level Panel of Eminent Persons on the Post-2015 Development Agenda.* United Nations Publications.

U.S. Securities and Exchange Commission. 2024. "SEC Adopts Rules to Enhance and Standardize Climate-Related Disclosures for Investors." Press release, March 6.

World Benchmarking Alliance. 2018. "World Benchmarking Alliance Launches to Help Business Measure Progress against the U.N. Sustainable Development Goals." Press release, September 24.

WBCSD (World Business Council for Sustainable Development). 2023. *Vision 2050: Time to Transform. How Business Can Lead the Transformation the World Needs.* WBCSD Publications.

PART I

Business Actors

TWO

What Next for Sustainable Development?

Business, Courage, and the Need to Accelerate

PAUL POLMAN

"When we try to pick out anything by itself, we find it hitched to everything else in the Universe."

—John Muir

The word *historic* is overused, but it does aptly describe the meeting of world leaders at the United Nations in September 2015, which saw the Sustainable Development Goals (SDGs) adopted as the successor to the expiring Millennium Development Goals. The SDGs are a blueprint for a world in which we have eradicated extreme poverty and created more equitable economic models that respect and protect our planet. They are a moral framework for action and an economic imperative, backed by every UN member state. They are a global rallying cry to "leave no one behind" at a time when, within and across our societies, we are too often growing apart.

While there is no hierarchy, Goal 17 is especially important. It is an addition that I and others who served on the Secretary-General's High-Level Panel of eminent persons on the Post-2015 Development Agenda strongly advocated in the drafting phase of the SDGs.[1] Goal 17 commits

1. UN (2015).

the world to delivering the other sixteen goals through a revitalized global partnership of multiple stakeholders, including the business community.[2] Humanity's greatest areas of challenge, including poverty, health, education, inequality, climate change, and conflict, are inextricably interlinked: we must move on all or risk failing on each. Each goal is "hitched" to every other, to borrow John Muir's language. If our challenges are intertwined and our fates are interconnected, it follows that our response must be collective. Neither governments nor business alone will rescue humanity, nor can we expect civil society to fix broken economic models. We must harness the best in all of us.

Better Business, Better World

The private sector has a key role to play. The SDGs need business, and business needs the goals. Having been part of their development, I understood fully that seventeen goals and 169 targets were a lot for many businesses to comprehend, and helping companies embrace the framework was my main focus. Soon after it was adopted, we therefore launched the Business and Sustainable Development Commission and asked Lord Mark Malloch-Brown, a former UN deputy secretary-general, to chair it. I was glad he accepted.[3]

Drawing on a series of global consultations and commissioned papers, in 2017 the commission published its flagship *Better Business Better World* report.[4] We wanted to encourage companies to look at the SDGs not just through a risk or cost prism but through an opportunity or investment prism. We wanted to help them integrate the goals into their core strategies, to improve their agility, resilience, innovation, and trust, in a world of increasingly complex and volatile problems. And we wanted to show business leaders that partnering with others to achieve this vision would allow the kind of progress that no single C-suite could achieve alone.

The commission concluded that the SDGs are a means by which companies and industries can renew their social license to operate while

---

2. For a description of Goal 17 ("Strengthen the means of implementation and revitalize the Global Partnership for Sustainable Development"), see the website at https://sdgs.un.org/goals/goal17.

3. See the website of the Business and Sustainable Development Commission—RELX SDG Resource Centre (https://sdgresources.relx.com/bsdc).

4. Business and Sustainable Development Commission (2017).

entering thrilling new markets. It found that achieving the goals by 2030 in just four economic systems—food, agriculture, and land use; cities; energy and materials; and health and well-being—could unlock opportunities worth up to U.S. $12 trillion a year and create 380 million new jobs.[5] In the years since, these numbers have only gone up. More than ever, the SDGs offer the business opportunity of a lifetime. We increasingly see that companies that embrace them, that work to address society's bigger challenges with a multistakeholder, longer-term focus, tend to perform better. In 2023, for example, the IBM Institute for Business Value conducted a survey of five thousand C-suite executives across twenty-two industries and twenty-two countries about sustainability's business impact, with a special focus on companies that embed sustainability deep into their organizations, including their strategy, workflows, organization, and decisions. It found that "those companies that embed sustainability (embedders) are 52% more likely to outperform their peers on profitability, with a 16% higher rate of revenue growth."[6] An earlier study by the McKinsey Global Institute and FCLTGlobal showed that companies operating with a true long-term mindset made critical decisions, such as investing more in research and development, and, as a result, had 47 percent higher revenue growth and faster-growing market caps.[7]

Exponential Problems versus Linear Solutions

The good news is that many companies now recognize the benefits of embracing more sustainable business models and are taking action to implement them. Many more executives understand that there is no business to be done on a dead planet, and that they cannot succeed in societies that fail. Indeed, many already face daily the negative consequences of humankind's collective failure to act. Embracing a sustainable business model is not easy, particularly as the scale of the transition needed in all economies is enormous, and the time to act is getting shorter and shorter. It starts with companies focusing on their own business operations and value chains and putting their own house in order. Of course, there are

---

5. Business and Sustainable Development Commission (2017), 26–41.
6. IBM Institute for Business Value (2024), 2.
7. McKinsey Global Institute (2017).

still the usual laggards and free riders, and those companies that benefit most from the status quo will often defend it at all costs. Even among those companies that are taking action, many still have low ambitions, whether the target is carbon reduction, or diversity and inclusion, or extending decent wages and human rights protections through their supply chains. They are playing not to lose rather than playing to win. Even among those making big commitments, still not enough are actually "walking the talk" with meaningful, measurable action. Certainly, the UN has identified a rise in so-called "SDG washing," or the selective reporting of positive contributions while avoiding mention of negative impacts.[8]

Despite all this, however, today we see levels of corporate awareness and activism with respect to issues of planetary health and societal cohesion that are unrecognizable compared with the situation a decade ago and that are continuing to increase. Over a thousand companies representing just over a third of the global economy, along with a majority of financial institutions, have introduced, or committed to introduce, decarbonization targets aligned with best science.[9] Exciting new markets are growing, such as markets in electric vehicles, solar panels, battery storage, and more, as industry and investors bet on safer and cleaner products and technology. The acceleration of new technologies, regulatory advances, and growing signals from the marketplace, not least from a company's own employees, are all helping drive needed reforms.

Even more important is collective action, which is essential to achieve the scale of change that no single business can deliver alone. Here, too, new coalitions are emerging in diverse industry sectors, from aviation and shipping to food and fashion, with CEOs putting aside traditional rivalry to collaborate on bigger common problems. In the same fashion, there are now plenty of examples of positive advocacy whereby the business community calls out political timidity and, at key moments, pushes for regulatory ambition. That said, conventional self-serving lobbying is alive and kicking. There will always be companies that privately or through their trade associations lobby ministers and officials to enact harmful policies that preserve the companies' own interests, which are often at odds with

---

8. United Nations Global Compact and Accenture (2023).
9. Science Based Targets (2022).

their public positions on environmental and social issues. Nonetheless, in recent times courageous and forward-thinking CEOs have been instrumental in helping secure some landmark global and regional policy and legislative wins, such as the COP15 Agreement on Protecting Biodiversity, the High Seas Treaty, the EU's nature restoration targets, and more. On biodiversity alone, hundreds of companies have argued for tougher rules, including, for example, mandatory reporting on businesses' reliance on, and impact on, natural ecosystems.[10] In such debates, we increasingly hear business voices making connections between environmental damage, justice, and broader societal stability, and recognizing that all are at stake.

The business community still has a mountain to climb, but we are light years away from the corporate disinterest and skepticism about sustainable development that dominated business practices when my generation of business leaders was coming up. Today the challenge is not that the private sector isn't moving. Advances in technology, signals from the market, and evolving legislation are encouraging most if not all companies to move in one way or another. Rather, the challenge is that the problems we are creating, with our predominantly linear and extractive consumption model, are growing faster than we are applying solutions. Humanity is in a race with multiple crises that threaten our very existence, and we are currently losing and in danger of being overwhelmed. Notwithstanding some important strides, notably in global access to health care, not a single SDG is on track to be delivered by the 2030 deadline.[11] Our most burning challenges—climate change, nature loss, and widening inequality—are exponential. The worse they get, the faster they go. And we're simply not doing enough. We're still trying to beat exponential problems with incremental and linear solutions, and it doesn't work.

Look at the investments being made. In 2023, global investment in renewable energy skyrocketed to $1.8 trillion, an all-time high.[12] The International Energy Agency named solar the "star performer" on the basis that more than $1 billion would go into solar investments each day, "edging this spending above that in upstream oil for the first time."[13] These are tremendous leaps, and they should be celebrated and applauded. Yet they need to be

---

10. Hillsdon (2022).
11. United Nations (2023).
12. BloombergNEF (2024).
13. IEA (2023b), 12.

at least two to three times bigger. UN economists estimate the cost of achieving the SDGs to be between $5.4 trillion and $6.4 trillion per year between now and 2030.[14] And as these problems get worse, the cost of addressing them goes up, and with it the number of people who will suffer, especially in emerging markets, where access to capital is even more difficult.

We can take action on climate, Goal 13, as an example. Deloitte predicts that unchecked climate change could cost the global economy $178 trillion between 2021 and 2070, and that the human costs would be far greater.[15] By contrast, acting rapidly to achieve net zero emissions over the same period could increase the size of the world economy by $43 trillion.[16] With respect to Goal 12, responsible consumption and production, the Food and Land Use Coalition calculates that the broken global food system costs $12 trillion a year in damage to people and planet.[17] On the other hand, reforming the system so that it provides food security and healthy diets for a growing global population while also tackling climate change, biodiversity, health, and poverty challenges could unlock $4.5 trillion a year in new business.[18] If people claim that we cannot afford to spend what is needed today, just consider that we currently spend $1.8 trillion a year in perverse subsidies that actually encourage climate change, land degradation, and deforestation.[19]

We have got ourselves stuck in a vicious downward spiral when what's needed is an upcycle of virtuous improvement. We need to begin closing the growing gap between our problems, which are racing away from us, and the solutions we are applying. *Our problems are exponential, and therefore our response must be exponential too.* Getting to this point will require a step change from the private sector, and from all other parts of society. Collectively, we need to attack our challenges with renewed ambition, focus, and collaboration because this is how we will achieve speed and scale. For the remainder of the 2030 Agenda and whatever will follow, we urgently need to accelerate effective solutions.

---

14. United Nations Conference on Trade and Development (2023).
15. Deloitte (2022).
16. Ibid.
17. Food and Land Use Coalition (2019).
18. Ibid.
19. B Team and Business for Nature (2022).

Tailwinds and Barriers

The question is, how? How do we galvanize more corporate leaders, to do more? How do we create the critical mass of companies that can, in turn, push their industries toward positive tipping points and help derisk the political process where it is stalled? How do we implement the right policy frameworks and enforcement mechanisms, quickly and at scale?

I have never met a CEO or executive who actively wanted their business to destroy the planet or send more children to bed hungry. Yes, there are undoubtedly some bad actors, as can be found in all walks. For the most part, though, business leaders struggle to embrace more sustainable business models because they lack the skills, means, knowledge, incentives, and time to do so effectively. On any given day they have a multitude of issues to contend with to keep their companies running, from managing internal staffing to keeping up with latest developments in AI, geopolitics, and the global economy. They are continually torn between thinking about the business's immediate needs versus its long-term health, and too often short-term interests win the day. If we are going to empower and motivate more C-suites to break the deadlock, it is important to understand and address the tailwinds and barriers at play.

On the positive side, several converging forces are making it more logical and appealing than ever for companies to embrace the SDGs. For a start, the costs of inaction are becoming ever more real and more expensive. Much of the technology needed has come online faster than anticipated. Stanford professor of civil and environmental engineering Mark Z. Jacobson, for example, argues that we already have "95% of the technologies we need [to fix the climate]. . . . The ones we don't have include long-distance aircraft and ships and some industrial technologies, but we know how to transition those technologies. We also need to address non-energy emissions as well, but we know how to do that, as well."[20] Others argue that with the technologies available today, combined with other measures such as increasing energy efficiency and greater use of renewables, we could make 80 percent of the emissions cuts needed by 2030, and fast developments in AI will be a key enabler.[21]

---

20. Jacobson (2023).
21. IEA (2023a), 13.

Important legislative shifts are boosting corporate confidence over the direction of travel. Europe is increasingly leading, thanks to legislation such as its Taxonomy, Carbon Border Adjustment, and Green Deal.[22] The United States is seeing a major shift of investments behind the Inflation Reduction Act and CHIPS Act,[23] and many other countries are similarly adopting legislation to enact more sustainable requirements.[24] Standard setting is advancing, with the Task Forces on Climate and now Nature-Related Financial Disclosures, the SEC's environmental disclosure requirements, the International Sustainability Standards Board, and others, and we are increasingly seeing convergence there as well. Last but not least, although multilateralism is not enjoying its finest hour, global agreements, including the Oceans and Biodiversity treaties, have been big wins, and the Global Plastic Treaty negotiations, scheduled to conclude at the end of 2024, are backed by high-ambition countries and businesses pushing for a bold instrument. While the annual COP climate negotiations have not fully produced the needed level of ambition, we are inching forward on reducing reliance on fossil fuels, providing climate financing for poorer nations, and recognizing the need for a just and people-centered transition.

We also see some encouraging signals from the financial market, with trillions of dollars of assets under management being committed to decarbonizing portfolios.[25] There is increasing evidence that the companies that lead in this transition also benefit from higher valuations.[26] This is not surprising: being better positioned for the economy of the future and more in synch with the needs of society drives opportunities, motivates employees, and rewards partners and communities throughout the value chain. Together, these currents, combined with the fact that business leaders are human beings with their own children and grandchildren to answer to, are helping many companies onto a better path.

---

22. On Taxonomy, see the European Commission website at EU taxonomy for sustainable activities - European Commission (europa.eu). On the Carbon Border Adjustment, see Carbon Border Adjustment Mechanism - European Commission (europa.eu). On the European Green Deal, see The European Green Deal - European Commission (europa.eu).

23. White House (2022); U.S. Department of the Treasury (2023).

24. United Nations Environment Programme (2019).

25. See the website of the Glasgow Financial Alliance for Net Zero (https://www.gfanzero.com/about/).

26. Cherel-Bonnemaison et al. (2021).

However, it is not a simple story. Many companies are still struggling to pivot. The SDGs are an attractive long-term bet, but they are a bet nonetheless. Financing often high upfront costs and investing in new technologies is hard enough at the best of times, especially in the cash-strapped emerging markets and poorer nations most exposed to environmental and social risk and instability. It is even harder when so much of the policy and funding landscape still points in the wrong direction.

In many countries, political commitment to the vision embodied in the SDGs is inconsistent and polarized. Inevitably, as the deep flaws in our destructive and exploitative economic system become more obvious, the vested order that benefits from that system is coming out to protect it, and the gloves are off. We need look no further than the continued attempts to thwart climate progress by the oil and gas industry and those who profit from it, which attempts are directly connected to political attacks on so-called "woke capitalism." An already struggling multilateral system originally designed to deal with issues of interdependence is being further weakened by its outdated designs and rising geopolitical tensions, making it less effective. All this offers little encouragement to company leaders still sitting on the fence and wondering which way to jump.

Short-sighted investors don't help, of course. Nor does the fact that in many areas we are still debating and developing clear standards for companies to follow. Notwithstanding the excellent work of organizations such as the World Benchmarking Alliance, the Global Reporting Initiative, and Just Capital, which measure, track, and compare companies' behavior on issues such as human rights and the fair treatment of workers, overall, we still lack common metrics to assess businesses' progress on implementing most of the SDGs, as well as mechanisms to ensure transparency and accountability around negative externalities.

Put it all together, the tailwinds and the barriers, and it is not hard to see why many more companies are moving, but equally many are not, or not quickly enough. The obstacles facing business leaders are real and challenging, but let's also be clear: none is insurmountable. The blocks and bottlenecks are ultimately either technical issues that should be within the reach of human intellect to solve or else matters of human willpower, which are also in our power to change. A future in which we fail is one we simply cannot entertain, and the momentum that is building—in technology, regulation, societal attitudes, corporate action—gives immense cause for hope. At last, we have a tremendous platform to build on, and the greatest incentive to do so: our safety and survival. For all humankind's frailties, our species has so far managed to avoid either annihilation or extinction, even if at times we have come terrifyingly close, and we will resolve our current predicament too. The issue is speed and scale. What matters, and it matters immeasurably, is how quickly we can step up, and how much further suffering we can avoid—suffering that will inevitably be worse for the most vulnerable people on the planet.

The Net Positive Mindset

To successfully accelerate and scale up corporate action for the rest of the 2030 Agenda and beyond, we need to be crystal clear on our situation. When the SDGs were launched in 2015, we did not know how quickly we were approaching negative tipping points in our environments and societies. We could not fully appreciate the dangers of crossing our planetary boundaries; six of the nine identified by the Stockholm Resilience Centre have now been breached, threatening Earth's stability.[27] Nor did we understand that when human well-being is considered alongside these biophysical limits, we have even less room for maneuver.[28]

We are starting to understand these things now. And it is time that, together, we realize that companies and governments trying to fix these problems by being "less bad" isn't going to work; it's just a slower suicide. We have this knowledge, and it is up to us to leave this world better than we find it. Not a bit better but better overall, and this means fundamentally reimagining and rebuilding the broken systems that got us here. For companies of every size, from multinationals to startups and the small and medium-size enterprises in between, it means striving to have a positive impact. The concept can be applied across other societal goods, beyond climate and the environment: Is your company contributing to making the world more just, more compassionate, more truthful? Think of food companies moving, for instance, to regenerative agriculture, which repairs the

---

27. The nine boundaries are: novel entities, climate change, biosphere integrity, land-system change, freshwater change, biochemical flows, stratospheric ozone layer depletion, atmospheric aerosol loading, and ocean acidification. The first six have been breached. Stockholm Resilience Centre (https://www.stockholmresilience.org/research/planetary-boundaries.html).

28. Rockstrom et al. (2023).

soil and sets millions of smallholder farmers onto a better trajectory, and beverage companies replenishing more water than they use, particularly in the most water-stressed areas. Think of banks actively improving financial inclusion among those who are poor. It's what my co-author and I call being a "net positive" company in our book, *Net Positive: How Courageous Companies Thrive by Giving More Than They Take*.[29] The aim is to be able to answer an overall yes to two simple questions: Am I profiting from helping solve the world's problems, rather than from creating them? And is the world therefore better off because my business is in it?

These ideas have been gaining traction in recent years. They are a natural evolution for the SDGs, and a direct consequence of our failure to implement them sooner. In essence, we are talking about more businesses adopting a net positive mindset, also known as a just and regenerative mindset, which we are beginning to find in the most forward-thinking companies. This way of thinking goes much deeper than asking how a business can minimize its environmental impact or prevent human rights abuses and instead gets to the heart of recognizing our interdependence with other people, other living beings, and ecosystems. By recognizing this interdependence, companies open the door to a future in which they can not only survive but thrive, by taking action to help regenerate, replenish, and renew our world, thereby creating the conditions for all people to flourish.

Adopting a just and regenerative approach means understanding that humans are a fundamental part of nature, and that the rights and potential of all people must be upheld. It challenges us to go beyond our current extractive models of consumption and toward economic models that improve the fundamental quality of life of all living beings and ecosystems. When we embrace this view, we see clearly the false division between environmental and social issues: a thriving planet cannot be one that contains widespread human suffering, and a thriving human population cannot exist on a dying planet. The regenerative, or net positive, mindset is the route to long-term, inclusive prosperity and a source of great hope.

If enough leaders embrace this mindset, and quickly, collectively we still have a chance. Embracing net positive can potentially unlock the greater and faster private sector action we need, in three critical ways.

First, a net positive mindset pushes companies to find their ambition, and to accelerate their transition to safer and more equitable business

---

29. Polman and Winston (2021).

models. If more companies accelerate, we will see more would-be leaders step up to join the best-in-class in their industries. This in turn will create the critical mass of leaders needed to lift sector norms.

When a company adopts and internalizes a net positive mindset, that company naturally begins to operate for the longer-term benefit of the business and wider society. It strives to create positive returns for all stakeholders, including employees, customers, suppliers, future generations, and the planet itself. Shareholders are rewarded as a direct result of this longer-term, multistakeholder model. Crucially, once a business embraces net positive, it allows the people in that company to take ownership of many more of the impacts and consequences of the business, whether those impacts are intended or not. This might be the greenhouse gas emissions or child labor the company is indirectly responsible for in its value chain. It might be the unintended but cruel and degrading uses of its products, or its impact on mental health or social cohesion. If *more* companies take *more* responsibility for *more* of these issues, we can collectively attack complex problems with far greater success.

Second, the net positive mindset unleashes collaboration: renewing and regenerating our societies and planet is inevitably a team sport. Human beings are capable of impactful partnership, and there are already some high-potential coalitions in place to help advance the SDGs.

The First Movers Coalition, for example, was established in 2021. It is a private sector–led initiative to create a clear demand signal for emerging climate technologies. In its first two years, members committed U.S. $16 billion to emerging technologies by 2030.[30] The Fashion Pact is a collective of more than sixty CEOs and 160 brands representing a third of the global fashion industry; these CEOs and brands are working together on issues from creating a market for low-impact materials to supporting farmers' livelihoods and tackling textile pollution in the oceans.[31] Through the Global Energy Alliance for People and Planet, philanthropies, governments, investors, technology companies, and implementation partners are tackling energy poverty and working to speed the green energy transition in emerging economies.[32] Collective action is essential for scaling up

---

30. First Movers Coalition (2024).
31. See The Fashion Pact website (https://www.thefashionpact.org/about-us/).
32. See the Global Energy Alliance for People and Planet website (https://energyalliance.org/).

solutions and transforming whole value chains. It is still the exception; we need it to become the rule.

Third, adopting a net positive mindset helps lead a company away from secretive and self-interested lobbying and toward a more constructive kind of advocacy. In the end, we will not achieve economic transformation without governments putting in place the right frameworks and enforcing them. If a company's goal is to improve the world, its leadership is more likely to argue for ambitious and sensible regulations that level the playing field and are in the long-term interest of wider society. It is more likely to engage in the major debates, where we desperately need more business voices at the table, not least on questions of finance and reform of our multilateral institutions.

More of this kind of net positive advocacy is now happening, and we need more still that is transparent and accountable. The more business leaders and governments can work together, providing one another with reciprocated confidence, the more both sides will be pushed to higher ambition. Such partnering in pursuit of a higher ambition exposes the regressive alliances between political elites and self-serving corporate interests that continue to hold us back. And it helps rebuild much-needed trust in business as well as in our institutions. This trust will be an essential glue for our societies as we seek to successfully guide them through these uncertain and sometimes dizzying times.

Courageous Leadership

There is no single lever that we can pull to lift corporate activities from "less bad" to net positive. There's no button that can accelerate companies, build collective action, or boost positive advocacy, all of which are needed to begin catching up with and tackling our shared problems. There is, however, one ingredient that is needed to deliver any and all of this. It is leadership. Courageous leadership.

Not all crises are created equal. I would argue that, at its root, our biggest problem is not really a climate crisis or an economic crisis or an inequality crisis. Ultimately, we are caught in a leadership crisis. Systems change is undoubtedly an exhausting, complicated, and difficult process, but what stands between us and the vision encapsulated in the SDGs is not technology or legislation or complexity or even money. All these things can be dealt with or found, if we are willing. The deciding factor in humanity's fate will be the behaviors and actions of human beings. While it is a nerve-wracking thought, this situation is brilliantly adjustable because change is in our hands.

When the global community first launched the SDGs, we knew that the private sector would need to help deliver them and that business leaders would need to step up. What we could not have articulated clearly then, but know today, is the *kind* of leadership that is required: ambitious and purpose-driven leadership. Cooperative rather than purely competitive leadership. Empathy, compassion, and an ability to put long-term shared interest over immediate self-interest. Leaders who understand that in a world of exponentially growing problems, moving slowly is as good as falling behind, and who see that by putting ourselves in service of others, we ultimately serve ourselves.

As we look to 2030 and beyond, the task before us appears immense. We are already working harder than ever to accelerate and scale up solutions, yet we must work much harder still. The process of transitioning our economies will get more difficult before it gets easier, and there has never been a less predictable and more demanding time to build a company. Equally, there has never been a more rewarding or important moment to be in business and to play a part in reshaping industries, markets, and economies so that they finally serve the billions of people who engage with or inhabit them and the planet that hosts us all. The challenge and beauty of systems transformation are that it begins with human transformation. The root of the word "courage" is *cor*, Latin for heart. We begin with ourselves.

We can take heart from realizing that the direction of travel is set. The SDGs are still the destination, and finally we are on the move. Even if we do not yet have every answer, ultimately we know what we need to do. The test for today's leaders is whether they can go faster, and go together. No one has said it better than Kenyan activist and Nobel Peace Prize winner, the late Wangari Maathai: "In the course of history, there comes a time when humanity is called to shift to a new level of consciousness, to reach a higher moral ground. A time when we have to shed our fear and give hope to each other. That time is now."[33]

---

33. Maatthai (2024).

REFERENCES

B Team and Business for Nature. 2022. "Financing Our Survival: Building a Nature-Positive Economy through Subsidy Reform." February.

BloombergNEF. 2024. *Energy Transition Investment Trends 2024*. New York, January.

Business and Sustainable Development Commission. 2017. *Better Business Better World*. London, January.

Cherel-Bonnemaison, Celine, Gustav Erlandsson, Ben Ibach, and Peter Spiller. 2021. "Buying into a More Sustainable Value Chain." New York: McKinsey & Co.

Deloitte. 2022. *The Turning Point: A Global Summary*. Chicago, June 20.

First Movers Coalition. 2024. "First Movers Coalition Impact Brief." Prepared for the annual meeting of the World Economic Forum, January.

Food and Land Use Coalition. 2019. *Growing Better: Ten Critical Transitions to Transform Food and Land Use*. September.

Hillsdon, Mark. 2022. "How Business Helped Drive 'Historic' Agreement for Nature at COP15." Reuters, December 21.

IBM Institute for Business Value. 2014. *Beyond Checking the Box: How to Create Business Value with Embedded Sustainability*. Armonk, NY: IBM Corporation.

IEA (International Energy Agency). 2023a. *Net Zero Roadmap: A Global Pathway to Keep the 1.5 °C Goal in Reach. 2023 Update*. Paris.

———. 2023b. *World Energy Investment 2023*. Paris.

Jacobson, Mark Z. 2023. "We Don't Need 'Miracle' Technologies to Fix the Climate. We Have the Tools Now." *Guardian*, February 7.

Maatthai, Wangari. 2004. "Nobel Lecture." Oslo, December 10.

McKinsey & Co. 2021. "Buying into a More Sustainable Value Chain." September.

McKinsey Global Institute. 2017. "Measuring the Economic Impact of Short-Termism." Discussion Paper. New York: McKinsey & Co.

Polman, Paul, and Andrew Winston. 2021. *Net Positive: How Courageous Companies Thrive by Giving More Than They Take*. Harvard Business Press.

Rockstrom, Johan, Joyeeta Gupta, Dahe Qin, et al. 2023. "Safe and Just Earth System Boundaries." *Nature* 619:102–11.

Science Based Targets. 2022. *SBTI Monitoring Report 2022*.

UN (United Nations). 2023. *The Sustainable Development Goals Report 2023: Special Edition. Towards a Rescue Plan for People and Planet*. New York: United Nations Publications.

———. 2015. "The UN Secretary-General's High-Level Panel of Eminent Persons on the Post-2015 Development Agenda."

United Nations Conference on Trade and Development. 2023. "Annual Cost for Reaching the SDGs? More Than $5 Trillion." New York, September 19.

United Nations Global Compact and Accenture. 2023. *SDG Stocktake: Through the Eyes of the Private Sector*.

United Nations Environment Programme. 2019. "Dramatic Growth in Laws to Protect Environment, but Widespread Failure to Enforce, Finds Report." Press release, January 24.

U.S. Department of the Treasury. 2023. "The Inflation Reduction Act and U.S. Business Investment." Press release, August 16.

White House. 2022. "Fact Sheet: CHIPS and Science Act Will Lower Costs, Create Jobs, Strengthen Supply Chains, and Counter China." Press release, August 22.

THREE

Strengthening Small Businesses to Support Sustainable Development

NDIDI OKONKWO NWUNELI

Small and medium-size enterprises (SMEs) are pivotal in advancing sustainable development, not only because of their substantial numbers but also because they are recognized as key drivers of employment and innovation. According to the International Labour Organization (ILO), more than 90 percent of all enterprises can be classified as SMEs, and micro and small enterprises account for 70 percent of employment worldwide and for a large share of new job creation.[1] The World Bank estimates that in emerging economies, seven in ten formal jobs are created by SMEs and that in these markets, formal SMEs create up to 40 percent of national income (GDP).[2] The bank notes further that "these numbers are significantly higher when informal SMEs are included."[3]

---

1. "SMEs typically have fewer than 250 employees. In many countries, more than 90% of all enterprises can be classed as SMEs, and a large share of those can be classed as micro firms, with fewer than ten employees" (ILO 2019).
2. World Bank Group (2019).
3. Ibid.

SMEs have a major role to play in shifting markets to more environmentally sound forms of economic progress. Research by the Organization for Economic Cooperation and Development (OECD) finds that despite SMEs' "significant environmental footprint" and the challenges posed to them by environmental degradation, "SMEs and entrepreneurs are, and can be even more of, a source of innovation and solutions by developing the technologies needed to address environmental challenges."[4]

Furthermore, SMEs are recognized as critical players in the global supply chains and distribution channels of larger companies and as drivers of innovation, competition, and growth more broadly.[5] They are often referred to as the "hidden middle" in these value chains because their issues are rarely included in policy debates.[6] For these various reasons, SMEs are positioned to be critical players and stakeholders in the transformation needed for sustainable development. The commitments that large companies are making to decrease their Scope 3 emissions, for example, will be difficult to realize without engaging the SME vendors, suppliers, or service providers in their value chains and supporting those smaller businesses' efforts to decrease their own emissions.[7] In turn, SMEs have a role to play in enabling larger companies to implement more inclusive business models that use market-based and commercially viable approaches to integrate low-income producers, workers, suppliers, distributors, retailers, and consumers into corporate value chains.[8] Such models can support livelihoods and economic opportunity, improve access to affordable products and services, and help tackle poverty.

Indeed, SMEs are critical to the fulfillment of the Sustainable Development Goals (SDGs). Although linkages and contributions can be identified across all 17 SDGs, their role is especially important to SDG 8, which aims to "promote sustained, inclusive and sustainable economic growth, full and productive employment and decent work for all."[9] They also have a key contribution to make toward achieving sustainable industrialization and innovation, the aim of SDG 9.[10] But SMEs face significant hurdles that constrain

---

4. OECD (2021).
5. WEF (2021).
6. AGRA (2019).
7. Ashcroft (2023).
8. IFC [2024].
9. Global Goals (n.d.).
10. United Nations Global Compact (2023).

their ability to fully assume their critical roles in sustainable development. Their engagement in this endeavor hinges on the creation of an enabling environment, complete with conducive policies, financial support, training, and community support. This chapter explores the challenges that SMEs face on their journey to serving as sustainability champions and discusses how to integrate SMEs more strategically in this quest.

Challenges Faced by SMEs in Supporting Sustainable Development

Small businesses face a variety of well-documented constraints that impede their ability to grow and survive, which in turn limits their contributions to sustainable development. They struggle to access reliable and affordable financing and risk management tools and to acquire and retain personnel with appropriate skills and talents, especially in managerial and technical capacities. When they are able to overcome challenges in accessing market information, data, and knowledge, they may face disproportionally high risks in adopting new technologies, practices, and business models.[11] SMEs are also most affected by shocks, climate change, and economic downturns. For example, during the COVID-19 pandemic, 34 percent of small businesses in the United States and 42.7 percent in South Africa closed, and relatively fewer bounced back compared to large companies in their sector.[12]

In addition to this well-known list of challenges, small businesses are increasingly facing the more recent challenge of proactively and effectively adopting environmental, social, and governance (ESG) standards and climate-smart principles. As a result of their limited financial and human resources, SMEs often struggle to incorporate ESG practices into their business processes, even when they are the most affected by the negative impacts of climate change. They are also increasingly being held to emissions and ESG standards stipulated by national governments or their larger business partners while being least often consulted in shaping policies and targets. Though SMEs have a vital interest in market alignment with ESG principles and the SDGs, they often face hurdles in registering their own contributions to realizing the relevant priorities.

11. WEF (2021).
12. On the 34 percent figure, see Ghosh (2021); on 42.7 percent, see Nsomba et al. (2021).

Supporting SMEs' Efforts to Contribute to Sustainable Development

According to the SME Climate Hub 2022 survey, SMEs are committed to reducing their energy consumption and waste, investing in employee education, and upgrading facilities and equipment.[13] However, the challenges outlined above, especially the lack of knowledge, human capital, and funding, are significant barriers to "greening" their operations.[14] As a result, the UN Global Compact estimates that only 54 percent of the compact's SME participants have set measurable sustainability goals, in contrast to 86 percent of the large-company participants.[15] There is likely some self-selection in these figures insofar as companies that voluntarily choose to sign up for the UN Global Compact already have made a commitment to sustainable development. Anecdotal evidence suggests that the disparities in participation rates in the broader SME community may be even more pronounced than the difference just noted between SMEs overall and larger companies.

A range of actions can help boost SMEs' resilience and their impact on sustainable development. Larger companies, industry associations, foundations, development partners, and governments should engage with SMEs directly or with their representative business bodies on high-priority sustainability issues. Some recommendations are discussed below.

Take an Ecosystem Approach

An ecosystem approach to engaging SMEs is crucial to enable them to fully embrace their roles in sustainable development. The siloed approaches often used by UN agencies, the development sector, governments, private sector, and different civil society interest groups commonly have not worked because they typically address only one aspect of SMEs' challenges and needs, without fully understanding their operations and where bottlenecks might lie. These siloed approaches dissipate limited resources and funding and increase the complexity and number of relationships and interventions that SMEs or their associations need to navigate. To better coordinate

---

13. SME Climate Hub (2022).
14. Jouven and Schmidt (2022).
15. United Nations Global Compact (2023).

development actors' involvement with respect to the sustainability goals of SMEs, engagement should strive to be multidimensional, integrating the aims of equity and diversity in the workplace with sustained growth through financing and innovation and an environmental sustainability focus that incorporates ESG principles and related climate actions.

SME support strategies should attempt to tackle barriers and bottlenecks by *working with value chain and industry associations* at local, state, federal, and regional levels to drive sustained transformation. For example, the Advancing Local Dairy Development in Nigeria (ALDDN) program, implemented by Sahel Consulting, convenes actors from across the Nigerian dairy ecosystem.[16] In light of the complexity of the industry, the team designed the program with an ecosystem-sustainability orientation from the outset. It incorporated interventions to address gender, climate, smallholder livelihood, and nutrition challenges and supported the Commercial Dairy Ranchers Association of Nigeria (CODARAN) in taking the lead to ensure continuity beyond the programmatic interventions.[17]

An ecosystem approach also demands that data on SMEs be collected by sector, shared in a transparent and accountable manner, and made accessible, to guide policy and programmatic interventions. The Food Systems Dashboard, developed by a consortium of partners, including the Global Alliance for Improved Nutrition (GAIN), the Columbia Climate School, the Cornell College of Agriculture and Life Sciences, and the Food and Agriculture Organization of the UN, provides a good example of a *data repository* that serves as the basis for strategic action in areas with the weakest performance.[18] The dashboard provides ecosystem data at state, country, and regional levels and thus serves to inform the interventions of SMEs and their industry associations in the food industry. Similar data collated for other sectors could also help inform the efforts of industry and regional associations to track SME commitments to help drive environmental performance, ensure decent work, close gender employment and pay gaps, and actively support diversity and inclusion, with a focus on female and youth engagement. When SMEs commit to collating their

---

16. Sahel Consulting is funded by the Gates Foundation and was cofounded by the author. See Sahel Consulting [2024].

17. See, e.g., CODARAN (2020).

18. See the website of the Food Systems Dashboard (https://www.foodsystemsdashboard.org/). The dashboard has received funding support from the Rockefeller Foundation, of which the author is a board member.

own data and setting clear targets, they can increase their transparency and accountability and achieve their own critical objectives.

Foster Links between SMEs and Larger Companies

Building and strengthening small business linkages in the supply chains, operations, and distribution channels of larger companies is a key way to achieve more inclusive and sustainable development. Strengthening linkages has the potential to create a variety of mutual benefits, including reduced procurement, production, and distribution costs and risks. It can also improve large companies' productivity and access to markets while enhancing skills, standards, technical capacity, job creation, and access to finance, technology, and markets for participating SMEs.[19] Such linkages can also serve as pathways for spreading ESG standards, practices, and business models along local and global value chains.

Large companies can help foster linkages by undertaking the following types of engagement with SMEs:

- *Sourcing from, subcontracting to, and procuring from small enterprises.* Engaging SMEs on these matters might take the form of smallholder farmer schemes, local content programs, and removing barriers to the provision of raw materials and components to larger manufacturers or finished products to larger retailers.
- *Distributing or franchising through small enterprises.* Larger companies can work with SMEs to distribute consumer goods and services to the local communities in which the SMEs operate. These communities may be remote and difficult for larger companies to reach.
- *Selling affordable products and services to small enterprises.* Larger companies can provide smallholder farmers and small-scale manufacturers with key inputs and productivity tools. The latter might include financial services, transport and logistics, digital technologies, utilities and infrastructure, seeds and fertilizers, production equipment, and education and training.[20]

Large companies can also support SME training, financing, and business development programs through individual or collective initiatives beyond

---

19. Nelson (2006).
20. Ibid. See also Nelson (2010), 66–70.

their own value chains, either in their industry sector more broadly or in the communities and countries where they operate. There is untapped potential for larger companies and their industry groups to engage in policy dialogues, advocacy efforts, and partnerships with governments and SME business associations, with these efforts aimed at strengthening the enabling environment for SME development. In this way large companies can specifically support SMEs in adopting ESG standards and practices.

A growing number of large companies are supporting SME capacity building for sustainability.[21] For example, Ikea, through its IWAY initiative, has outlined a robust code of conduct for its suppliers around environmental, social, and working conditions.[22] It also provides a community for learning and support to enable its suppliers to meet its high ESG standards. Further, the Ikea Foundation has made a sizable investment in the provision of clean and renewable energy through the Global Energy Alliance for People and Planet, in partnership with the Rockefeller Foundation and the Bezos Earth Fund.[23] These organizations are working with public, private, and nonprofit actors to address energy poverty by investing in innovation and scaling up clean solutions.

Walmart, through Project Gigaton, which the company launched in 2017, supports small businesses in its supplier network in actively setting targets and taking measurable actions to reduce emissions in six areas: energy use, natural resource consumption, waste production, packaging, transportation, and product use and design.[24] According to Walmart, as of 2024, 5,900 suppliers have signed up for the project, and the practical impacts are evident.[25]

Eni, the Italian energy group, introduced a digital platform, Open-es, which provides smaller enterprises with knowledge and a community of support for the sustainability transition.[26] It also provides tools for them to measure and report on their progress and to build new supply chain partnerships. In 2024 the platform included over 22,000 companies in 103 countries, the vast majority of which were SMEs.[27]

21. Al-Saleh (2023).
22. Ikea Global [2024].
23. See Global Energy Alliance for People and Planet, "Who We Are" (https://energyalliance.org/). (The author is a trustee of The Rockefeller Foundation.)
24. Walmart Sustainability Hub (2024).
25. Ibid.
26. See the Open-es website (https://www.openes.io/).
27. Ibid. The figures are as given on the website as of August 12, 2024.

Industry associations and nonprofits are also working to support SMEs in transitioning their sustainability practices, serving as climate and sustainability champions, and advocating for a more robust policy environment, funding, and training for SMEs in these areas. The SME Climate Hub, for example, through its free Carbon Calculator for businesses and Climate Fit, an online training course, is equipping small businesses with the knowledge, skills, and support needed to reduce their emissions and undertake strategic climate-related actions.[28]

African Food Changemakers, a digital hub for African SMEs in forty African countries, supports SMEs through its Building Resilience Against Climate and Environmental Shocks (BRACE) program.[29] This initiative aims to empower "[agricultural] and food SMEs, through training and technical support, to implement sustainable solutions for scaling their agribusinesses in the face of climate change."[30] In addition to a robust eLearning curriculum, the program exposes African agricultural and food-producing SMEs to local and regional best practices and connects them to a support community.

The business case for large companies to support SMEs in enhancing diversity and inclusion (D&I) initiatives is compelling.[31] Customers prioritize services or products from brands invested in D&I, and there is a direct impact on job creation and economic development. The MIT *Sloan Management Review* reports that, in the U.S. context, "directing $1 million in procurement spending toward diverse suppliers can create as many as 10 new jobs," which in turn "[drives] at least $124,000 in economic impact through tax revenues, helping to build local communities where the suppliers operate."[32] Similar multipliers are likely to apply in other geographies.

Of the Fortune 100 companies that have explicit D&I initiatives, however, only 59 percent source from diverse suppliers, and when they do, the

---

28. See SME Climate Hub, "About Us" (https://smeclimatehub.org/about-us/). The figures are as given on the website as of August 12, 2024.
29. African Food Changemakers, "Building Resilience Against Climate and Environmental Shocks" (https://brace.afchub.org/).
30. African Food Changemakers, "Home" (https://brace.afchub.org/). (The author is the founder of the BRACE platform.)
31. Swette and Boyo (2021).
32. Ibid.

share is limited to about 10 percent of their suppliers and services.[33] Similarly, according to Gartner, ethnicity/race is considered by 75 percent of supply chain organizations as part of their D&I strategies and objectives, but only 40 percent of them have specific interventions in this regard.[34] There is a severe gap between announced or documented objectives and the actions being taken by large companies. There is also considerable concern that with the overturn of affirmative action in U.S. college admissions, the focus on D&I will wane in the absence of sustained engagement, strategic interventions, data transparency and accountability, and clear objectives for achieving results.[35] The implications of such country-specific debates around D&I have potentially significant consequences for other SMEs around the globe that might interact with companies in the world's larger economies.

For their part, it is imperative that SMEs embrace D&I principles and set targets for gender equity in their workforce, as well as engage other underrepresented groups. Industry and value chain associations and local governments can support these efforts by providing centralized D&I consulting, job placement resources, and pipeline support to ease the costs for SMEs that cannot afford dedicated teams.

Develop Talent and Workforce Capabilities

A skilled and informed workforce that fully embraces a sustainability mindset and adopts the requisite practices is critical to the achievement of the SDGs. SMEs as the most numerous category of employers of labor must be actively engaged to develop their workforce talent and capabilities.

The process for engaging SME talent is complicated by the sheer number of SMEs operating in the informal economy. The ILO estimates that 208 million adults are unemployed and that more than two billion people operate in the informal economy.[36] The Business and Sustainable Development Commission estimated in 2017 that sustainable business models could generate economic opportunities creating 380 million jobs by 2030.[37] But nearly one in four (23.5 percent) young people are not in

---

33. Ibid.
34. Gartner (2022).
35. Sidley Austin LLP (2023).
36. Seppo (2023).
37. Business and Sustainable Development Commission (2017).

school, employment, or training.[38] This is especially concerning on the African continent, where, according to the World Bank, only three million new formal wage jobs are created annually, while 12 million youth enter the workforce.[39] Clearly, the disconnect between the high number of unemployed adults and companies' need for talent, cited as a significant challenge by SME leaders, shows that substantial education, skill, and capacity gaps persist at all levels. These gaps are especially notable in middle and senior management roles.[40]

Many companies, including small businesses, frustrated by the inadequate work readiness skills provided by formal educational institutions, are designing and developing their own training programs for entry-level personnel. Accordingly, some best practices are emerging among individual companies and industry associations that should help accelerate the achievement of SDG 8 and foster decent work that is inclusive and equitable. City and state governments are also introducing robust youth skills and job readiness interventions, especially in information and communications technology and digital capabilities, other vocational areas, and, more recently, in the clean energy sector and climate-smart interventions.[41]

AACE Food Processing & Distribution offers a promising example.[42] It is a spice- and snack-processing company operating in Ogun State, Nigeria, with 150 full-time employees. The majority are first-time job seekers; 60 percent are women, and 90 percent are less than thirty years old. In addition to providing a robust training program, nutritious meals, health insurance, and an adult literacy program for its team members, AACE supports the farmers in its supply chain and trains and upskills women to serve as distributors. AACE also trains its team members in sustainability principles and operates a robust internal recycling and circularity system. Thousands of business models like that of AACE Foods operating at scale could make a significant dent in the quest for decent work. This is a situation where SMEs could fruitfully take the lead.

---

38. ILO (2023).
39. World Bank Group (2023).
40. WEF (2021).
41. See, e.g., the web pages of the C40 City Alliance on the Global Green New Deal and the C40 Youth Hub (https://www.c40.org/).
42. See the website for AACE Food Processing & Distribution (https://aacefoods.com/). (The author is a cofounder of AACE Foods.)

Improve Access to Financing

The substantial gap that SMEs face in accessing financing creates challenges for SME growth and sustainable development at three levels. First, the funding available to SMEs is insufficient. Second, when financing is available, it is relatively costly. Third, there is a lack of funding and risk management instruments targeted specifically to supporting SMEs in adopting more sustainable practices.

Globally, micro enterprises and SMEs, or MSMEs, face serious financing gaps, estimated at $1.2 trillion for companies in the formal sector and $6 trillion for those in the informal sector.[43] This gap is particularly pronounced in emerging economies, where the vast majority of these businesses still operate in the informal economy, and among women entrepreneurs, who continue to face additional hurdles and biases that limit their access to financing.

Many small enterprises opt to stay in the informal economy, which is characterized by low productivity, low pay, and no benefits, out of concern for multiple taxation and onerous reporting requirements by local, state or federal government. The resulting lack of legal formality and a credit history limits their ability to obtain financing from banks and other institutions.

Various solutions have emerged to ease enterprises' transition from the informal to the formal economy for most entrepreneurs. Some examples are tax reforms in Colombia, policy tracking and reforms in Kenya, and one-stop-shop registration and business operations support in Nigeria.[44] However, these local or country-specific solutions do not sufficiently address the persistent funding gaps that exist for most small businesses, especially in developing economies.

There are also considerable disparities between funding available for female-owned versus male-owned businesses, with some countries reporting 2 percent or less of venture capital funding going to female entrepreneurs.[45] Similarly, only 2–3 percent of total global funds across private equity and venture capital flow to women fund managers, who, even with their limited resources, are more likely to fund women-owned SMEs and provide additional support to enable them to grow their business.[46]

---

43. Liu (2018).
44. UN DESA (2022), 15.
45. Masterson (2024).
46. Gender Smart (2021).

The Goldman Sachs 10,000 Women Initiative is one example of a pioneering initiative that supports women entrepreneurs in emerging markets to build skills and obtain the support and funding to scale up their operations.[47] The One Million Black Women: Black in Business initiative, also supported by Goldman Sachs, is committing $10 billion in direct investment capital and $100 million in philanthropic support to address the systemic barriers that have prevented Black women from thriving in business and the workforce.[48]

Where financing is available, it is costly in terms of fees and interest rates, which often are in the double digits. Despite the emergence of grant facilities, preferential rates, loan guarantee programs, and capacity-building interventions and the evolution of challenge, venture, and impact funds, the gaps persist. They are often associated with cumbersome application and selection processes and the fact that most of these funds are dollar- or euro-denominated, which exposes SMEs in developing and emerging economies to currency devaluation risks, making these financing options unattractive.

The challenges of availability and cost of financing are arguably even greater when it comes to SMEs adopting more sustainable models of doing business. There is often additional cost, investment, or risk associated with adopting sustainability standards, technologies, practices, or business models. This is the case even for the largest corporations, but it can be highly risky or even prohibitive for SMEs.

There is an urgent need for a radical transformation of the global financing landscape to address the needs of SMEs, especially those led by women and youth and those that have an explicit goal or business model focused on addressing social and environmental challenges and needs in a sustainable manner.

The Way Forward to 2030 and Beyond

SMEs are crucial to sustainable and equitable development and to the achievement of the SDGs. Several key actions have the potential to mobilize SMEs as informed and committed champions of change leading to 2030 and beyond.

47. See Goldman Sachs [2024a].
48. See Goldman Sachs [2024b].

A first priority is to *set and communicate clear expectations for SMEs*. In many contexts, ESG and sustainability requirements are clear for large companies but relatively opaque for small businesses. This is especially relevant in the agriculture and food landscape. For example, definitions of regenerative agriculture and how to practice and measure impact are still being refined, among other challenges faced by small-scale farmers and enterprises operating in this sector.[49]

A second priority is to *finance the sustainability transition at local levels*. Funding is needed to subsidize and incentivize SMEs' technological and operational transitions from diesel to solar energy or renewable waste and water management. The technology and funding to track baseline data and to fill the technology gaps is also crucial. As part of this effort, governments, bilateral and multilateral agencies, large companies, financiers, and philanthropists must *shift resources to local organizations*. They must actively track what percentage of their funds currently goes to local SMEs and SME support organizations and set clear commitments and targets for shifting 90 percent to local organizations by 2030, with only 10 percent going to intermediaries. This is especially relevant for intervention funds that are being channeled to close gaps in skills, capacities, funding, employment practices, and technology. Anecdotal evidence suggests that the majority of those funds continue to be channeled to international NGOs and large organizations that can meet the procurement requirements stipulated by funders.[50] Local organizations can usually deliver impact at a fraction of the cost of external entities. In addition, they can ensure greater resilience as external entities typically do not have the staying power to support small local businesses, especially during times of conflict and crises. Many proxies and strategies exist that can be utilized to find appropriate local organizations capable of supporting SME growth, resilience, and climate action on a more sustained basis and at scale.

A third priority is to *provide shared services to SMEs*. Because most SMEs cannot afford a sustainability officer or even a team, there is the potential for shared ESG support services modeled on existing shared audit or accounting services. Business incubation hubs, accelerators, and small-business development services offered by governments, industry associations, and nonprofit

---

49. See, e.g., Bambridge-Sutton (2023).
50. See, e.g., the Publish What You Fund web page "Localization" (https://www.publishwhatyoufund.org/projects/localization/).

organizations should incorporate the role of a "shared sustainability officer" in their offerings to SMEs to strengthen their capacities and enable them to "green" their operations.

A fourth and related issue is the need to act systematically within sectors. As outlined earlier in this chapter, there is untapped potential to take a more *coordinated ecosystem approach* to engaging with and serving SMEs in specific locations or sectors. Partnerships with local, state, and national governments will be critical for sustained actions in addressing the gaps that most SMEs face in accessing skills and talent, finance and risk management tools, technology, data, and markets. Government partnerships and leadership can be further enhanced with the support of large private sector companies and philanthropists.

Fifth, it is critical to *incorporate the perspectives of small businesses*, especially those in emerging markets, into global debates on sustainable development. Policy development, design, and implementation should incorporate the needs and realities of small companies rather than cater only to the large companies with government relations departments and ESG teams that can influence national, state, and local governmental policies. In addition, national, regional, and global industry associations should include seats on their boards for small businesses to ensure that the needs, voices, and concerns of SMEs are woven into policy agendas focused on ESG, sustainability, and development issues.

When, for example, governments, and companies set ambitious standards for supply chains and distribution channels to meet ESG and sustainability requirements, *they must not create new hurdles and barriers that prevent SMEs from meeting these standards* and hence from participating in key value chains and markets. This is especially relevant in countries and regions that have stipulated ambitious new guidelines for business operations. Examples include Germany through the German Act on Due Diligence in Supply Chains and the EU through the Corporate Sustainability Due Diligence Directive.[51] As these and other standards and mandatory reporting requirements are introduced and become the norm, an array of

---

51. On the German Act on Due Diligence in Supply Chains, see Burghardt-Kaufmann et al. (2023); on the Corporate Sustainability Due Diligence Directive, see the European Commission's web page "Corporate Sustainability Due Diligence" (https://commission.europa.eu/business-economy-euro/doing-business-eu/sustainability-due-diligence-responsible-business/corporate-sustainability-due-diligence_en).

funding, innovation, data, and capacity-building interventions must be implemented to ease the transition for small businesses so that their inability to comply does not further exclude them from supply chains. It is also imperative that the same standards not be rigidly applied to all SMEs operating in different parts of the world. Many SMEs might find it harder to comply because of their diverse business environments, cultural norms, and pace of change. SMEs operating in emerging economies often need longer lead times for the sustainability transition.

Ultimately, all stakeholders must commit to *replicating and scaling up what works*, not simply boosting their organization's work. This demands the active sharing of best practice examples of interventions and initiatives that are working at scale and rallying together to support the further replication or scaling up of those initiatives. Research has shown, for example, that investing in women-led and diverse businesses and organizations can generate important results.[52] However, raising funds and support for interventions in this area has proved difficult, and this must change. All stakeholders must also be honest about projects and programs that are not working and be willing to learn from and even end them. Understanding what types of interventions, business linkages, and collective action can support SMEs in building resilience, equitably scaling up their operations, and embracing climate actions will help create decent jobs and more efficient supply chains. SMEs can then not only survive and thrive as businesses but also become more effective instruments through which to accelerate progress toward achievement of the SDGs.

REFERENCES

AGRA (Alliance for a Green Revolution in Africa). 2019. *Africa Agriculture Status Report 7: The Hidden Middle: A Quiet Revolution in the Private Sector Driving Agricultural Transformation*. Nairobi.

Al-Saleh, H. 2023. "Why Big Business Must Support SMEs for Growth and Net Zero." World Economic Forum, January 6.

Ashcroft, S. 2023. "Scope 3: Big Business 'Must Help SMEs Decarbonize.'" Supply Chain Digital, May 3.

---

52. See, e.g., Baselga-Pascual and Vähämaa (2021), Revenga and Shetty (2012), Turban et al. (2019), and Weaver and Heinzel (2024).

Bambridge-Sutton, A. 2023. "How Do We Measure the Success of Regenerative Agriculture?" Food Navigator Europe, December 19.

Baselga-Pascual, L., and E. Vähämaa. 2021. "Female Leadership and Bank Performance in Latin America." *Emerging Markets Review* 48 (September): 100807.

Burghardt-Kaufmann, A., C. Connellan, S. Kueper, et al. 2023. "Due Diligence in Supply Chains: Update on Corporate Human Rights and Environmental Due Diligence Requirements in the EU and Germany." White & Case, January 11.

Business and Sustainable Development Commission. 2017. *Better Business Better World: The Report of the Business & Sustainable Development Commission.* London.

CODARAN (Commercial Dairy Ranchers Association of Nigeria). 2020. "Sahel and CODARAN Hold Virtual Dairy Conference on Catalyzing Local Dairy Development in Nigeria." Press release, November 20.

Gartner. 2022. *Supply Chain's Focus on DEI Grows in 2022.* Stamford, CT: Gartner.

Gender Smart. 2021. *A Guide to Investing in First-Time Women and Diverse Fund Managers.* Samata Capital, January.

Ghosh, I. 2021. "34% of America's Small Businesses Are Still Closed Due to COVID-19. Here's Why It Matters." World Economic Forum and Visual Capitalist, May 5.

Global Goals. n.d. "Goal 8: Decent Work and Economic Growth." London: Project Everyone and the Global Goals Campaign.

Goldman Sachs. [2024a]. "10,000 Women." Goldman Sachs | 10,000 Women | An Initiative to Provide Business & Management Education to Female Entrepreneurs in Emerging Markets.

———. [2024b]. "One Million Black Women: Black in Business." Goldman Sachs | Goldman Sachs | Black in Business.

IFC (International Finance Corporation). [2024]. "Inclusive Business." Washington, DC: World Bank Group.

IKEA Global. [2024]. "IWAY: The IKEA Supplier Code of Conduct."

ILO (International Labour Organization). 2023. *Transformative Change and SDG 8: The Critical Tole of Collective Capabilities and Societal Learning.* Geneva.

———. 2019. *The Power of Small: Unlocking the Potential of SMEs.* Geneva.

Jouven, P., and A. Schmidt. 2022. "Survey: Small Businesses Face Recurring Barriers to Carbon Reduction." SME Climate Hub, February 23.

Liu, C. K. 2018. "Policy Brief: The Role of Micro-, Small and Medium-Sized Enterprises (MSMEs) in Achieving the Sustainable Development Goals (SDGs)." New York: United Nations, Department of Economic and Social Affairs.

Masterson, V. 2024. "Women Founders and Venture Capital: Some 2023 Snapshots." Geneva: World Economic Forum, March 28.

Nelson, J. 2010. *Expanding Opportunity and Access: Approaches That Harness Markets and the Private Sector to Create Business Value and Development Impact*. Cambridge, MA: Harvard Kennedy School.

———. 2006. *Building Linkages for Competitive and Responsible Entrepreneurship: Innovative Partnerships to Foster Small Enterprise, Promote Economic Growth and Reduce Poverty in Developing Countries*. Vienna: United Nations Industrial Development Organization (UNIDO); Cambridge, MA: Harvard Kennedy School.

Nsomba, G., N. Tshabalala, T. Vilakazi, et al. 2021. *Analysis of the Impact of COVID-19 on Micro, Small and Medium-Sized Enterprises in South Africa*. Geneva: UN DESA Development Account Project, coordinated by UNCTAD.

OECD (Organization for Economic Cooperation and Development). 2021. "No Net Zero without SMEs: Exploring the Key Issues for Greening SMEs and Green Entrepreneurship." *OECD SME and Entrepreneurship Papers* no. 30, 6. Paris: OECD Publishing.

Revenga, A., and S. Shetty. 2012. "Empowering Women Is Smart Economics." *Finance & Development* 49 (1): 40–43.

Sahel Consulting. [2024]. "Advancing Local Dairy Development in Nigeria."

Seppo, M. 2023. "Time to Act for SDG 8: What Will It Take to Ensure Decent Work for All?" Geneva: International Labour Organization, August 3.

Sidley Austin LLP. 2023. "U.S. Supreme Court Ends Affirmative Action in Higher Education: An Overview and Practical Next Steps for Employers." Washington, DC, August 2.

SME Climate Hub. 2022. "New Data Reveals Two-Thirds of Surveyed Small Businesses Concerned over Navigating Climate Action." Press release, February, 23.

Swette, K., and T. Boyo. 2021. "How Procurement Can Strengthen Diversity and Inclusion." MIT *Sloan Management Review*, May 20.

Turban, S., D. Wu, and L. Zhang. 2019. "When Gender Diversity Makes Firms More Productive." *Harvard Business Review (online)*, February 11.

UN DESA (United Nations Department of Economic and Social Affairs). 2022. *Best Practices: Formalization of Micro-, Small and Medium-Sized Enterprises (MSMEs) in Africa*. New York: United Nations, Department of Economic and Social Affairs.

United Nations Global Compact. 2023. *SME Engagement Strategy 2021–2023*. New York: UN.

Walmart Sustainability Hub. [2024]. "Project Gigatron."

Weaver, C., and M. Heinzel, "Why Women's Representation Matters: Evidence from Gender Mainstreaming in the World Bank." Blog post, Center for Global Development, August 15.

World Bank Group. 2023. "The World Bank in Africa: Overview." Washington, DC.

———. 2019. *Small and Medium Enterprises (SMEs) Finance*. Washington, DC.

WEF (World Economic Forum). 2021. *Future Readiness of SMEs: Mobilizing the SME Sector to Drive Widespread Sustainability and Prosperity*. Geneva.

FOUR

Key Actions for Corporate Boards in Accelerating Sustainable Development

EMILY FARNWORTH AND ELDRID HERRINGTON

Corporate boards have an essential role to play in ensuring that business executives are strategic and accountable in the way they manage their company's sustainability performance and engagement with stakeholders. The effectiveness of independent or non-executive directors, who do not run day-to-day operations or have a material financial stake in the company, is particularly important.

This chapter outlines some of the key trends driving the evolution of corporate governance that are relevant to the role of boards in governing sustainable development in the context of their own company's business operations and broader value chain. It introduces a framework for board action and recommends ways in which board directors and policymakers can help accelerate the integration of climate and other sustainability risks and opportunities into boardroom mandates and structures.

The Evolution of Corporate Sustainability Governance

The norms, rules, and regulations that determine corporate governance practices have evolved over recent decades while retaining the core concept of fiduciary duty. In the context of sustainable development, the legal interpretation and scope of fiduciary duty are evolving. This change is taking place largely in response to two systemic shifts that are underway. The first is a renewed focus on corporations' and directors' responsibilities to stakeholders, including but not limited to shareholders. The second major shift is the growing relevance of environmental, social, and governance (ESG) principles and technology-related risks and opportunities for companies in almost all industry sectors.

Variations in company ownership structure, sector, and size all affect how a board might understand stakeholders' interests and sustainability issues alongside financial returns. Good governance is key to the delivery of value creation irrespective of difference in ownership structure, that is, whether the company is a family-run firm, a small to medium-size enterprise (SME), a state-owned enterprise (SOE), or a large, publicly listed multinational corporate entity. In many regions of the world, such as Asia and South America, family firms or SMEs dominate economic activity. In others, SOEs dominate. Understanding the levers that most effectively drive changes in corporate behavior is critical, but some principles and themes are common and relevant for all boards.

The Reemergence of Stakeholder Governance

In 1973 the World Economic Forum published the Davos Manifesto, which held that "the purpose of professional management is to serve clients, shareholders, workers and employees, as well as societies, and to harmonize the different interests of the stakeholders."[1] Drawing on research by the forum's founder, Klaus Schwab, this was one of the early efforts explicitly to outline a model of stakeholder governance. In recent decades the focus of corporate boards in many jurisdictions has primarily been on meeting shareholder interests. This shareholder-primacy orientation was influenced by seminal work in the 1970s by academics such as Milton Friedman and Michael Jensen.[2] However, in many jurisdictions it is

---

1. Schwab (2019).
2. *HBR* (2022).

common practice rather than the letter of the law that has created a sense that shareholders are the only stakeholders that need to be considered by boards.

As a better understanding of the impact businesses have on society and the environment has evolved, the voices of other stakeholders have become increasingly important. These various stakeholders range from employees and customers to host communities, governments, and civil society organizations. In a growing number of cases, major institutional investors and shareholders themselves are calling for measurable and credible evidence of business risk management and value creation beyond purely financial performance and metrics.

More recent definitions and emerging good practice of corporate governance emphasize the importance of stakeholders in shaping and driving risk and value within companies. The role of stakeholders, both internal and external, is pivotal in determining how resources are used, conflicts are resolved, and, ultimately, how risk is managed and value is created and shared across the organization.

Hanson and others present an encompassing definition, understanding corporate governance as "the set of mechanisms used to manage the relationship among stakeholders and to determine and control the strategic direction and performance of organizations."[3] This perspective shifts the emphasis from just internal alignments to the broader dynamics of stakeholder relationships.

In addition to an increased focus on stakeholders, including but not limited to shareholders, there is also a growing emphasis on boards being more accountable for overseeing strategy and long-term value creation, not just short-term performance. Currently, most jurisdictions have some requirement for boards to consider the long-term value of their company's business activities.[4]

Growing Environmental and Social Awareness and the SDGs

Although company law and guidance on good corporate governance have not always been a barrier to boardroom discussions of the business impact—and opportunity—of considering environmental and social

---

3. Hanson et al. (2017), 292.
4. Mulholland and Farnworth (2022).

factors as part of business strategy, failure to assign financial value to these factors has often kept ESG discussions out of the boardroom.

The 1987 publication of *Our Common Future*, also known as the Brundtland Report, by the World Commission on Environment and Development, first introduced the concept of sustainable development.[5] The next milestone was the United Nations Conference on Environment and Development, also known as the Earth Summit, held in Rio de Janeiro in 1992, which focused on the interdependence of social, economic, and environmental factors and encouraged international cooperation in this sphere.[6] At the same time, major companies were increasing efforts to promote sustainable development, both individually and through organizations such as the International Chamber of Commerce, the World Business Council for Sustainable Development, and the UN Global Compact. By 2015, a core group of business leaders were playing a proactive role in the development of the Sustainable Development Goals (SDGs), and many leading companies had started to report publicly on their performance on sustainability measures and to make commitments to address social and environmental issues. In many cases, however, these matters did not become a priority in corporate boardrooms until they started to create financially material business risks and opportunities.

What Does Sustainable Development Mean for Corporate Governance?

Corporate boards need to understand the growing environmental and social risks and opportunities that have an impact on their financial success. The SDGs provide a useful framing for companies to use and adapt within their evolving corporate governance structures and management systems to support the delivery of the goals.

Linking Environmental and Social Issues to Financial Impact

Today, there is a plethora of frameworks designed to help businesses make sense of what the SDGs mean for them from an operational

---

5. WCED (1987).
6. For more on UNCED, see the website at https://www.un.org/en/conferences/environment/rio1992.

perspective.⁷ Despite these developments, until recently the identification and management of environmental and social issues remained, on the whole, a management concern without significant integration into boardroom discussions in relation to corporate governance and business growth and development.

A major catalyst for change was the growing corporate awareness of the economic, financial, operational, and strategic risks of climate change. In 2006, the publication of Lord Nicholas Stern's report, *The Economics of Climate Change*, shone a light on what he called the "greatest market failure the world has ever seen." He was referring to the lack of action being taken to address climate change given that, based on his analysis, "the benefits of strong and early action far outweigh the economic costs of not acting."⁸

Organizations such as the Boston-based advocacy organization Ceres and the UN, which offered Principles for Responsible Investment (PRI), along with some institutes of directors, started to develop guidelines for corporate boards and directors to address risks to business associated with climate change and other environmental alterations.⁹ The dial shifted significantly again in September 2015 when Mark Carney, then governor of the Bank of England, made his "Tragedy of the Horizon" speech in which he told his audience, "The challenges currently posed by climate change pale in significance compared with what might come."¹⁰ The Financial Stability Board (FSB) put Mark Carney in charge of the newly created Task Force on Climate-Related Financial Disclosures (TCFD) that same year, to develop recommendations on the information that businesses and their boards needed to share with investors related to the level of risk that climate change posed to their financial performance.

With the Paris Agreement on climate change having been adopted by 196 countries at the UN's Climate Change Conference (COP21) in 2015, and with increasingly clear signals of the potential financial devastation to the global economy from the effects of climate change, publication of the final recommendations of the TCFD in June 2017 provided a significant step forward for board engagement on climate action.¹¹ The release of the final recommendations of the Taskforce on Nature-Related Financial

7. Demastus and Landrum (2023).
8. Stern (2006), viii.
9. See Ceres (2022) and UN (2022).
10. Carney (2015).
11. TCFD (2017).

Disclosures (TNFD) in September 2023 added a further layer of guidance on how boards and businesses can better understand their impact on nature and biodiversity and, correspondingly, the impact that the declining health of nature and biodiversity can have on business.[12] In advance of COP29, scheduled for November 2024, 320 companies have announced their intent to implement the recommendations of the TNFD.[13] This figure complements the more than 3,800 companies that are now reporting under TCFD, all requiring board-level oversight and accountability.[14]

Strengthening Stakeholder Engagement

A broad range of external stakeholders is taking an interest in and forming a view of business practices that do not take into account environmental and social impacts. Awareness of the impact human activity is having on the environment and, as a result, on people's health and livelihoods has led to substantially increased efforts on the part of nonprofit organizations (NPOs) to influence business activities, ranging from activists' campaigns or lawsuits against companies to engaging directly with businesses to improve awareness and capacity.[15] These NPOs and activists are increasingly calling for board oversight of business impacts and requesting engagement with board directors.

Alongside the need to engage with a broader set of stakeholders, boards also need to recognize and respond to the changing perspectives and expectations of existing and potential stakeholders. Notably, major institutional investors and shareholders are increasingly focused on managing ESG-related risks to their portfolios and ensuring their money is being applied to generating profits that align with long-term value creation.[16] Likewise, regulators are starting to implement mandatory corporate disclosure requirements on ESG issues, requiring increased board oversight.

Responding to Increasing Complexity

Against the backdrop of increased scientific understanding, shifting policies, and expanded stakeholder expectations, the role of board directors, especially independent or non-executive directors, has become more

---

12. TNFD (2023).
13. TNFD (2024).
14. FSB (2022).
15. Partelow, Winkler, and Thaler (2020); Willetts (2018), 72.
16. Samans and Nelson (2022b).

complex, sophisticated, and multidisciplinary. Changing environmental and social realities—well documented by the Stockholm Resilience Centre's work on planetary boundaries, and which map onto the SDG agenda—have become important considerations for board discussions.[17] This is happening alongside, and increasingly influencing, discussions of more traditional boardroom topics such as competition and market dynamics, corporate strategy, and enterprise risk management.[18] Understanding what this means for short-term performance, let alone the long-term future of a business, is complicated. Not all the answers are available, and therefore the judgment of board directors is increasingly important.

Corporate boards are increasingly aware of climate change and its potential impact on their business, but quantification of the impact is challenging, and in some cases data are completely lacking. Inevitably, the current approach treats climate change, and the environment more generally, in the same way as other business inputs that need quantification before suitable governance and management solutions can be designed. There is merit to this approach, and eventually metrics, measurement systems, accounting rules, and verification processes will be necessary to develop a robust approach to managing these issues, just as businesses use metrics and processes today to make financial and commercial decisions. However, the complexity of these nonfinancial issues, the speed with which the natural world is changing, and the interrelated consequences of that change create a challenge for board members, who may need to make strategic decisions in the absence of hard data. Making such decisions requires skills, experience, and habits of mind different from those of many traditional non-executive directors, who are used to making decisions based on hard facts and a more linear understanding of long-term strategy and business propositions. It requires an understanding of environmental, social, and technological trends as well as economic, financial, and political trends, potential scenarios, systems dynamics, and the often complex emerging solutions. In some cases it involves bold but considered risk-taking wherein a "fail fast" mentality can support innovation.

Taking a Long-Term View

Effective governance for sustainable development requires boards and management to take a long-term view. As Paul Polman has commented,

---

17. See, e.g., Richardson et al. (2023).
18. Ibid.

"Increasingly, companies are starting to understand that you need to be restorative, reparative, regenerative. And this is really what net positive leaders do. Net positive leaders take responsibility for their total impact on the world, lead with transparency, and focus on the long term."[19]

Board directors can be important stewards of this focus on the long term. In most corporations, non-executive directors have a longer-term tenure than CEOs and executive directors and therefore can afford to adopt a longer-term perspective. This is valuable in the context of decision-making with sustainability in mind. For example, the average tenure of an executive director in a UK FTSE 100 company is a little over four years, and approximately the same is true for executive directors of the U.S. S&P 500, where average tenure decreased from six to 4.8 years between 2013 and 2022.[20] By contrast, non-executive directors often serve for ten years or more.[21] In some jurisdictions, such as the UK and Australia, they are no longer considered to be independent after this period.[22]

The focus on long-term value creation is at the heart of the role of boards. This has always been the case, but becoming sustainable in its fullest sense can sometimes challenge short-term profit making, causing a clash with decisions to deliver long-term value. This conundrum is testing the mettle of boards and driving a need for a stewardship approach to corporate governance. This situation requires the board to think through a full range of increasingly complex and long-term risks and opportunities and, despite the attendant uncertainties, to choose the option most likely to deliver return on investment and value to all stakeholders in the long term while still meeting the short-term performance expectations of investors and other stakeholders.

The current moment in time may be one of the most difficult as we are in the midst of a disruptive transition that will produce winners and losers, especially in the energy and digital sectors. The potential losers often cling to business-as-usual profit-generating models and unfortunately, in some cases also try to influence political and policy agendas in their favor. More focus on the economic and scientific facts and a better understanding of the technological solutions that are viable and affordable today are critical to enable better decision-making in the boardroom. The question is

19. Polman (2023).
20. Chen (2023).
21. Barker (2023).
22. Ibid.

whether current non-executive directors are equipped for such a dramatic combination of complexity and transition, which challenges many incumbent business models that have worked for decades and creates a need for visionary leadership to prioritize long-term value creation.

Family-owned businesses may have some advantage in this respect because their boards typically think in terms of several generations. The intergenerational issues associated with climate change in particular are creating different approaches to risk-taking in the business decision-making of younger family shareholders because they anticipate bearing the brunt of climate change effects.[23]

Some multinational corporations are also thinking more explicitly about future generations and corporate purpose, particularly in the consumer products sector. However, stricter greenwashing regulations are creating increased litigation and reputational risks, where even the sustainability champions face risks if they rely too heavily on style over substance in their marketing tactics.

Evolving Good Governance Practices for Sustainability

In 2019, as a result of board-level discussions on how to implement the governance requirements of the TCFD, the World Economic Forum published a report titled *How to Set Up Effective Climate Governance on Corporate Boards*.[24] The report included a set of eight guiding principles and supporting questions that boards may want to address to strengthen their climate governance capabilities. Although directed toward climate governance, these principles are relevant for effective sustainability governance more broadly. The guiding principles are summarized in box 4.1.

The principles provide non-executive directors with a framework for their board discussions on climate and have spurred the development of peer groups around the world, which are part of an international network, the Climate Governance Initiative.[25] As of April 2024 the initiative had thirty-one chapters working in more than seventy countries and reaching

---

23. Bauweraerts, Arzubiaga, and Diaz-Moriana (2022); Sharma and Sharma (2021).
24. WEF (2019).
25. See the Climate Governance Initiative's web page, "What If Every Company Had a Climate Target and a Plan to Meet It?," at https://climate-governance.org/.

Box 4.1. Principles for Effective Climate Governance on Corporate Boards

In 2019, a joint team of the World Economic Forum and the audit and consulting firm PwC published a report, *How to Set Up Effective Climate Governance on Corporate Boards*. The report included the following eight guiding principles, which continue to be relevant for board-level conversations and decision-making on climate-related issues:

1. **Climate accountability:** Boards should be accountable for a company's long-term resilience regarding potential changes in the business landscape as a result of climate change.

2. **Command of the subject:** Boards should have a relevant mix of knowledge, skills, and experience to make decisions based on a strong understanding of climate-related threats and opportunities.

3. **Board structure:** Boards should determine the most effective way to integrate response to climate issues into their structures and committees.

4. **Material risk and opportunity assessment:** Boards should ensure management assesses the short-, medium-, and long-term materiality of climate-related risks and opportunities and that actions and responses are proportionate to the level of materiality.

5. **Strategic and organizational integration:** Boards should ensure climate issues systematically inform strategic investment planning and decision-making processes and are embedded in an organization's management of risk and opportunities.

6. **Incentivization:** Boards may want to consider including climate-related targets and indicators in their incentive schemes for both company executives and non-executive directors.

7. **Reporting and disclosure:** Boards should ensure the consistent and transparent disclosure of material climate-related risks, opportunities, and strategic decisions to investors and, where necessary, regulators, with the same disclosure governance as financial reporting.

8. **Exchange:** Boards should ensure regular dialogues with peers, policymakers, investors, and other stakeholders to stay informed on climate-relevant methodologies, risks, and regulatory requirements.

Source: WEF (2019).

some 100,000 members. Based at Hughes Hall, the University of Cambridge, the initiative supports ongoing capacity building and information sharing across the network to enable continuous learning and implementation of good practices. There are some interesting observations and examples of good practice emerging, as well as areas that will require boards to become more sophisticated and efficient in determining the role of independent board chairs and non-executive directors separately from the role of executive management teams. The current blurring of responsibilities is in some cases causing boards to get distracted by the details, particularly around sustainability disclosure requirements, and to allot insufficient time to strategy.

The following section outlines some of the most relevant principles and lessons for effective sustainability governance that are emerging across different jurisdictions and industries.

Focus on Material Sustainability Risks and Opportunities

A critical area of focus for any board is to understand, as far as possible, the material sustainability risks the business is facing as a result of its current business model and operations and the operations of its broader value chain. The business risks associated with climate change, biodiversity loss, social inequality, and other sustainability issues are often the top motivator for companies to take action on the SDGs. Mitigation of risk, from physical impacts to reputational damage, is a powerful driver. Adherence to evolving industry norms and standards, capturing market share, and establishing good will are additional motivators for boards to engage on these topics.[26]

Investors are going through the same process of understanding the material financial risks to their investments caused by a changing environmental and social landscape.[27] This effort at understanding is driving increased requests for data, disclosure, and transparency from companies and greater investor engagement with corporate boards on sustainability topics.

Sustainability issues need to be assessed to understand their materiality in terms of both the business's impact on the environment and society and

---

26. Chakravorti (2015).
27. Betti, Consolandi, and Eccles (2018).

the financial impact of environmental and social issues on the business.[28] The concept of "double materiality" has evolved from the TCFD and emerging EU requirements for disclosure. Double materiality requires companies to consider not only the impact that environmental and social issues have on the business (single materiality) but also the impacts that the company has on society and the environment.

The 2023 final recommendations of the TNFD also refer to double materiality, a key concept the board must understand to determine what actions need to be taken to mitigate risk. This double materiality approach is likely to be applied to climate and other sustainability issues in the future.

Assessing risk is critical, and successful businesses complete this task well, including by developing enterprise risk management systems, policies and processes to identify and mitigate risk. However, this is only the starting point when it comes to governing effectively for sustainable development. Risk assessment alone is not enough. Boards also need to consider the potential business opportunities created by the company addressing systemic environmental and social issues and trends or by the company mitigating risks more radically than current regulation requires or their competitors are doing. Viewing risks through an opportunity lens can enable more creative thinking about future technologies, products, services, and business models and can motivate board members who have a longer-term vision.[29]

Asking the management team questions not only about the short-term financial risks and opportunities but also about the long-term ones, based on trends in policy and public attitudes, can provide more visibility for the changes a business may need or decide to make in the short term. Awareness of such risks and opportunities can also spur innovation. As one academic has concluded, "Innovating for sustainable development is actually quite close to the processes of 'traditional' innovation."[30] Innovation and "intrapreneurship"—fostering innovation within the company, for example by sponsoring, recognizing, and incentivizing innovative approaches to achieving sustainability goals—can be an effective way for the business to transform a problem into an opportunity. This way of thinking needs to be driven from the top to succeed and to ensure a change in corporate culture, and this is an area where boards can play a more influential role.[31]

28. Khan, Serafeim, and Yoon (2015).
29. Van Tulder and van Mil (2022).
30. Chakravorti (2015).
31. Nelson, Jenkins, and Gilbert (2015).

Align Corporate Purpose and Strategy with Sustainability Goals

Even good processes that assess the sustainability risks and opportunities associated with a business can quickly become a management tool rather than a governance or strategy tool. The board needs information and tools to help directors expand curiosity, ask probing questions, and encourage discussions that support broader corporate purpose and strategy creation. Some of this information will come from management and employees. At the same time, as Bob Eccles comments, "Senior management and the board need to engage with shareholders and other stakeholders on the company's statement of purpose and its commitments to the SDGs. Through engagement, the company will learn whether it is meeting the expectations of those on whom its own long-term sustainability depends."[32]

A recent survey found that many board directors feel they are not spending enough time in meetings discussing strategy, both generally and with respect to sustainability.[33] One reason for this lacuna is the overwhelming amount of information on sustainability issues that results from risk assessment, disclosure, and reporting requirements.

Yet a core role of boards is to shape purpose and strategy, and to take a stewardship approach rather than becoming tied too closely to current management systems, norms, and ways of thinking. Boards should articulate the purpose and vision for the company and hold management and themselves accountable for delivery on that purpose and vision. Framing strategy in terms of the SDGs ensures reference to global norms and can also provide an opportunity to map out and identify business value propositions in terms of universal values. And focusing on corporate purpose and strategy requires that boards take a longer-term perspective.

The financial benefits of taking a long-term view on value creation are starting to emerge. Ariel Fromer Babcock's research indicates that "long-term companies outperform on financial metrics, including revenues, profitability, and stock price. They also fare better on several nonfinancial metrics, including job creation. As a recent study of large public companies in the United States found, from 2001 to 2014 long-term companies cumulatively grew their revenues 47 percent more on average than their shorter-term peers, with less volatility. During the same period, these long-term companies similarly outperformed on measures of economic

---

32. Eccles (2019).
33. BCG, INSEAD, and Heidrick & Struggles (2023).

profit, cumulatively besting peers by 80 percent, with earnings growth that was also 35 percent higher. Companies seeking the performance advantages that come from long-term thinking should have a ready partner in their corporate board."[34]

Director liabilities associated with not taking long-term risks into consideration have also begun emerging. As the World Economic Forum points out, boards are "ultimately accountable to shareholders for the long-term stewardship of the company. Accordingly, the board should be accountable for the company's long-term resilience with respect to potential shifts in the business landscape that may result from climate change. Failure to do so may constitute a breach of directors' duties."[35]

Ensure Effective Oversight and Accountability for Sustainability Performance

Developing a clear purpose and strategy based on sound analysis of sustainability risks and opportunities in the short, medium, and long term will be effective only if the strategy is implemented with clear targets, metrics, incentives, and accountabilities for delivery—and consequences for not delivering. This calls for creating appropriate structures for oversight and accountability for the board itself and between the board and management internally, and for strengthening external board and director accountability mechanisms.

At the level of the board itself, one notable development has been the establishment of sustainability committees operating alongside the more traditional audit, compensation and nominations, and governance committees. There are pros and cons to delegating sustainability oversight to a board committee. While a committee can ensure more detailed coverage of a wide range of sustainability topics than is possible with the limited time of the full board, there is the risk of key topics being siloed or sidelined from corporate strategy, planning, and capital allocation decisions. Many boards are adopting a hybrid model whereby the most material environmental and social risks and opportunities are addressed by the full board, with the

---

34. Babcock (2019).
35. WEF and PwC (2019).

broader range of issues and oversight and reporting requirements being addressed at the committee level.[36]

Boards are increasingly holding management teams to account for setting sustainability-related goals and targets and the company's performance on achieving these targets. To this end, boards are using such mechanisms as incorporating sustainability results into the regular reporting of financial and operational results to the board, the explicit integration of sustainability goals into business planning, strategy, and capital allocation discussions, and including progress on sustainability goals in executive compensation formulas and succession planning.

In terms of external board accountability for sustainability performance, mandatory disclosure requirements and changes in corporate law are moving in this direction. Collective and personal accountability are critical, and directors' liability is currently being tested under company law in many jurisdictions, as the work of the Columbia Law School's Sabin Center for Climate Change Law, the London School of Economics and Politics, and other institutions is showing.[37] The question is whether more needs to be done to require boards or named directors to be held legally accountable for climate or broader sustainability impacts. The lack of progress in delivering reduced emissions, for example, despite well-used monitoring, reporting, and target-setting standards, makes it clear that something needs to change.

Recommendations and Conclusion

Scientific research and evidence are providing increasingly clear information about what is happening to the environment and society. Yet the lack of broad economic and political agreement on the business and societal costs of environmental degradation and societal inequality is a key reason for the lack of progress toward achieving global goals, despite the existential risk to humanity if some of them are not reached.[38]

---

36. Samans and Nelson (2022a).
37. The Sabin Center's Global Climate Change Litigation database is available at https://climatecasechart.com/non-us-climate-change-litigation. The London School of Economics and Politics' database, compiled by the Grantham Research Institute on Climate Change and the Environment, is available at https://www.lse.ac.uk/granthaminstitute/legislation/.
38. Steffen et al. (2014); Richardson et al. (2023).

There is no doubt that awareness of sustainability risks and opportunities is increasing in many corporate boardrooms. The challenge for boards, and in particular chairs and non-executive directors, is to ensure that their oversight and decision-making keep up with the rapidly changing landscape. Institutional investors are also recognizing the impact of sustainability on their own fiduciary duties, and their governance is evolving in a similar way to companies' in the "real economy."[39] The need for increased board engagement with investors has never been more important, as is director engagement with a wider range of stakeholders.

The following three recommendations outline actions that corporate boards can take, both individually and collectively, to enhance their role of stewardship beyond compliance, and to engage in the next generation of SDGs, after 2030.

1. Strengthen Board-Level Sustainability Competence and Governance Structures

Almost all boards can benefit from increasing the level and diversity of their sustainability-related skills, experiences, and capabilities. Some of this improvement will emerge naturally as a younger generation of corporate executives takes on board roles, having led companies and business units over the past few decades of growing awareness and integration of sustainability risks and opportunities into core business activities. More boards are also appointing directors with subject matter expertise in the sustainability issues that are most material to their company or industry sector. At the same time, the drive for climate and sustainability competence on boards is producing a formal requirement for experience in such matters at a national and international level, through changes in stock exchange listing requirements, Institute of Directors (UK) certification programs, and company law. In Southeast Asia, for example, the Singapore Stock Exchange Group now requires that all board directors adhere to enhanced SGX sustainability reporting rules by undertaking an approved course.[40]

Through networks such as the Climate Governance Initiative, Ceres, and associations of directors, boards can access and contribute to the growing body of research, insights, and examples of how different governance

---

39. UN (2021).
40. The Singapore Stock Exchange's Capacity Building and Training program is available at https://www.sgx.com/sustainable-finance/capacity-building-training.

structures and models of stakeholder engagement are influencing sustainability governance. Regular board evaluations and reviews can also play a role in making progress. These evaluations can be done internally or through an independent party, such as a professional board search and advisory firm, law firm, or academic institution.

2. Support Regulations and Accounting and Incentive Mechanisms That Enhance Sustainability Governance

Boards, associations of directors, and other corporate governance networks can play a leadership role in supporting the development of regulations and accounting, disclosure, and incentive mechanisms that enhance rather than undermine sustainability governance. In some cases, these mechanisms may involve mandatory board oversight and reporting, such as the evolving disclosure requirements in the United States, Europe, Australia, and other countries, which are covered elsewhere in this volume. In other cases they may be in the form of policies that apply financial incentives for progress or disincentives for behaviors that undermine sustainability governance.

Associations of directors and their equivalent bodies and networks can support efforts to increase the evidence base for smart climate and sustainability policies and regulations. Working in partnership with institutional investor networks has the potential to be even more effective in advancing this agenda. One example is the Inevitable Policy Response (IPR) consortium and platform hosted by the Principles for Responsible Investment in partnership with others. The PRI describes the initiative as "a climate transition forecasting consortium commissioned by the PRI which aims to prepare institutional investors for the portfolio risks and opportunities associated with an acceleration of policy responses to climate change."[41] Such a platform is valuable also for board directors and corporate governance networks.

Helping to fund initiatives that either track evolving policies and incentives, or research the effectiveness of such policies and incentives, or advocate for their implementation is an area where boards and executive leadership teams can be more proactive. Examples range from networks

---

41. See the web page for the Inevitable Policy Response at https://www.unpri.org/sustainability-issues/climate-change/inevitable-policy-response (accessed April 28, 2024).

such as Ceres and the We Mean Business Coalition to initiatives such as the Carbon Pricing Leadership Coalition and show a growing number of academia-based sustainability policy research programs.[42]

3. Engage in Large-Scale Collaboration and Platforms That Support It

Linked to recommendation 2 is that the scale of change needed to achieve the SDGs requires the most influential companies to participate in large-scale collaboration to overcome system-level market failures and governance gaps. Boards of directors have a role to play in providing both support and oversight for the collaborative initiatives that their management teams consider to be the most likely to achieve effective outcomes and change. Some of these initiatives focus on addressing a particular set of sustainability challenges; examples here are the Forest and Climate Leaders Partnership and the Partnership for Global Infrastructure and Investment. Others bring together a critical mass of companies in a specific industry sector that is crucial to achieving progress, such as transport, energy, mining, agriculture, and the built environment.

Board engagement in this area may include helping management address the emerging challenge of anticompetition or antitrust regulation being aimed at pre-competitive industry coalitions that focus on addressing climate and other sustainability issues.[43]

Boards can also be more proactive in questioning management personnel on their participation in trade and industry associations or research programs that may be undermining or at odds with the company's publicly stated sustainability goals. A vanguard of boards and the companies they govern is now reporting publicly on affiliations with such business groups.

All of these areas ultimately come down to actualizing SDG 17—"Strengthen the means of implementation and revitalize the Global Partnership for Sustainable Development."

In conclusion, corporate boards of directors can play a vital role in strengthening the sustainability capabilities and governance of their own companies while also contributing to the broader enabling environment

---

42. See also Eccles and Mulliken (2021).
43. Gasparini et al. (2022).

of policies, regulations, and collaborative platforms that are needed to make good sustainability governance mainstream. It will also be essential for policymakers and regulators to respond to create the rules and frameworks necessary to provide clarity and consistency to ensure all businesses play their role.

REFERENCES

Babcock, A. F. 2019. "The Long-Term Habits of a Highly Effective Corporate Board." Harvard Law School Forum on Corporate Governance, April 19.

Barker, R. 2023 "Governance Explainer—Board Tenure." Institute of Directors, June 2.

Bauweraerts, J., U. Arzubiaga, and V. Diaz-Moriana. 2022. "Going Greener, Performing Better? The Case of Private Family Firms." *Research in International Business and Finance* 63 (101784).

BCG, INSEAD, and Heidrick & Struggles. 2023. *The Role of the Board in the Sustainability Era.*

Betti, G., C. Consolandi, and R. G. Eccles. 2018. "The Relationship between Investor Materiality and the Sustainable Development Goals: A Methodological Framework." *Sustainability* 10 (7).

Carney, M. 2015. "Breaking the Tragedy of the Horizon—Climate Change and Financial Stability." Speech, Lloyd's of London, September 29.

Ceres. 2022. *Guidance for Engaging on Climate Risk Governance and Voting on Directors.* Boston.

Chakravorti, B. 2015. "What Businesses Need to Know about the Sustainable Development Goals." *Harvard Business Review*, November 20.

Chen, J. 2023. "CEO Tenure Rates." Harvard Law School Forum on Corporate Governance, August 4.

Demastus, J., and N. E. Landrum. 2023. "Organizational Sustainability Schemes Align with Weak Sustainability." *Business Strategy and the Environment* 33 (2): 1–19.

Eccles, R. 2019. "A New Business Case." In *Sustainable Development Goals 2019*, 55–57. https://www.sustainablegoals.org.uk/.

Eccles, R., and J. Mulliken. 2021. "Carbon Pricing Might Be Your Company's Biggest Financial Liability." *Harvard Business Review*, October 7.

FSB (Financial Stability Board). 2022. "2022 TCFD Status Report: Task Force on Climate-Related Financial Disclosures." Press release, October 13.

Gasparini, M., et al. 2022. "When Climate Collaboration Is Treated as an Antitrust Violation." *Harvard Business Review*, October 17.

Hanson, D., M. A. Hitt, R. D. Ireland, and R. E. Hoskisson. 2017. *Strategic Management: Competitiveness and Globalisation*, 13th ed. Melbourne: Cengage AU.

HBR (*Harvard Business Review*). 2022. "4 Business Ideas That Changed the World: Shareholder Value." Podcast, October 20.

Khan, M. N., G. Serafeim, and A. Yoon. 2015. "Corporate Sustainability: First Evidence on Materiality." *Accounting Review* 91 (6): 1697–724.

Mulholland, E., and E. Farnworth, eds. 2022. *Primer on Climate Change: Directors' Duties and Disclosure Obligation: In support of the Principles for Effective Climate Governance*, 2nd ed. Oxford: Commonwealth Climate and Law Initiative.

Nelson, J., B. Jenkins, and R. Gilbert. 2015. *Business and the Sustainable Development Goals: Building Blocks for Success at Scale*. Cambridge, MA: Harvard Kennedy School.

Partelow, S., K. J. Winkler, and G. M. Thaler. 2020. "Environmental Non-Governmental Organizations and Global Environmental Discourse." *PLoS ONE* 15 (5).

Polman, P. 2023. "Paul Polman Calls on US Business to Lead with Courage." PaulPolman.com, September 20.

Richardson, K., W. Steffen, W. Lucht, et al. 2023. "Earth beyond Six of Nine Planetary Boundaries." *Science Advances* 9 (37).

Samans, R., and J. Nelson. 2022a. "Corporate Governance and Oversight." In *Sustainable Enterprise Value Creation*, 103–40. Geneva: Palgrave Macmillan.

———. 2022b. *Sustainable Enterprise Value Creation*. Geneva: Palgrave Macmillan.

Schwab, K. 2019. "Davos Manifesto 1973: A Code of Ethics for Business Leaders." World Economic Forum, December.

Sharma, P., and S. Sharma. 2021. *Pioneering Family Firms' Sustainable Development Strategies*. Cheltenham: Edward Elgar.

Steffen, W., W. Broadgate, L. Deutsch, O. Gaffney, and C. Ludwig. 2014. "The Trajectory of the Anthropocene: The Great Acceleration." *Anthropocene Review* 2 (1): 1–18.

Stern, N. 2006. *The Economics of Climate Change: The Stern Review*. London: Her Majesty's Treasury, October.

TCFD (Task Force on Climate-Related Financial Disclosures). 2017. *Final Report: Recommendations of the Task Force on Climate-Related Financial Disclosures*. Basel.

———. 2022. *2022 Status Report*. Basel.

TNFD (Task Force on Nature-Related Financial Disclosures). 2024. "320 Companies and Financial Institutions to Start TNFD Nature-Related Corporate Reporting." Press release, January 16.

———. 2023. *Recommendations of the Task Force on Nature-Related Financial Disclosures*. London.

UN (United Nations). 2022. "Climate Risk: An Investor Resource Guide." Principles for Responsible Investment. UNPRI.org, January 21.

———. 2021 *A Legal Framework for Impact*. Principles for Responsible Investment. UNPRI.org.

van Tulder, R., and E. van Mil. 2022. *Principles of Sustainable Business: Frameworks for Corporate Action on the SDGs.* New York: Routledge.

Willetts, P. 2018. "NGOs as Insider Participants: Evolution of the Role of NGOs at the United Nations." In *Handbook of Research on NGOs*, ed. A. Kellow and H. Murphy-Gregory, 56–94. Cheltenham: Edward Elgar.

WCED (World Commission on Environment and Development). 1987. *Our Common Future.* Oslo: United Nations.

WEF (World Economic Forum). 2019. *How to Set Up Effective Climate Governance on Corporate Boards: Guiding Principles and Questions.* Geneva.

FIVE

Industry and Multisector Alliances to Achieve System-Level Impact

JANE NELSON

Over the past three decades, the number of companies that have begun voluntarily reporting on their sustainability activities and performance has grown significantly.[1] And, since 2015, many of the same companies have started to report specifically on their commitments to support

---

1. KPMG International (2022). KPMG has undertaken a regular survey of corporate sustainability reporting since 1993. The 2022 report covered 5,800 companies from fifty-eight countries, territories, and jurisdictions and reviewed trends in corporate reporting on sustainability performance (since 1993 and 1999), the SDGs (tracked since 2015), and carbon emissions (tracked since 2015) across different industries. As of 2022, 96 percent of the world's largest 250 companies by revenue were reporting publicly on their sustainability-related performance, up from 35 percent in 1999 (p. 13 of the report), with some 74 percent of the largest 250 companies reporting explicitly on their contribution to the SDGs, up from 43 percent in 2017 (p. 57) and 80 percent reporting on carbon targets, up from 67 percent in 2017 (p. 39). The advent of mandatory reporting requirements will continue to enhance the credibility and comparability of such reporting.

As outlined later in this chapter, the World Benchmarking Alliance has developed a method for tracking the SDG-related performance of two thousand influential corporations (the SDG2000) across seven key systems, which also draws on publicly reported corporate data.

the 17 Sustainable Development Goals (SDGs) and the 2015 Paris Agreement.[2] In addition to multinational corporations with global reach and large national companies, more small and medium-size enterprises (SMEs) from diverse industries and jurisdictions are starting to support the SDGs.[3] Voluntary actions undertaken by individual firms, while moving toward achievement of the goals, are in aggregate insufficient to achieve the system-level transformations needed for the private sector to be able to support governments in delivering the 2030 Agenda.

While leadership within individual firms and the creation of operational partnerships in firms' own value chains and communities remain fundamental to progress, more ambitious, larger-scale collective action is required. A critical mass of companies working together on a precompetitive basis at the industry level and in large-scale, multisector alliances will be essential to support more inclusive and sustainable development. Such alliances, while complex and challenging to establish and sustain, have an important role to play in helping to overcome some of the systemic obstacles that are impeding the progress of business engagement with the SDGs.

Systemic obstacles to achieving the SDGs and to expanding the contribution of the private sector include a variety of governance gaps, market failures, and trust deficits. These range from the lack of enabling policies, regulations, political will, and industry-wide norms and standards to insufficient resources, innovation, incentives, and market demand from consumers, customers, investors, and other market actors.[4] Lack of public trust in large corporations and governments is another impediment to making progress on the type of deep-seated political, economic, and technological changes and often trade-offs that are needed in many jurisdictions and sectors.[5] A related factor is the absence of effective consultative and governance mechanisms for systemwide coordination on setting common goals and priorities and then holding relevant institutions accountable for their delivery. Few of these system-level challenges can be

2. Ibid.
3. UNDESA (2020).
4. WBCSD (2021).
5. Edelman Trust Institute (2024). The Edelman Trust Barometer is a useful source of trends and insights into public trust of different sectors and institutions. In its twenty-fourth year, the 2024 report surveyed the views of 32,000 respondents from twenty-eight countries, with respondents selected to be "representative of the general population across age, gender, region and ethnicity/nationality (where applicable) within each country" (p. 2).

addressed by any one company acting on its own. In many cases they cannot be addressed even by governments in the absence of broader stakeholder consultation and coordination, often at multiple levels.

Parts II and III of this book provide examples of initiatives by financial actors, policymakers, and regulators aimed at addressing some of these systemic governance, policy, and market obstacles to business engagement in achieving the SDGs. Large-scale business-led alliances among companies and between business, governments, and civil society offer another important set of mechanisms for overcoming these obstacles and scaling up the contribution and impact of business.

This chapter focuses on a subset of precompetitive, industry-led alliances and multisector platforms that are combining a variety of approaches to effect more inclusive and sustainable change in crucial systems such as energy, food, hard-to-abate industries, and finance. Hard-to-abate industries are those that are energy- and capital-intensive and difficult to decarbonize for financial or technological reasons; they are also heavy emitters of greenhouse gases.[6] These alliances aim simultaneously to shape markets, increase the adoption of industry-wide norms and standards, mobilize resources, and advocate for policy reforms at global, value chain, and local levels. The chapter outlines evolving models of large-scale collective action, identifies some of the operational and strategic challenges to implementation, and provides recommendations for the way forward.

Operational, Project-Level Partnerships to System-Level Collective Action

The formation of sustainability partnerships and the practice of collaboration among business and other sectors are not new. In addition to introducing the term "sustainable development," the seminal report of the World Commission on Environment and Development, published in 1987, explicitly called on governments to increase cooperation with industry, noting that "industry is on the leading edge of the interface between

---

6. Categorizations of hard-to-abate industries vary, but the list usually includes iron and steel, cement and concrete, aluminum, glass and chemicals, aviation, shipping, heavy trucking, certain food and agricultural commodities, and some land uses. See International Energy Agency (2020).

people and the environment. It is perhaps the main instrument of change that affects the environmental resource bases of development, both positively and negatively. Both industry and government, therefore, stand to benefit from working together more closely."[7]

Almost thirty years later, SDG 17 calls on all actors to "encourage and promote effective public, public-private and civil society partnerships" alongside other joint actions aimed at "strengthen[ing] the means of implementation and revitaliz[ing] the Global Partnership for Sustainable Development."[8]

Over this period, likely thousands of individual companies have established or participated in a wide variety of sustainability partnerships. Large companies in particular can point to their engagement in multiple different partnerships, often with diverse partners, goals, and timelines, in numerous different locations and with different levels of activity. These partnerships range from global alliances to supply chain coalitions to local community groups and may combine both philanthropic and core business resources and motivations. Likewise, the number of industry-level collaborative efforts to support sustainable development at scale is growing. It is fair to assume, for example, that most of the 25,000+ firms that are members of the United Nations Global Compact are participating in partnerships to support the SDGs.[9] To cite just one instance, the SME Climate Hub, which is itself supported by a coalition of business groups and financial institutions, is partnering with some eight thousand SMEs to enable climate action by small businesses.[10]

Despite the numerous individual examples and case studies and the substantial anecdotal evidence on corporate-led partnerships for sustainable development, it is difficult to track or evaluate their number, scope, or impact. There is no commonly agreed-on way to categorize the different types of sustainability partnerships that involve business, nor is there any reliable and comprehensive database. This lacuna makes it impossible to assess the total numbers of such partnerships, let alone evaluate their

---

7. United Nations (1987).

8. UNDESA (n.d.). For additional historical background on frameworks for UN, government, and business partnerships for sustainable development, see United Nations (2015).

9. For the list of participants in the United Nations Global Compact, see the website at https://unglobalcompact.org/what-is-gc/participants.

10. For information on participants in the SME Climate Hub, see the web page "Our SMEs" at https://smeclimatehub.org/our-smes/.

effectiveness, whether on an individual company or partnership basis, comparatively, collectively, or cumulatively. Yet there is little doubt that partnerships have a role to play as catalysts of change for sustainable development, and there is value to better understanding their different models, challenges, and relative effectiveness.

Categorizing Business Partnerships and System-Level Collective Action

As part of an effort to characterize different forms of business sustainability partnerships, work that was supported by the Business and Sustainable Development Commission, I previously identified five levels of collaboration that large companies were engaging in with the aim of scaling up their impact in managing sustainability risks and opportunities.[11] These were:

- *Cooperation with business partners along specific value chains.* Partnerships of this kind are often one-on-one partnerships with the limited goal of addressing an operational or strategic challenge within a specific value chain.
- *Project-level financing and implementation partnerships.* Such partnerships usually entail one or a few companies partnering with one or a few governments, financial institutions, research organizations, or nongovernmental organizations (NGOs) to share risks, costs, or resources in developing new technologies, products, services, or delivery models with explicit sustainability goals, or to increase philanthropic support and donations for humanitarian goals.
- *Industry-level, precompetitive business alliances.* These alliances typically involve a group of companies working together within or across an industry to drive sectorwide change.
- *Multistakeholder institutions, platforms, or networks among groups of companies, governments, or civil society organizations (CSOs).* These large-scale alliances are aimed at overcoming governance gaps and market failures to achieve widespread change.
- *Coordination between different levels or types of partnership.* These efforts aim to align or proactively coordinate the actions of separate partnerships with the goal of achieving a multiplier effect to support systemic change at scale.[12]

---

11. Nelson (2017). See also Grayson and Nelson (2013) and Nelson (2013).
12. Nelson (2017).

This chapter focuses on the last three of these partnership approaches, in which businesses interact with other businesses and stakeholders or with broader networks. While many thousands of smaller partnerships at the operational, individual supply chain, community, and project levels can cumulatively contribute to sustainable development outcomes, it is these large-scale alliances that are most likely to drive system-level transformation, the challenges of establishing and sustaining them notwithstanding.

Others have sought to categorize large-scale, transformative partnerships according to the ambitions of the alliances in question. The World Resources Institute, for example, has divided transformative partnerships into two broad categories. Those in the first category, described as *enabling partnerships*, aim "to shift policies and practices to move actors more quickly to a sustainable development pathway. To do so, they may form roundtables or voluntary commitments to set sustainability standards; they may focus on sharing knowledge or advice; or they may look to create market conditions such that commercial investments are feasible in the future."[13] Those in the second category, described as *market-driven partnerships*, "use the power of market signals and forces to drive sustainable change by launching a commercially viable product or service."[14]

In a similar vein, Lambin and coauthors from Stanford University have identified what they describe as three "upscaling pathways" whereby coalitions of public, private, and civil society actors align their motivations to drive sustainability transition at scale.[15] These pathways can be summarized as follows:

- *Market power pathway:* This pathway entails leveraging a dominant private actor's market power or that of a small group of dominant private actors that are willing to work with civil society and government actors to drive change along their supply chains.
- *Public policy integration pathway:* In this pathway, CSOs or progressive actors from the private sector design and pilot voluntary sustainability initiatives, after which government adopts elements of successful initiatives into legal mandates, thereby making these initiatives applicable to all actors in a jurisdiction and considerably bolstering their integration.

13. Li, Gray, and Dennis (2020).
14. Ibid.; United Nations Global Compact and Accenture Strategy (2018).
15. Lambin et al. (2020).

- *Government-led pathway:* Here, governments lead transformations, but government actions are reinforced by private action as a result of willing and capable policymakers coordinating effectively with civil society and private actors.[16]

The Role of Systems Leadership by Individuals and Institutions

The models of large-scale collective action and coordination outlined in the previous section involve business actors, both individuals and institutions, engaging to varying degrees with each other and with governments, financial institutions, and CSOs in a particular system or ecosystem. Engagements may be within or across industry sectors or development sectors or may occur among a complex set of value chains. Engagements may occur simultaneously in place-based national, subnational, and city- and community-level systems. Such interactions and systems are rarely static. Effective engagement is usually a dynamic and adaptive process. It involves collective efforts to identify and cultivate a shared vision for change, map and mobilize relevant stakeholders, and understand systemic obstacles to achieving change and specific pathways for addressing these obstacles, and then aligning interests, incentives, and accountability mechanisms in a manner that doesn't stifle widespread innovation and action by individual actors.[17]

The obstacles to engagement and change are often similar, regardless of the system, sector, or jurisdiction in question. A two-year consultative process led by the World Business Council for Sustainable Development to survey the views of corporate leaders, policymakers, and sustainability experts identified five broad types of constraints to achieving greater scale and systemic impact:[18]

- policy and regulatory gaps,
- differences in norms and values,
- lack of sufficient or accurate data and information flows,
- inadequate or misallocated capital and financial flows, and
- lack of incentives to support technology development and implementation.

---

16. Ibid. The titles of the pathways are as in the original report; the descriptions are paraphrased.
17. Nelson and Jenkins (2016).
18. WBCSD (2021).

The same obstacles to systemic change have been identified by other studies and through practitioner experience. Drawing on the extensive literature examining systems change and systems thinking, Kania, Kramer, and Senge have described six interdependent conditions of systems change, namely, policies, practices, resource flows, relationships and connections, power dynamics, and mental models.[19] They comment that these "six interdependent conditions typically play significant roles in holding a social or environmental problem in place. . . . The interaction can be mutually reinforcing or it can be counteracting."[20] The conditions can also be affected by biases in the underlying models, such as race and gender biases, which means changemakers must be acutely attuned to the sorts of power dynamics that turn relationships in one direction or another.[21]

In short, system-level collective action aimed at accelerating and scaling up the transition to sustainable development requires participants to address more than one of these obstacles or conditions simultaneously. Participants, whether business leaders or other actors, need to understand the feedback loops between them and the related trade-offs, synergies, and cobenefits. They also need to understand the key stakeholder groups with the ability to influence the agenda, whether in a supportive or in an obstructive manner, and the roles of power dynamics, values, incentives, and vested interests.

None of this is easy, and new leadership skills and capabilities will be needed by both individuals and institutions. The type of linear, command-and-control leadership that has often characterized public and private sector leadership in the past is no longer fit for purpose. Effective collective action calls for what has been referred to as systems leadership on the part of participating individuals and institutions.[22]

Prioritizing Collective Action for Key Systems, Sectors, and Actors

A key question that needs to be addressed is, what are the systems and pathways that are most important strategically for achieving the SDGs? Relatedly, who or what are the key industry sectors and companies that have the

---

19. Kania, Kramer, and Senge (2018).
20. Ibid
21. Ibid
22. In addition to Kania, Kramer and Senge (2018) and Nelson and Jenkins (2016), see also Dreier, Nabarro, and Nelson (2019).

greatest potential to drive change in these systems, alongside other institutional actors, such as governments (at different levels) and CSOs?

An Emerging Focus on Key Systems and Transformation Pathways

In the introduction to a special feature on sustainability transitions in consumption-production systems published in 2023 by the *Proceedings of the National Academy of Sciences*, the organizers note the following: "The ultimate stage on which the pursuit of sustainability is played out is now generally understood to be that of the globally intertwined, coevolving and extraordinarily complex nature-society system. On that stage, people seek to meet their needs for food, shelter, energy, health, etc. by tapping the earth's resources and human ingenuity in ways mediated by markets and other institutions, politics, and power."[23] The special feature focuses on innovations and developments in three production-consumption systems—electricity, mobility, and food—and on emerging cross-cutting themes, including interactions between different production-consumption systems.[24]

In 2021 the International Institute for Applied Systems Analysis (IIASA) "embarked on a new strategy to develop and apply systems science to support transformations to sustainability."[25] Built on nearly half a century's worth of scientific research, the 2021–2030 strategy focuses on three core systems or domains, which the IIASA recognizes are often incompatible—production and consumption, biodiversity and ecosystem services, and equitable and resilient societies—as well as on four key drivers of sustainable development, namely, governance and institutions, technology and innovation, economy and society, and population and behavior.[26]

The emerging focus on systems approaches to support sustainable development is not the domain solely of the scientific and academic community. Several business-led or business accountability organizations are realigning their programs to focus on key systems or pathways as the most effective way to engage business in accelerating and scaling up the transition to sustainable development.

The World Business Council for Sustainable Development (WBCSD), for example, has identified nine transformation pathways that its members

---

23. Geels, Kern, and Clark (2023).
24. Ibid.
25. IIASA (2020b).
26. IIASA (2020a).

consider to be "at the heart of what is needed to realize a world in which 9+ billion people live well, within planetary boundaries," and where business plays a central role in either supporting or undermining systemic change.[27] These pathways are energy; transportation and mobility; living spaces; products and materials; financial products and services; connectivity; health and well-being; water and sanitation; and food.[28] As the WBCSD recognizes, "While business can take a leading role, it must work on and design systems transformations, together with scientists, policy makers, financiers and investors, innovators and consumers. Only collaboration at unprecedented levels will create the impact and speed needed."[29] This points to the need for more ambitious models of collective action and alliances.

A systems approach has also been adopted by the World Benchmarking Alliance (WBA). Initiated in 2018 as a multistakeholder alliance, the WBA set out to benchmark the impact of major corporations on each of the 17 SDGs.[30] Following several years of consultation, the alliance shifted its focus from the 17 SDGs to seven systems transformations, stating, "The 2030 Agenda requires that we challenge our current thinking and no longer act in silos. We have learned over the course of global stakeholder consultations involving more than 10,000 people that we cannot assess progress issue by issue, SDG by SDG, given that all areas are interrelated."[31] Although not identical to the transformation pathways identified through the WBCSD's global consultative process, there is substantial overlap in the seven systems transformations that have been identified by the WBA, namely, social, decarbonization and energy, food and agriculture, nature and biodiversity, digital, urban, and financial.[32]

These examples reflect a growing body of both academic research and practitioner action and coalition building focused on identifying key stakeholders, drivers, and obstacles—research and experience that will be essential for determining progress in complex and often context-specific, but clearly defined systems.

---

27. WBCSD (2021). The author served on the External Review Committee for this report.
28. Ibid., 8.
29. WBCSD (2024.)
30. WBA (n.d.a).
31. WBA (2019).
32. WBA (n.d.b).

Identifying and Mobilizing Key Industry Sectors, Value Chains, and Companies

It follows from the evolving focus on key systems and transformation pathways that certain industry sectors, value chains, and companies within these sectors will have a particularly important role to play in moving society toward more sustainable models of economic growth and development.

Although not a perfect match, there are obvious industry sectors that align directly with such systems as energy, food and agriculture, transportation and mobility, the urban and built environment, products and materials, financial products and services, digital and connectivity platforms, and health. Within these sectors, it is also possible to identify specific value chains and companies that have a high or disproportionate impact—for better or worse—on the achievement of key SDGs.

The WBA has developed the concept of "keystone companies." The alliance proposes that "the largest companies in a given industry can operate similarly to keystone species in ecological communities. That means that they can have a disproportionate effect on the structure and the system in which they operate."[33] This observation aligns with the "market power" upscaling pathway identified by Lambin and coauthors and discussed earlier in the chapter, which relies on leveraging the market power of a dominant private actor or of a small group of dominant private actors that are willing to work with civil society and government actors to drive change along their supply chains and arguably in the system more broadly.[34]

The WBA has identified, and continues to refresh on an annual basis, what it calls the SDG2000, a list of the two thousand companies "with the greatest potential to transform systems and influence outcomes on the SDGs."[35] Five principles for selection are used, reflecting a company's dominant position in global production revenues or volumes within a particular sector, its control of production and/or service provision, its ability to connect systems through its network of subsidiaries and supply chains, its influence on global governance processes and institutions, and its global footprint, particularly in developing countries.[36]

---

33. WBA (2021).
34. Lambin et al. (2020).
35. WBA (2021), 18.
36. Ibid.

The WBA has used this approach to develop a set of benchmarks to compare the sustainability performance and accountability of influential companies in the seven systems transformations that it has identified. For the decarbonization and energy system, for example, it is developing comparative benchmarks on performance and accountability for major companies in oil and gas, electric utilities, automotives, transport, buildings, heavy industries, and food and agriculture.[37]

The concept if not the terminology of "keystone companies" is being used by other sustainability-oriented corporate benchmarking and accountability initiatives. These initiatives are usually structured as multistakeholder nonprofit organizations, independent of the companies they assess and benchmark, that aim to research, influence, and incentivize the most influential companies in the most important sectors and systems.

Examples include the Access to Medicines Foundation, which benchmarks the most impactful value chains and companies in the health sector with the goal of driving both competition and stakeholder pressure for improving access to and affordability of essential medicines, vaccines, and health diagnostics services.[38] The Access to Nutrition Initiative takes a similar approach of researching, benchmarking, identifying lessons and good practices, and engaging stakeholders such as investors and policymakers to influence key companies in the food and beverage sector to improve access to more nutritious and affordable foods.[39] In their inaugural Corporate Climate Stocktake in 2023, the We Mean Business Coalition and its partners focused on "keystone companies" and sectors by assessing "300 of the world's largest emitters" and providing "a data-based analysis of eight key transition sectors: power, road transport, concrete and cement, steel, shipping, agriculture, aviation, and hydrogen."[40]

These multistakeholder coalitions are mostly examples of nonprofit platforms aimed at influencing and driving corporate behavior from the outside rather than being led and driven by keystone companies themselves. Yet the model of the most influential companies in the most important sectors taking the lead themselves on a voluntary basis is one with encouraging examples and untapped potential. Today, most industry

37. Urlings et al. (2023).
38. See the home page of the Access to Medicines Foundation at https://accesstomedicinefoundation.org/.
39. See the Access to Nutrition Initiative's mission statement at https://accesstonutrition.org/mission-vision-values/.
40. We Mean Business Coalition (2023).

sectors can point to examples of a core group of influential companies and business leaders jointly establishing precompetitive coalitions that aim to proactively and collectively address systemic obstacles to sustainable development on an industry-wide basis.

Examples of industry-led, market power–driven coalitions that aim to support more inclusive and sustainable development include the Responsible Business Alliance, which describes itself as "the world's largest industry coalition dedicated to responsible business conduct in global supply chains" and, together with its Responsible Minerals, Labor and Factory Initiatives, has "more than 500 members with combined annual revenues of greater than $7.7 trillion, directly employing over 21.5 million people, with products manufactured in more than 120 countries."[41] Other examples include CEO-led initiatives such as the Consumer Goods Forum, the International Council on Mining and Metals (ICMM), the Extractive Industries Transparency Initiative (EITI), the Global Sustainable Tourism Council, the ICTI Ethical Toy Program, the Global System for Mobile Communications Association (GSMA), the Fashion Pact, and a variety of commodity- or value chain–specific alliances, to name a few.[42] The approach and efficacy of each coalition vary, so it is important to consider the determining factors for success.

Emerging Practice and Insights from System-Level Alliances

Whether large-scale alliances are business-led and consist only of companies working collectively on a precompetitive basis or are structured as multisector or multistakeholder entities and networks characterized by business leader engagement alongside policymakers and civil society leaders, they share similar approaches to accelerating and amplifying change toward sustainable development. Key shared activities of such coalitions include the following:

- *Setting industry standards, goals, and commitments:* This type of activity may include establishing industry-wide norms and standards that all members either must adhere to or demonstrate

---

41. See the Responsible Business Alliance web page "About the RBA" at https://www.responsiblebusiness.org/about/rba/.

42. The author has served as an adviser to or has served on boards related to some of these industry alliances, including ICMM, EITI, and the ICTI Ethical Toy Program.

they are on a pathway to meeting; "setting ambitious shared goals or roadmaps for achieving specific social or environmental objectives (or the SDGs more broadly)"[43]; establishing a common mechanism for companies to report and benchmark their performance against these standards, goals, and roadmaps; and sharing lessons and good practices within the industry.

- *Accelerating or scaling up innovation and market development:* Activities in this category could include supporting precompetitive R&D consortia for essential technologies, products, or services that have the potential to meet social and environmental needs and creating or strengthening markets or value chains for essential technologies, products, or services. Companies can compete once the markets are created or strengthened, but often benefit from working together at the outset to make markets and market-based solutions commercially viable.
- *Undertaking joint policy advocacy and government engagement:* Activities of this kind undertaken jointly seek to influence the broader enabling environment for sustainable business.[44]

Increasingly, as outlined earlier in the chapter, the most effective coalitions aim to simultaneously address some combination of the above goals, recognizing that a holistic approach is needed to tackle root cause obstacles and drive system-level change and is preferable to working on individual obstacles on their own in isolation from each other. But approaches addressing multiple goals simultaneously are not easy to craft, and take sustained time and effort to implement and sustain. In a study of more than fifty corporate-led sustainability alliances, the Boston Consulting Group (BCG) found that "approximately 30% were able to address root causes to deliver at-scale social and environmental benefits. The remaining 70% were either focused on mitigating negative societal and environmental impacts without addressing root causes or targeting root causes but not yet able to scale their initiatives. And of those alliances that have a real impact, half are more than 15 years old—demonstrating that it takes time for an alliance to become a truly effective vehicle for collective action."[45]

43. Samans and Nelson (2022).
44. These goals draw on previous work by the author, including Samans and Nelson (2022) and Nelson (2010, 2013, 2017).
45. Young, Beck, and von Szczepanski (2022).

Despite the challenges of establishing and sustaining large-scale collective action and alliances, there is untapped potential for these alliances to be mobilized in supporting sustainable development. Two broad types of collective-action alliance with strong potential are those focused on driving sectorwide transformation within key industry sectors or production-consumption systems such as energy, food, mobility, or the built environment and those focused on driving place-based systems change at national, subnational, or city (or smaller) levels. Each type is discussed next.

Alliances to Drive Sectorwide Transformation

Precompetitive, industry-led or sector-specific alliances that seek to integrate setting standards, goals, and commitments, accelerating or scaling innovation and market development, and engaging with governments on policy issues warrant increased attention and support. The BCG analysis found that the vast majority of the industry sector coalitions BCG surveyed, 82 percent, were focused on enabling sustainable operations through setting industry standards. Fewer than 50 percent were primarily concerned with shaping the context for sustainability by influencing regulations and shaping customer preferences, and fewer than 15 percent sought to drive innovation through spurring joint R&D and catalyzing funding for innovation.[46] There is thus room for further progress, especially with respect to driving innovation, attracting private sector funding, and creating markets to meet the SDGs.

Two recently established alliances that aim to achieve sectorwide transformation through multifocus pathways are the First Movers Coalition and the Glasgow Financial Alliance for Net Zero, both of which were created as large-scale, public-private collective action platforms as part of the process leading to the COP26 climate conference in Glasgow in 2021. While both are relatively new and face operational and strategic challenges, they offer interesting models to observe, learn from, and potentially emulate and adapt going forward.

FIRST MOVERS COALITION (FMC). The FMC was created as a joint effort by the U.S. government, under the auspices of the special presidential envoy for climate, and the World Economic Forum. Its participants have the

46. Ibid., 4.

shared objective of scaling up technological innovation and decarbonization in the following hard-to-abate industry sectors: aviation, shipping, trucking, aluminum, cement and concrete, steel, and carbon dioxide removal. As outlined by the Forum, "One of the challenges in decarbonizing these sectors is that around 50% of the reductions needed to achieve net-zero emissions by 2050 need to come from technologies not yet commercially available at scale. . . . FMC is designed to build early demand for decarbonized solutions through purchasing commitments made by members, to help accelerate the adoption of breakthrough near-zero emissions technologies and reach commercial scale by 2030."[47]

Three years after its establishment, the FMC has more than ninety members from top global corporations that have made purchasing commitments. Those commitments are sending a demand signal for near-zero emission products and services amounting to some $16 billion in aggregate demand by 2030 and an estimated 31 million tonnes of carbon dioxide equivalent in annual removals.[48] At the same time, in addition to companies making purchase commitments, the Forum has recognized the importance of undertaking parallel efforts to mobilize concessional capital, blended public-private finance, and derisking mechanisms to unlock commercial private capital for further expanding these markets. It has also developed a government engagement strategy to advocate for supportive policies, incentives, standards, and mandates.

In short, the FMC is taking a holistic and multidimensional approach to overcome both governance gaps and market failures. It aims to enable its corporate members to "become part of a wide ecosystem of partners advancing the supply, financing, and deployment of innovative emerging climate technologies via bankable projects and offtake agreements, supported by access to financing solutions, development of critical infrastructure and government support."[49]

Building on the early lessons of the industry-focused FMC, in December 2023 at COP28 the Forum launched a First Movers Coalition for Food, supported by the government of the UAE and an initial twenty companies.[50] The First Movers Coalition is expected to take a similar

---

47. WEF (2024b).
48. Ibid. See also WEF (2024a).
49. WEF (2024a, 2024b).
50. WEF (2023).

approach with companies and other actors in the value chains of the commodities beef cattle, dairy, rice, row crops, soy, and palm oil, which are estimated to account for up to 70 percent of the global agrifood systems' greenhouse gas (GHG) emissions, in addition to having a major impact on freshwater use, nature, human rights, and livelihoods.[51] At its launch, the partners set a shared goal of creating "a combined procurement commitment with an estimated value of $10–$20 billion by 2030."[52]

GLASGOW FINANCIAL ALLIANCE FOR NET ZERO (GFANZ). GFANZ is another system-level collective action platform with the goal of "coordinat[ing] efforts across all sectors of the financial system to accelerate the transition to a net-zero global economy."[53] Established in April 2021 by UN Special Envoy on Climate Action and Finance Mark Carney and the COP26 presidency, in partnership with the UNFCCC Race to Zero campaign, GFANZ is today the world's largest coalition of financial institutions publicly committed to support this transition. As of mid-2024, it was composed of more than 700 financial institutions in more than fifty countries and eight sector-specific alliances bringing together asset owners, asset managers, banks, financial service providers, investment consultants, venture capital firms, and export credit agencies.[54]

Like similar system-level coalitions, GFANZ has a multilevel and multidimensional approach to influencing company performance and sector transformation. From the outset, it has aimed to expand the number of financial institutions that have made public, measurable commitments to help fund the energy transition through their own operations. At the same time, it is coordinating these institutions to collectively address sectorwide challenges associated with the net zero transition. In addition to supporting participating companies and sector initiatives to develop credible net zero pathways and action plans, the alliance is engaged in joint efforts to mobilize climate finance for emerging markets and developing countries and to develop credible voluntary carbon markets. It also aims to influence governments on defined public policy reforms, working at the level of global governance as well as through national and regional chapters.

51. Ibid.
52. Ibid. See also WEF (2024c).
53. See the GFANZ web page "About Us" at https://www.gfanzero.com/about/.
54. Ibid.

GFANZ's efforts have not been without challenges or critics from both ends of the political spectrum. The more common criticisms are that the targets set for member financial institutions are either too ambitious or not ambitious enough and that the methods being used to track progress are either too demanding or too opaque and easy to manipulate.[55] Politics weighs in as well: participating financial institutions may face threats of litigation because they continue to fund fossil fuel expansion while the very same institutions risk being sued in certain U.S. states and jurisdictions for publicly committing to meet ambitious climate targets in the first place. Merely participating in the collaborative format may draw threats of antitrust action. These factors have influenced the withdrawal of major insurance companies from the Net-Zero Insurance Alliance and increased the pressure on other financial institutions to withdraw.

The range of challenges and the types of criticisms that GFANZ faces illustrate the enormous complexity of trying to undertake collective action to advance systems change and the multiple layers and interdependencies of economic, political, cultural, methodological, and technical factors that need to be understood and navigated. While not a reason to retreat from collective action—indeed, collective action is one of the most important approaches available for driving and sustaining sectorwide transformation—it is important to be realistic about the time and effort needed to achieve this transformation.

Alliances focused on supporting sustainable development in essential systems and sectors offer one high-potential avenue for change. Another pathway to broaden and amplify business engagement in sustainable development goes through place-based alliances, which may be aligned with one or more essential sectors but organize around a specific jurisdiction or spatial area as the core structure.

Alliances to Drive Place-Based Transformation

Place-based transformation can happen at any jurisdictional or spatial level, from the local community level to towns and cities, subnational regions, industrial clusters, corridors, landscapes, and states up to the federal level within countries. They can also occur across national borders on a regional level. There is an opportunity to convene key stakeholders and

---

55. Pellegrino (2023); see also Reclaim Finance (n.d.).

decision-makers, including businesses, at any one of these levels for the purpose of agreeing on a shared vision and the goals, pathways, and resources needed to influence progress on one or more of the SDGs or in the complex production-consumption systems outlined earlier in the chapter.

Engaging the private sector more strategically in well-structured and ideally multiyear country-level platforms and city-level coalitions offers two interesting pathways for accelerating and scaling up place-based solutions to sustainable development.

COUNTRY-LEVEL PLATFORMS. Country-level platforms bring together key groups of stakeholders, including decision-makers and funding entities, in government, business, civil society, and sometimes the donor community around a shared national or subnational agenda, which may be issue- or sector-specific or focused on supporting a broader sustainable development agenda.

The 2030 Agenda and the Paris Agreement both call for state-led processes to establish national action plans and review progress. As part of the 2030 Agenda, UN member states are encouraged to conduct voluntary national reviews (VNRs), described as "regular and inclusive reviews of progress at the national and sub-national levels, which are country-led and country-driven."[56] The Paris Agreement similarly requires governments to establish "climate action plans to cut emissions and adapt to climate impacts"[57] and to update these plans every five years in the form of Nationally Determined Contributions (NDCs).[58] As of late 2024, the UN High-Level Political Forum on Sustainable Development reported that 406 VNRs had been presented, with many countries having presented multiple reviews.[59] Meanwhile, the UN's 2023 NDC Synthesis Report indicates that 168 NDCs had so far been published, representing 195 parties to the Paris Agreement.[60]

The process of developing and implementing a national sustainable development strategy or climate action plan, including the development of

---

56. Voluntary national reviews are described in United Nations High-Level Political Forum on Sustainable Development [2024a].
57. See the 2022 one-page summary on Goal 13 at https://unstats.un.org/sdgs/report/2022/goal-13/.
58. See the United Nations Climate Action web page, "All About the NDCs," at https://www.un.org/en/climatechange/all-about-ndcs.
59. United Nations High-Level Political Forum on Sustainable Development [2024a].
60. United Nations Climate Action (2023).

VNRs and NDCs, offers a convening mechanism for governments to engage with national companies of all sizes and sectors alongside other nonstate actors. There is currently no comprehensive review available of the different types of convening mechanisms and no analysis of the nature, scope, or scale of business sector engagement in the countries where such mechanisms exist. Anecdotal evidence suggests that when private sector engagement does happen, it tends to be in the form of one-off or irregular consultations rather than more structured strategic and multiyear advisory councils, national pacts, or resource mobilization platforms.

Evolving models exist that are worth reviewing in more detail to assess their effectiveness and applicability to other countries. One example is Sustainable Iceland, a cooperation platform established by the Iceland prime minister's office in December 2022.[61] Supported by a Sustainability Council, chaired by the prime minister, and consisting of "other ministers in the government, and representatives from the business sector, trade unions, local authorities, the Icelandic parliament, civil society and NGOs," the platform's tasks include formulating the country's sustainable development strategy, identifying goals and indicators, and engaging in consultation and coordination, among other activities.[62]

Kenya's SDG Partnership Platform offers another country-level example. Established with support from the UN in 2017, this country-level alliance "convenes and connects leadership from Government, development partners, private sector, philanthropy, civil society, and academia to create 'SDG Accelerator Windows;' to catalyze SDG partnerships, financing and innovations in alignment with Government development priorities."[63] The private sector is officially represented by the Kenya Private Sector Alliance and a core group of leading Kenyan and multinational companies. Participants jointly prioritize initiatives within the government's Big Four Agenda, which is focused on manufacturing, food and nutrition security, universal health, and affordable housing.[64]

In some countries, national business associations have taken a systematic and multiyear approach to mobilizing their members to support the SDGs

---

61. See the Government of Iceland's web page "Sustainable Iceland" at https://www.government.is/topics/sustainable-iceland/.
62. Ibid.
63. SDG Partnership Platform (2023).
64. Republic of Kenya State Department for Planning (2022).

and to engage strategically with their government. One example is Japan's Keidanren, with its membership comprised of more than 1,500 representative companies, 106 nationwide industrial associations, and the regional economic organizations for all 47 prefectures. In 2015, Keidanren created its Society 5.0 for the SDGs platform, which offers a useful model for business engagement on the SDGs at a country level.[65] Chile's ACCIÓN Empresas is another example; it has worked with other Chilean business groups and the government to produce the first national Voluntary Business Report for Sustainable Development as part of the country's VNR.[66]

More analysis is needed of the different models of country-level platforms that aim to drive sustainable development at a national level or in specific sectors within a country. Whether these platforms are led by government and structured to systematically include business or are led by business associations and focused on influencing or supporting government priorities, they have the potential to broaden and amplify impact, but their effectiveness and the challenges they face need to be better understood. Research by Engberg and Linn points to some of the factors that enable country platforms to be effective in pursuing a scaling agenda for achieving the SDGs, ranging from whether they have a longer-term vision of outcome goals to their scope, organizational structures, resourcing mechanisms, and governance models.[67]

CITY-LEVEL COALITIONS. The subnational alliance is another place-based format that offers significant potential for mobilizing companies and business associations to work with municipal or state governments and other stakeholders in expanding joint efforts on sustainable development.

Since the Local Agenda 21 model was implemented after the Rio Earth Summit in 1992, city-level coalitions have continued to evolve as effective multistakeholder platforms for working toward systemic change. Coalitions such as the Resilient Cities Network, the C40 Cities consortium, and the long-standing ICLEI Local Governments for Sustainability network all offer interesting models for mobilizing public and private resources around a shared agenda for sustainable development.

---

65. See the home page of Keidanren SDGs at https://en.keidanrensdgs.com/homeen. See also Inoue (2019).
66. WBCSD (2023). See also Gobierno de Chile (2023).
67. Engberg and Linn (2023). See also the Global Community of Practice on Scaling Development Outcomes website at https://scalingcommunityofpractice.com/.

Within municipalities, industrial clusters or business parks where companies from different industries and value chains are colocated offer another convening mechanism to facilitate implementation of sustainability initiatives such as circular economy models, carbon capture and storage hubs, and shared training and workforce development programs. As the World Economic Forum notes, these clusters "provide opportunities for scale, sharing of risk and resources, and aggregation and optimization of demand," yet "often, industrial clusters' impact is limited due to the lack of cooperation and common vision from co-located companies and governments."[68] They can also be an effective platform for engaging and building the sustainability capacity and impact of SMEs.

In recent years, a growing number of cities have started to produce voluntary local reviews.[69] Like the national reviews, these local reviews show that the private sector is not always engaged in a structured or strategic manner. More analysis of business engagement models at the city level or in voluntary industrial clusters and business parks could help identify good practices and opportunities for replication.

Conclusion and Recommendations

As the examples in this chapter illustrate, large-scale business-led or multistakeholder alliances have untapped potential to drive system-level sustainability transitions. Building and sustaining these alliances is a complex and challenging process. Success is far from assured as they face both operational and strategic challenges.

Operationally, large-scale alliances have high transaction costs and require a substantial commitment of resources by participating companies and other partners, both financial and in the time and skills commitment of key decision-makers. Even when major commitments of time, talent, and funds are made at the outset, it can be difficult to sustain this level of commitment over the years to decades needed to drive systems transformation. Changes in leadership in a company, government entity, financial institution, or foundation often result in the prioritizing of new projects rather than a recommitment to the alliances championed by a predecessor.

---

68. WEF (2024d).
69. UN-Habitat (2024).

Strategically, precompetitive industry alliances may face antitrust litigation. This has been a particular challenge in recent years for corporate-led climate and ESG coalitions, especially in the United States. As Gasparini and coauthors comment, "Alliances and their members must always remember that no matter how good their intentions are, certain actions can expose them to antitrust enforcement threats or sanctions. Although rules vary by jurisdiction and are constantly changing, politicians opposed to decarbonization can allege antitrust behavior or violations of fiduciary duty, and their allies can engineer outright boycotts."[70]

Measuring and attributing impact is also difficult in complex, large-scale, multidimensional and multistakeholder alliances. Difficult, but not impossible. In their edited volume, *Partnerships for Sustainability in Contemporary Global Governance*, Andonova, Faul, and Piselli propose a theoretical framework that "specifies distinct pathways to partnership effectiveness. These include (i) the attainment of a partnership's self-declared goals; (ii) the creation of value for partners; (iii) productive collaboration inside a partnership; (iv) the impacts of a partnership on affected populations; (v) its influence on collaboration and institutions outside a partnership."[71]

Despite the challenges of building and sustaining business-led or multistakeholder alliances, these alliances offer a valuable and to date inadequately deployed mechanism for increasing impact and driving systemic change in sustainable development. This type of framework warrants further analysis, experimentation, and engagement on the part of business leaders and policymakers. In this regard, the following three recommendations are worth considering in developing a post-2030 agenda.

Take a Systems Approach Focused on Key Sectors and Corporations

A post-2030 global policy goal framework could take more of a systems approach to identifying the sectors, pathways, and actors, including corporate actors, that will be most influential in scaling up solutions to sustainable development.

As outlined in this chapter, complex production-consumption systems are at the core of meeting many essential human needs. This includes expanding access to affordable, adequate, and safe food, energy, health

---

70. Gasparini et al. (2024).
71. Andonova, Faul, and Piselli (2022).

care, housing, mobility, financial services, and digital connectivity—as well as being central to job creation and improving livelihoods. The same systems, however, are also the largest sources of GHG emissions, water use, and impacts on nature. In many cases they are the causes of human rights abuses, unsafe and insecure working conditions, and inequality.

For better or worse, private sector actors play an essential role in most of these systems, and business leaders in most industry sectors increasingly recognize the need to participate in efforts to make these systems more inclusive and sustainable. Large-scale collective actions and alliances offer important mechanisms for doing so.

As outlined earlier in the chapter, a relatively small number of corporations—two thousand or so—have a disproportionate influence in supporting or undermining sustainable development. They should be a core focus for engagement by policymakers and civil society actors in the future, in terms of establishing and spreading norms and standards, mobilizing resources to support increased investment and innovation, and improving corporate accountability. At the same time, it will be important not to ignore the contribution of millions of smaller enterprises and not to miss opportunities to enhance their engagement.

Focus on National or Subnational, Place-Based Coalitions to Engage Business in Sustainable Development Strategies

National and subnational governments could be more systematic in engaging business associations, sector-based trade and industry groups, SMEs, and corporate sustainability or responsibility coalitions to jointly define priorities and pathways for delivering on the SDGs and climate commitments.

The creation of multiyear sustainability advisory councils, national pacts, or resource mobilization platforms that explicitly include private sector leaders on a sustained basis could facilitate the implementation of norms and standards, establish mutually agreed-on goals and commitments, identify different sources and types of funding, and clarify relative roles, responsibilities, and accountabilities.

Nationwide sectoral alliances, city-level coalitions, and industrial clusters offer high potential for testing and supporting the broad application of innovative technologies, products, services, business models, and financing mechanisms; for influencing policy reforms; and for creating market demand to support sustainable development.

Mandate Industry- and Corporate-Level Reporting and Accountability Mechanisms

Increased corporate accountability and transparency are essential to assessing impact, understanding risks, and building trust between companies and other stakeholders.

The evolution of mandatory—and double materiality—sustainability reporting requirements for individual companies has high potential to propel more responsible business practices and greater corporate impact for sustainable development. At the same time, there is the potential to explore collective reporting and accountability mechanisms through national business associations or sector-based trade and industry groups. Governments could encourage or require such business organizations to provide an annual or biennial report on the contribution their members are making collectively to supporting priority sustainability goals. Such a process not only could serve to enhance stakeholder understanding of the role that key industries or groups of companies are playing in supporting or undermining sustainable development, it could also provide a mechanism for shared learning, competitive benchmarking, and greater collaboration.

In summary, precompetitive collective action by companies in key systems, sectors, and jurisdictions, as well as multisector or multistakeholder alliances, offers tremendous potential for increasing the scale and impact of the business contribution to sustainable development. Such actions and alliances warrant greater analysis, attention, and investment on the part of leaders in both the public and the private sector.

REFERENCES

Andonova, L. B., M. V. Faul, and D. Piselli, eds. 2022. *Partnerships for Sustainability in Contemporary Global Governance: Pathways to Effectiveness.* London: Routledge.

Dreier, L., D. Nabarro, and J. Nelson. 2019. *Systems Leadership for Sustainable Development: Strategies for Achieving Systemic Change.* Corporate Responsibility Initiative Report 80. Cambridge, MA: Harvard Kennedy School.

Edelman Trust Institute. 2024. *2024 Edelman Trust Barometer: Global Report.* New York.

Engberg, E., and J. F. Linn. 2023. "A Concerted Push to Achieve the SDGs Needs a Practical Scaling Approach." Commentary. Washington, DC: Brookings Institution, October 5.

Gasparini, M., K. Haanaes, E. Tedards, and P. Tufano. 2024. "The Case for Climate Alliances." *Stanford Social Innovation Review*, Fall.

Geels, F. W., F. Kern, and W. C. Clark. 2023. "Sustainability Transitions in Consumption-Production Systems." In "Special Feature: Sustainability Transitions in Production Consumption Systems." *Proceedings of the National Academy of Sciences* 120 (47).

Gobierno de Chile. 2023. *Objetivos de Desarrollo Sostenible 2030: Informe Nacional Voluntario.* Santiago. https://hlpf.un.org/sites/default/files/vnrs/2023/VNR%202023%20Chile%20Report.pdf.

Grayson, D., and J. Nelson. 2013. *Corporate Responsibility Coalitions: The Past, Present and Future of Alliances for Sustainable Capitalism.* London: Greenleaf Publishing; Redwood City, CA: Stanford University Press.

International Energy Agency. 2020. "The Challenges of Reaching Zero Emissions in Heavy Industry." Paris.

IIASA (International Institute for Applied Systems Analysis). 2020a. *Reducing Footprints, Enhancing Resilience: Systems Science for Transformations to Sustainability. IIASA Strategy 2021–2030.* Laxenburg.

———. 2020b. "Strategy 2021–30: Reducing Footprints, Enhancing Resilience." Laxenburg.

Inoue, T. 2019. "Keidanren's Initiatives on Delivering the SDGs." Tokyo: Keidanren (Japanese Business Federation).

Kania, J., M. Kramer, and P. Senge. 2018. *The Water of Systems Change.* Boston: FSG.

KPMG International. 2022. *Big Shifts, Small Steps: Survey of Sustainability Reporting 2022.* New York.

Lambin, E. F., H. Kim, J. Leape, and K. Lee. 2020. "Scaling Up Solutions for a Sustainability Transition." *One Earth* 3 (1): 89–96.

Li, S., E. Gray, and M. Dennis. 2020. *A Time for Transformative Partnerships: How Multistakeholder Partnerships Can Accelerate the Sustainable Development Goals.* Washington, DC: World Resources Institute.

Nelson, J. 2017. *Partnerships for Sustainable Development: Collective Action by Business, Governments and Civil Society to Achieve Scale and Transform Markets.* Corporate Responsibility Initiative Report 73. Cambridge, MA: Harvard Kennedy School (report commissioned by the Business and Sustainable Development Commission).

———. 2013. "Scaling Up Impact through Public-Private Partnerships." In *Getting to Scale: How to Bring Development to Millions of Poor People*, chap. 12. Washington, DC: Brookings Institution Press.

———. 2010. *Expanding Opportunity and Access: Approaches That Harness Markets and the Private Sector to Create Business Value and Development Impact.* Corporate Responsibility Initiative Report 46. Cambridge, MA: Harvard Kennedy School.

Nelson, J., and B. Jenkins. 2016. *Tackling Global Challenges: Lessons in System Leadership from the World Economic Forum's New Vision for Agriculture.*

Corporate Responsibility Initiative Report 67. Cambridge, MA: Harvard Kennedy School.

Pellegrino, S. 2023. "Explainer: What Is Gfanz and Is It Working?" *Capital Monitor*, March 16.

Reclaim Finance. n.d. "Glasgow Financial Alliance for Net Zero."

Republic of Kenya, State Department for Planning. 2022. *Third Progress Report of the Implementation of the Big Four Agenda. 2020/2021 FY*. Nairobi.

Samans, R., and J. Nelson. 2022. "Corporate Partnerships and Systemic Change." In *Sustainable Enterprise Value Creation*, chap. 7. London: Palgrave Macmillan.

SDG Partnership Platform. 2023. "Achieving the Sustainable Development Goals." Nairobi.

UN-Habitat. 2024. "Join the Global Movement of Voluntary Local Reviews." United Nations Human Settlements Programme.

United Nations. 2015. *Partnerships for Sustainable Development Goals: A Legacy Review towards Realizing the 2030 Agenda*. New York: UN.

———. 1987. *Report of the World Commission on Environment and Development: Our Common Future*. New York: UN.

United Nations Framework Convention on Climate Change. 2023. *2023 NDC Synthesis Report*. New York: UN. https://unfccc.int/ndc-synthesis-report-2023.

United Nations Global Compact and Accenture Strategy. 2018. *The UN Global Compact-Accenture CEO Survey, Special Editions: Transforming Partnerships for the SDGs*. New York: UN.

United Nations High-Level Political Forum on Sustainable Development. [2024a]. "Countries." https://hlpf.un.org/countries.

———. [2024b]. "Voluntary National Reviews." https://hlpf.un.org/vnrs.

UNDESA (United Nations Department of Economic and Social Affairs). 2020. *Micro-, Small, and Medium-Sized Enterprises (MSMEs) and Their Role in Achieving the Sustainable Development Goals*. New York: UN.

———. n.d. Goal 17.

Urlings, L., et al. 2023. *Do Intentions Translate into Reality? The Role of Companies in Transforming Seven Systems Needed to Put the World on a More Sustainable Path* (2023 update). Amsterdam: World Benchmarking Alliance.

WBA (World Benchmarking Alliance). 2021. *It Takes a System to Change the System: Seven Systems Transformations for Benchmarking Companies on the SDGs*. Amsterdam.

———. 2019. *Measuring What Matters Most: Seven Systems Transformations for Benchmarking Companies on the SDGs*. Amsterdam.

———. n.d. "How It Started." Amsterdam. www.worldbenchmarkingalliance.org/how-it-started.

———. n.d.b. "Seven Systems Transformations." Amsterdam.
WBCSD (World Business Council for Sustainable Development). 2024. "Vision 2050: Time to Transform." Geneva.
———. 2023. "Chile—ACCIÓN Empresas." Geneva.
———. 2021. *Vision 2050: Time to Transform*. Geneva.
We Mean Business Coalition. 2023. *Corporate Climate Stocktake 2023*. New York.
WEF (World Economic Forum). 2024a. "First Movers Coalition." Geneva.
———. 2024b. *First Movers Coalition: Status Report*. Geneva.
———. 2024c. "Food and Water—About." Geneva.
———. 2024d. "Transitioning Industrial Clusters: Unlocking the Potential for Collaboration." Geneva.
———. 2023. "First Movers Coalition for Food to Create up to $20 Billion Value Chain for Sustainable Farming." Press release. Geneva, December 1.
Young, D., S. Beck, and K. von Szczepanski. 2022. "How to Build a High-Impact Sustainability Alliance." Boston Consulting Group, February 14.

PART II

Financial Actors

SIX

Scaling Sustainable Finance

The Role of Asset Owners

SASJA BESLIK

As providers of capital, institutional asset owners are at the top of the investment chain. Pension funds, sovereign wealth funds, insurance companies, endowments, and foundations are all entrusted with vast pools of capital, making them pivotal actors in the pursuit of sustainable development. Their fiduciary responsibilities position them as influential voices in global markets, investment policies, and standards. How asset owners interpret and act on their fiduciary duty is crucial to shaping prosperous societies, including the pursuit of the Sustainable Development Goals (SDGs), net zero greenhouse gas emissions, and broader environmental, social, and governance (ESG) priorities.[1]

1. In this chapter, the terms ESG, SDG, and sustainability are used in conjunction and somewhat interchangeably, recognizing that each has its own origins, traditional audiences, and analytical reference points. For example, ESG principles have evolved over recent decades through extensive business community–focused discussions and debates, while the SDGs were forged through formal intergovernmental deliberations aiming toward broader societal outcomes. Overall, both frameworks have similar underlying ambitions around the need to

Tackling these major challenges necessitates alignment of interests among a myriad of stakeholders across the economic spectrum. It is difficult to align everyone's incentives. This ultimately begs the question: Who bears the mantle of responsibility to help vested interests interact harmoniously? The main influence in this paradigm is none other than the owners of capital. With changing financial regulatory frameworks, technological advances across industries, innovation, and the improving economic picture for low-carbon solutions, the global goals for 2030 could be within reach. Contrary to popular belief, this would also be the most profitable outcome for asset owners.[2]

Asset Owners' Framework and Duties

Asset owners operate within a framework governed by fiduciary duties or equivalent obligations and designed to ensure the diligent management of other people's assets in the best interests of beneficiaries.[3] The foremost fiduciary duties include:

- *Loyalty:* Fiduciaries must act in the best interests of beneficiaries, impartially weighing the interests of different beneficiaries and avoiding conflicts of interest.
- *Prudence:* Fiduciaries must exercise due care, skill, and diligence in their investments, adhering to the standard of an "ordinary prudent person."

Asset owners investing on others' behalf often cite fiduciary duties as the reason for not integrating the SDGs and ESG factors into their investment processes. Several barriers impede such asset owners from taking a more proactive approach. These barriers include the following:

---

align market actors and economy-wide actions with sustainable development practices and outcomes. See chapter 1, "For the World's Profit: Overview," in this volume for further discussion on this point.

2. Atz et al. (2022).

3. Here, "beneficiaries" refers to "entities that manage investments on behalf of participants, beneficiaries, or the organization itself, and include pension funds, endowments, foundations, and sovereign wealth funds" (https://www.gipsstandards.org/standards/gips-standards-for-asset-owners/).

- The perception that the SDGs and ESG factors do not enhance investment decision-making.
- Personal values and misconceptions, such as viewing ESG factors as purely ethical or believing that a focus on them compromises financial performance.
- Competing organizational priorities, such as risk management, which can lead to short-term performance-focused strategies.
- Perceptions of substantial additional resource requirements for making SDG- and ESG-related investments.
- The belief that fiduciary duties prevent a proactive approach to addressing long term the SDGs and ESG principles.
- The influence of investment consultants and products provided by investment managers, which may not align with asset owners' SDG and ESG needs.

For many asset owners, the upshot is outdated perceptions of fiduciary duty regarding material SDG- and ESG-related risks, limited clarity in defining the practice of SDG and ESG factor integration into investment decisions, and a lack of understanding about the relationship between ESG issues and investment performance.

These perceptions might lead, among other challenges, to a "climate change Minsky moment," that is, a sudden, crisis-level drop in asset market valuations triggered by the disparity between economists' optimism about global trends and the reality of the effects of global warming. Potential routes to such a moment could entail (1) large-scale physical asset destruction due to climatic events, resulting in the write-off of their financial value; (2) government policies restricting fossil fuel use in response to a growing realization of the severity of global warming, leading to the devaluation of physical assets; and (3) the devaluation of significant components of the fossil fuel energy system, such as coal mines and power stations, as a result of auditors imposing costs for decommissioning and remediation.

This type of market crisis represents only one form of uncertainty in the global financial system. The world's dynamism is characterized by unpredictable events that can quickly disrupt predictions in any direction. Disruptions can emerge from geopolitical conflicts, pandemics, shifting political landscapes, new national priorities, changing corporate interests, and many other factors. Asset owners need to be able to navigate these challenges in a manner that fulfills their core duties.

Asset Owner Types, Roles, and Nuances

Asset owners comprise a diverse group of institutions and individuals who invest capital on behalf of themselves or others. Many are proactive in contributing to global problem solving. But asset owners differ in their risk-return profiles, the amount of assets under management, and approach to sustainable investing. For that reason, they have different roles in and approaches to affecting the SDG trajectory.

PENSION FUNDS. Pension funds, which manage retirement savings for employees, typically have a long-term investment horizon. They aim to generate consistent returns to meet future obligations. This capital is very well-suited to sustainable investment strategies as pension funds by nature should have a long-term investment horizon. An alignment with sustainable investment is also intuitive: individuals save for retirement to be able to maintain a certain living standard when they leave the workforce. Financial returns would therefore not be the sole objective as future retirees would also want to make sure that the planet—and the environment in which they will spend the remaining years of their life—is in a good state.

The good news is that financial returns and positive outcomes for planet and people can go hand in hand. Sustainability is often fully consistent with investors' self-interest. For example, people living in coastal cities around the world may be worried about having to move because rising sea levels are expected to make their homes uninhabitable by the time they retire, and hence have a clear stake in the need for investments to mitigate greenhouse gas emissions. Similarly, early- or mid-career professionals living in warm or temperate climates may worry about intensifying extreme heat days that will disproportionately affect elderly people decades in the future. Anyone saving for retirement—and we all are—needs to be able to understand the interconnections between investment strategies and long-term well-being. Savers also need to be aware of the contradictions in, for example, investing in fossil fuels while making eco-friendly consumption choices in the local supermarket.

Pension funds can be quite large, especially those managed by governments or multinational corporations. Their scale allows them to influence markets and companies by promoting sustainable practices through their investment choices. Many pension funds have demonstrated strong commitments to sustainability while also achieving strong financial performance over time. The First Swedish National Pension Fund (AP1) has been placing significant emphasis on sustainable investments by integrating ESG factors into investment decisions. It has exclusion policies in place, and active engagement with companies in its portfolio. Other examples include the New Zealand Superannuation Fund, the California Public Employees' Retirement Fund (CalPERS), and PGGM, a Dutch pension fund service provider. ABP is the Dutch civil servants pension fund, one of the largest globally with a strong focus on sustainability. Because of the long-term investment horizon of pension funds, private equity and infrastructure are asset classes that suit these asset owners well. In the case of private equity, investors typically have a significant ownership stake and may even hold board seats, both of which allow significantly greater control over or influence on the management of the business compared to a minority investment in a publicly listed company.

SOVEREIGN WEALTH FUNDS. Sovereign wealth funds (SWFs), typically funded out of a country's foreign exchange reserves or commodity exports, vary widely in risk-return profiles. Some aim for maximum returns, while others prioritize long-term economic stability. Sustainability considerations can align with both objectives as they mitigate risk and promote stability. SWFs play a unique role, especially in the context of sustainability. They may be among the largest asset owners globally because of their government backing and so able to contribute significantly to global regulatory coordination efforts. Their sheer size makes them influential in sustainable finance as they can direct capital toward environmentally and socially responsible investments, and their approach and practices can influence how regulations are implemented. Norges Bank Investment Management (NBIM)—Government Pension Fund Global, also known as the Norwegian Oil Fund, is one of the largest sovereign wealth funds in the world. Even though the capital in the fund is partly generated by revenues from the oil and gas sector, the fund has a well-established commitment to ESG integration and sustainability. It actively engages with companies, promotes ethical investment practices, and places restrictions on investments in certain controversial sectors.

ENDOWMENTS AND FOUNDATIONS. Endowments and foundations are diverse, but they often prioritize capital preservation while generating income for their missions. Sustainable finance can align with their values and help manage portfolio risk in the long term. Their size varies greatly, from small family foundations to the multibillion-dollar endowments of universities and large nonprofit organizations. The influence they exert on sustainable finance depends on their size and commitment to sustainability. Harvard Management Company, the manager of Harvard University's endowment funds, actively pursues an ESG orientation in its investment processes while aiming for strong returns. Other examples include the Bill & Melinda Gates Foundation Trust and the Rockefeller Brothers Fund. The latter has a commitment to divest from fossil fuels, a position that has been significant and symbolic for the divestment movement.

INSURANCE COMPANIES. Insurance companies face various risks, primarily underwriting and investment risks. Sustainable investments can help them manage their portfolios by aligning the investments with ESG criteria, which can reduce certain risks, such as climate risk. Insurance companies can range from smaller regional insurers to global giants. Large insurance companies can exert a significant impact on sustainable finance through their investments and underwriting practices. Zurich Insurance, AXA, and Aviva are some examples of insurance companies that have made significant commitments to sustainability.

INDIVIDUAL INVESTORS. The scale of individual investors varies widely, from small retail investors to modest family offices and ultra-high-net-worth individuals with substantial capital to allocate. Individual retail investors typically have fewer assets to invest than larger institutional investors and, on their own, have less direct influence on other market actors. However, retail investors can have a significant collective impact through their investment strategies and shareholder votes, especially as they are increasingly demanding more ESG options. Meanwhile, high-net-worth individuals and sizable family offices often have privileged access to market actors and can often have a direct voice in investor deliberations as they customize sustainable investment strategies to align with their own risk-return preferences and individual values.

For all these types of asset owners, sustainability-focused strategies offer opportunities to promote sustainable practices. The influence each asset owner wields depends on its size, commitment to sustainability, and how it integrates ESG considerations into investment decisions. As more asset owners embrace sustainability, they collectively contribute to the global transition toward a more sustainable and responsible financial system.

For each of the categories listed above, several good examples exist of asset owners with large-scale AUM embracing sustainability. This development is promising but not yet predominant: despite all the global initiatives, net zero commitments, and trillions of dollars invested in ESG- and SDG-aligned strategies, a majority of companies worldwide are still focused narrowly on growth while suffering from the "tragedy of the horizon," as pointed out by former Bank of England Governor Mark Carney in the context of climate change and financial stability.[4] While many asset owners have made commitments to advancing the SDGs and engaging on material ESG issues, there remains a need for effective implementation of these commitments. Lofty investment beliefs or statements promoting sustainability and ESG principles frequently do not translate into actionable strategies for investment commitments and mandates.

In practice, asset owners engage in continuous dialogue with asset managers, discussing financial goals, risk appetites, and market conditions. In the typical scenario, asset owners, unless specifying custom solutions, must select the most suitable investment products from among those available from investment managers. Sometimes there is a mismatch between products available and asset owners' broader ambitions. Collaboration between the parties is essential for navigating market dynamics and addressing investors' needs.

Signals to the Market

Asset owners convey three distinct sets of signals to the financial system. These signals have considerable influence over financial market dynamics and the financial viability of SDG and ESG principles in the investment context:

- *Indirect Investment Signals*
  Indirect investment signals emanate from investment beliefs, principles, policies, and statements. They are widely perceived by the investment market as indicators of the issues the asset owner is concerned with.

4. Carney (2015).

- *Direct Investment Signals*
  Direct investment signals manifest in the emphasis placed on the SDGs or ESG concerns during the appointment and reappointment of investment managers and consultants. These signals are further codified in formal conditions in investment mandates.
- *Policy Signals*
  Policy signals are delivered by investors as they advocate for policy measures supporting responsible investment. While these signals indicate potential change, their weight is typically less than that of signals transmitted through investment mandates, particularly when regulatory change is probable but not immediate.

Table 6.1 illustrates how the market signals and the frameworks of asset owners can be applied, in both good and bad scenarios. The differences highlight a distinction between the personal ethics of individuals working as asset owners and the institutional ethics governing asset owners. Personal ethics encapsulate the moral compass of an individual. They encompass the individual's values, principles, and beliefs, which are inherently subjective, molded by cultural influences, personal experiences, and individual perspectives. Institutional ethics extend beyond individual convictions and form a collective set of principles guiding an organization as a whole, including its role in the broader societal landscape. In this institutional arena, decision-making adheres to more objective criteria, often formalized through policies, codes of conduct, and governance structures. Procedures can promote a focus on aligning actions with legal compliance, fiduciary responsibility, and the organization's mission and values. An institution's ethical framework may or may not transcend borders, consider ESG or SDG factors, or seek to align with global standards and societal expectations.

Challenges to Greater Progress

The magnitude of the global sustainable development challenge underscores the imperative for private and institutional investors to substantially augment their capital commitments. In this regard, the spotlight often turns toward developing countries. The coming years out to 2030 will need to see the deployment of roughly $2.5 trillion a year across

Table 6.1. How Asset Owners Send Signals: Examples of Good and Bad Practices

Signal	Poor practices	Good practices
Indirect investment signals	SDG and ESG issues are either absent or seen as separate from the investment philosophy and strategy. They are a "nice to have"; typically the focus is limited to operational issues and a narrow definition of materiality.	Commitment comes from the top, and integration of ESG and SDG principles into investment policy is clearly articulated. There is transparent reporting on material issues relating to sustainability. Key issues are carefully assessed and communicated. The organization collaborates with peers to generate collective calls to action.
Direct investment signals	Due diligence and selection processes focus on managing downside risks, with very little attention paid to the potential of investing aligned with ESG considerations. SDG alignment expectations typically are nonexistent.	There is systematic consideration of the SDGs and ESG principles in asset selection processes. Relevant guidelines exist governing investment mandates, such as baseline expectations for integration, exclusion lists, and desired engagement outcomes.
Policy signals	While stakeholder engagement might be prevalent, it is typically in the direction that would limit efforts to promote responsible investments, such as advocating for more conservative disclosure requirements.	A formal process exists to engage stakeholders. A clear voting policy is used to align investments with ESG principles and to influence companies to work toward realizing the SDGs. The organization supports and advocates for policies that encourage sustainability in the financial sector.

Source: Author's compilation.

developing economies alone to effectively address the SDGs.[5] Asset owners can become architects of change by directing investments toward sustainable investments, not least in infrastructure projects, offering a lifeline for developing countries striving for economic expansion while mitigating environmental impacts.

In the context of infrastructure investments, whether in developing or developed countries, meeting the colossal investment demands often requires public-private partnerships because of the intertwined interests of the public and private sectors. Neither sector alone can address the complex challenges posed by the development and upkeep of critical infrastructure. A focal consideration is the equitable sharing of risks. Innovative financing instruments, such as blended finance or green bonds, can play a pivotal role.

One significant practical issue that can easily impede progress toward SDG- and ESG-related investing arises from the misalignment between the extended-term return objectives of numerous funds and the imperative to achieve positive short-term returns, driven by quarterly or annual assessments and compensation structures for investors. Fund and institutional asset owners often maintain ten- to twenty-five-year outlooks for their expected returns, allowing them to align their decision-making and financial models accordingly. Entities such as pension funds, sovereign wealth funds, and most institutional asset managers bear a fiduciary responsibility to maximize returns. But in many instances, the time horizon for achieving this objective remains unspecified, leading to a disjunction between short-term and long-term return horizons.

Nonetheless, these very same asset owners frequently evaluate their internal teams and external investment managers on an annual basis, and their compensation frameworks are often tied to this short cycle. This situation creates a powerful incentive to optimize investing for immediate gains, which can, unfortunately, come at the expense of longer-term value. Long-termism needs to be rooted more firmly in our investment and regulatory culture: in the way we direct capital flows, how we regulate industries, and how we consume.

There are at least three other big challenges to asset owners wanting to pursue the SDGs and ESG principles through financing and investment: an unclear risk-reward balance, challenges to impact measurement, especially if trying to maximize sustainable impact, and debates over the

---

5. United Nations (2014).

returns achieved with SDG- and ESG-aligned investment strategies versus conventional approaches. Each is discussed below.

Unclear Risk-Reward Balance

Institutional investors rely on financial models and their risk-return preferences to make investment decisions. These models produce estimates of the "prices" for various types of "risks." Notably, the value of the risks is determined by the variables integrated into the models. To turn the common saying around, if it's not quantified, it's not managed.

Asset valuation models and decision frameworks often fail to incorporate evolving external factors, such as climate risks or other essential SDG-related criteria. This often results from the lack of a long-term perspective or from thinking that such risks will materialize only later, beyond the investment horizon. This posture can lead to a significant distortion of risk perceptions in financial and economic assessments, as reflected in asset valuations.

Among other sustainable development challenges, the impacts of climate change, including tipping points, extreme weather events, sea-level rise, and climate-related migration, are often excluded from the damage functions of economic and financial models. The connection between climate science and financial risk is complex, with the scientific literature and the economic literature often disagreeing on the extent of damage climate change may inflict on the economy and its timing. Some models project significant GDP losses or substantial declines in existing financial assets if climate change is not slowed or halted.[6] These downside estimates may even be conservative. The world's carbon budgets could be smaller than anticipated, and risks may materialize more swiftly. A faster pace of global warming may lead to more severe acute and chronic physical risks, potentially triggering multiple climate tipping points.

The tension between financial risk estimations and climate science projections is particularly evident in pension funds. To facilitate a transition to a climate-secure energy system, pension schemes must send appropriate investment signals to the market. These signals should indicate that a rapid, organized transition is in the financial interest of all, particularly scheme beneficiaries. Asset owners should prepare for potential scenarios such as stranded assets as a result of climate events, new policies and regulation, or

---

6. See, e.g., Kahn et al. (2021) and Karydas and Xepapadeas (2022).

devaluation of the fossil fuel system. However, if climate risk models underestimate the financial consequences of climate change, asset owners and trustees may lack incentives to take prompt action.

Challenges in Impact Measurement

In a time in which the consequences of climate change, social inequality, and governance lapses are increasingly evident, asset owners are confronted with a responsibility that extends beyond maximizing financial gains. The integration of ESG-related considerations into the investment strategies of pension funds, for example, can help manage long-term risks and achieve stable returns, but this is seldom sufficient to achieve positive societal and environmental outcomes. Impact measurement, therefore, becomes a tool for evaluating the tangible contributions of investments to these types of broader outcomes. From the standpoint of fiduciary duty, the question becomes not just one of maximizing returns but of maximizing sustainable returns. As stewards of significant financial resources, asset owners are increasingly recognizing that the long-term health of their portfolios is intertwined with the health of the planet and of society at large.

Defining and quantifying impact remains a persistent challenge for both the investment community and corporations tasked with delivering meaningful outcomes. As investors increasingly seek results beyond purely financial returns, it becomes imperative to establish a common definition and standardized measurement criteria. The concept of impact has diverse interpretations among different stakeholders, contributing to the intricacy of measurement. Furthermore, the SDGs were not originally formulated with investment objectives in mind, necessitating a retrofitting of investment strategies and products to align with these goals. Various initiatives, such as the Global Impact Investing Network and Impact Frontiers, strive to foster consensus among a broad spectrum of stakeholders on methods for measuring and reporting impact. Nonetheless, the ongoing absence of consensus further complicates the investment process, hindering the flow of investments that align with the SDGs.

Debates Surrounding the Advantages of Sustainable Investments

The ongoing discussion of the benefits of SDG- and ESG-aligned investment strategies versus conventional approaches to delivering superior returns continues to persist. Despite a growing body of empirical evidence supporting the financial gains to be realized from sustainable investing, skepticism remains. The debate is further compounded by varying regulatory approaches in different jurisdictions. For example, in some regions, fiduciary standards place a strong emphasis on economic interests, requiring that they take precedence in managing investments. In contrast, other jurisdictions, particularly in Europe, adopt a different perspective on fiduciary duty, suggesting that failure to consider sustainability factors in investment decisions could constitute a violation of fiduciary responsibility.

Many current regulatory scenarios introduce consistency but also the risk of groupthink. Scenario-based analysis may be taken too literally or out of context, fostering herd mentality instead of a comprehensive understanding of relevant challenges. Underlying model limitations, assumptions, and judgments often are not widely grasped, as evidenced by the current disclosures of financial institutions. Investors and regulators evaluating financial resilience must exercise caution and avoid placing undue reliance on overly optimistic model results.

Overall, the financialization of the global economy, still guided by neoclassical theory, remains on an unsustainable and nonresilient path. Short-term financial objectives too often supersede sustainability goals. Environmental and social constraints are still overlooked in assessments of financial and economic risks. Urgent measures are needed to rebuild finance on ecological foundations, align financial systems with ecological limits, and develop a sustainable finance theory that integrates the concepts of nature and sustainability into financial modeling.

What Asset Owners Can Do

It is important for asset owners to set up an effective framework that addresses the SDGs and ESG across the full investment value chain. This starts with three key action pillars:

Pillar 1. Embrace an Ambitious Vision

As an asset owner, it is crucial to think big and envision ambitious priorities that align with investment goals. This means credibly incorporating ESG criteria into the full spectrum of investments as a means to obtain a full set of information before making investment decisions, and to consider how a business may either align with or risk achieving the SDGs. Integrating climate risk and other SDG-related criteria that have a substantial impact on business risk can provide a more comprehensive, accurate, and impartial evaluation of risks and returns on invested capital. For instance, a real estate developer embarking on a project in an area prone to extreme weather events might overlook the associated climate risks. Failing to account for these risks could lead to an underestimated exposure and an overestimated expected return.

An investment strategy should also involve selecting investment areas that not only promise financial returns but also contribute positively to society and the environment. In building this strategy, asset owners and managers can start by identifying investment opportunities that resonate with the values and objectives of the organization and its stakeholders. Then one can consider sustainable and impact-focused investment themes, such as renewable energy, affordable housing, or clean technology, that could generate both financial returns and positive social and environmental outcomes. Scrutiny is essential in the asset manager selection process, as is making sure the ESG, or sustainability-related, information is well understood. This should help achieve a comprehensive risk assessment and opportunity set that leads to more accurate expectations on risk and return.

A compelling, aspirational vision needs to guide the investment strategy. Clear, descriptive language and visual storytelling can help articulate what the investments can achieve. Engaging with stakeholders, including investors, clients, and partners, can include inviting them to imagine the potential for broader impact and to help shape the investment narrative. This offers an opportunity to incorporate their ideas and values into the investment approach to ensure alignment.

Pillar 2. Start with Practical Steps

An asset owner can start by selecting specific investment projects that address urgent and evident needs within the chosen thematic areas. Asset owners committing to measuring the outcomes of these investments in a systematic way can leverage external standards and data available for this purpose. Perfect is the enemy of good here. It is important to define a process for impact measurement and reporting. As an example, using the guidance available from the Global Impact Investing Network and Impact Frontiers is a good start.[7]

---

7. See Global Impact Investing Network (2023) and Impact Frontiers (2021).

Investment projects should be aligned with the overarching investment vision and should identify tangible, achievable goals. For instance, if the focus is on renewable energy, it might make sense to begin with investments in solar or wind energy projects in areas with high energy demand. These initial investment projects can then be implemented in a way that demonstrates positive results, showcasing the financial viability and the social or environmental impact of the investment strategy. They can act as proof of concept and provide valuable insights for scaling up or down the investments. It is important to be open to learning from these initial projects and to using the knowledge gained to refine the investment strategy and inform the design of future investment strategy. This adaptive approach allows asset owners to fine-tune the asset allocation and risk management as they expand the impact investment portfolio.

Pillar 3. Rapidly Expand and Collaborate

In addition to learning, it is important for asset owners to gather the necessary resources to scale up impact investments. This may entail attracting additional capital from like-minded investors or utilizing financial instruments that support the goals, such as green bonds or impact funds. This might require collaboration with the private sector, nonprofit organizations, and other stakeholders. Partnering with organizations that share values and goals can amplify the impact of the investments. Contributing to the debate on the benefits of SDG-aligned investment strategies is important, as is showcasing ways to tackle relevant challenges. Collaboration in joint ventures, co-investments, or consortiums can help asset owners and managers achieve economies of scale and broaden their reach. Advocating for supportive regulations and policies that encourage impact investments in the chosen thematic areas can be beneficial, as can engaging policymakers and industry associations that help create an environment to foster long-term growth and political support for the chosen impact investments.

Collaborative initiatives such as the Net-Zero Asset Owner Alliance (NZAOA) offer a powerful platform for asset owners to unite in their commitment to drive positive change in the businesses they own. Through partnerships, asset owners can leverage their collective influence to push for sustainable business practices and actively engage with companies to encourage transparency and proper governance, and to better address material SDG or ESG topics. This not only enhances the long-term viability of investments but also drives a systemic shift toward a more sustainable and equitable global economy. NZAOA and similar partnerships exemplify how shared commitment among asset owners can catalyze positive change and drive the net zero transition while addressing broader societal challenges.

Governments form an important piece of the puzzle too, mainly because of their ability to set policies, mobilize resources, and create regulatory frameworks that support sustainability. Should the financial markets become overwhelmed by the effects of climate change, governments may even need to step in to bridge any income shortfalls. Asset owners need to scale up collaboration with governments for financing and implementation of SDG- and ESG-related initiatives. Examples of successful public-private partnerships that provide innovative solutions and bridge funding gaps include the EIT Climate-KIC (the European Institute of Innovation and Technology Climate Knowledge and Innovation Community), a public-private partnership supported by the EU. It focuses on driving climate innovation through entrepreneurship, education, and collaboration. The initiative brings together businesses, academic institutions, and public sector organizations to create sustainable solutions and scale up innovations that address climate change. The Nordic Green Bank (Nefco) is another example, an international financial institution established by the Nordic countries to promote green growth and sustainable development through financing and investment in environmental projects.

In the face of pressing global challenges and the urgency to achieve the SDGs, the role of asset owners and managers has never been more critical. By following this framework for investing proposed in this chapter, asset owners can not only achieve their financial objectives but also contribute significantly to sustainable development and societal well-being. This approach allows them to think big, start small, and scale up fast in the realm of global sustainable development.

REFERENCES

Atz, U., T. Van Holt, et al. 2022. "Does Sustainability Generate Better Financial Performance? Review, Meta-analysis, and Propositions." *Journal of Sustainable Finance & Investment* 13 (1): 802–05.

Carney, M. 2015. "Breaking the Tragedy of the Horizon: Climate Change and Financial Stability." Speech delivered at Lloyd's of London.

Global Impact Investing Network. 2023. *Guidance for Pursuing Impact in Listed Equities*. March.

Impact Frontiers. 2021. *Impact-Financial Integration: A Handbook for Investors*. May.

Kahn, M. E., et al. 2021. "Long-Term Macroeconomic Effects of Climate Change: A Cross-Country Analysis." *Energy Economics* 104 (105624).

Karydas, C., and A. Xepapadeas. 2022. "Climate Change Financial Risks: Implications for Asset Pricing and Interest Rates." *Journal of Financial Stability* 63 (101061).

United Nations. 2014. *World Investment Report 2014: Investing in the SDGs: An Action Plan*. New York and Geneva: UNCTAD, May.

SEVEN

Aligning International Banking Regulation with the SDGs

LILIANA ROJAS-SUAREZ

Banks play a central role in both the payments system and the provision of funding for firms and corporations. This role is particularly important in emerging markets and developing economies (EMDEs), where alternative sources of financing are scarce owing to underdeveloped local capital markets. Furthermore, an extensive literature emphasizes the pivotal role of a well-functioning financial system in development and poverty reduction. In essence, sound banking systems are imperative for achieving the UN's Sustainable Development Goals (SDGs).

To ensure financial stability, banking regulation addresses sources of fragility in the banking system. These sources include moral hazard issues stemming from deposit insurance, which could incentivize banks to take excessive risks, and the potential for panics (i.e., bank runs) to emerge, leading to liquidity problems and ultimately solvency crises. While regulations may differ across countries, there are global standards established by the Basel Committee on Banking Supervision (BCBS), the international body responsible for recommending best practices in banking regulations. Basel III, the current set of standards for banking regulation, was finalized in 2017, with full implementation set for 2028.[1]

Basel III represents the BCBS's response to the severe banking crises that originated in advanced economies and manifested in the global financial crisis of 2007–2008.[2] The new accord recommends that large, internationally active banks adhere to its standards. Only countries that are members of the BCBS are bound to adopt the accord. This group of countries is largely formed by advanced economies, but it also includes some large emerging markets, such as Brazil, China, and Turkey.

Although not mandatory, a large number of EMDEs are either implementing or considering implementing the recommendations of Basel III because of the perceived benefits with respect to ensuring financial stability. Past banking crises in EMDEs have had devastating consequences on development, motivating countries to follow the standards.[3] But countries also implement Basel III because adhering to these standards is considered a signal of good behavior, expected to positively influence the perception of creditworthiness by international investors and international credit rating agencies. Moreover, where implemented, the standards apply to all banks and not solely to the largest banks within the systems.

Assessments of the effectiveness of the Basel III regulatory framework recognize that it has contributed to the stability of banking systems worldwide. It is notable that despite the confluence of global shocks since the onset of the COVID-19 pandemic, EMDEs' banking systems have, with few exceptions, remained stable.[4] However, the regulatory framework is not free of unintended consequences, some of which may adversely affect progress toward achieving the SDGs.[5] This chapter deals with that issue but does not pretend to be exhaustive. While Basel III affects several SDGs, the chapter focuses on two: SDG 10 and SDG 8. Specifically, it argues that Basel III may (1) create incentives for banks to reduce financing

---

1. BIS (2022a).
2. Basel III was first introduced in 2010 and finalized in December 2017. See BIS (2011); BCBS (2010, 2017).
3. Beck and Rojas-Suarez (2019).
4. It is noteworthy that lack of compliance with the recommendations of Basel III was one of the major factors explaining the collapse of Silicon Valley Bank in the United States in 2023. See Gruenberg (2023).
5. See Beck and Rojas-Suarez (2019) for a comprehensive analysis of the unintended consequences of Basel III in EMDEs.

to small and medium-size enterprises (SMEs), thereby challenging the goal of SDG 10 to reduce inequality within countries, and (2) reduce the attractiveness of large international banks in financing infrastructure, thereby contravening SDG 8, on economic growth.

The rest of the chapter is organized as follows. The next section discusses how Basel III affects SMEs in EMDEs and offers recommendations to address identified issues. This is followed by a similar analysis of the impact of Basel III on infrastructure finance. The final section concludes.

Basel III and SDG 10: Dealing with the Financial Inclusion Issues of SMEs

The Problem

Capital requirements, aimed at helping banks absorb losses to reduce the likelihood of a bank failure, constitute a central component of Basel III. Specifically, the accord establishes that banks need to hold a minimum risk-based capital ratio of 8 percent:[6]

$$\text{Minimum capital requirement:} \frac{\text{Capital}}{\text{Risk-weighted assets}} = 8\%,$$

where every type of asset held by banks is assigned a weight according to its riskiness. To calculate minimum capital requirements, the value of the asset is multiplied by the relevant risk weight. The riskier the asset, the more capital banks need to hold.

Who sets the risk weights? Under certain stringent conditions, banks can use their internal models to estimate risk-weighted assets—the internal ratings–based (IRB) approach.[7] However, the simplest method, the standardized approach, in which banks' risk weights are specified by Basel III, is the one followed by most EMDEs.[8]

The implementation of Basel III in EMDEs has strongly supported banking sector stability in these countries. Nonetheless, there are some unintended consequences, one of which relates to the effects on credit to SMEs. There are two issues.

6. BCBS (2017).
7. Ibid.
8. Beck and Rojas-Suarez (2019).

FIGURE 7.1. **Minimum Capital Requirements Adopted in Selected Countries**

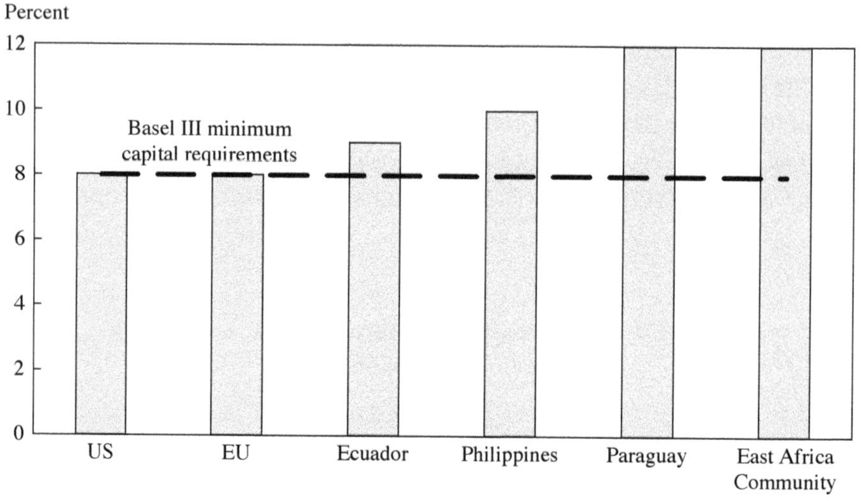

Percent

[Bar chart showing minimum capital requirements: US ≈8%, EU ≈8%, Ecuador ≈9%, Philippines ≈10%, Paraguay ≈12%, East Africa Community ≈12%. Dashed line indicates Basel III minimum capital requirements at 8%.]

Source: Author review of National Reports.

First, in contrast to advanced economies, many regulators in EMDEs have established minimum capital requirements several percentage points above those recommended by Basel III, a practice known as gold-plating (figure 7.1). This is done to reflect the higher overall risk in their economies. The idea is that showing higher capital ratios will provide assurances to local and international investors as to the strength of their financial systems. The problem is that although gold-plating doesn't differentiate between specific risks, it might affect the composition of banks' lending, potentially leading banks to concentrate their exposure in the sectors considered less risky by the standards, to the detriment of SMEs. Insofar as bank lending is the most important external source of SME financing in EMDEs, gold-plating could exacerbate these firms' significant funding constraints, especially in the current international financial environment where interest rates are expected to remain high for a prolonged period.[9]

---

9. According to the World Bank's Enterprise Surveys, almost 50 percent of small firms report being fully or partially credit constrained, twice the ratio of large firms that report facing credit constraints. See the results of "Biggest Obstacle" survey at https://www.enterprisesurveys.org/en/data/exploretopics/biggest-obstacle.

A second concern pertains to the credit risk weights attached to banks' exposures to SMEs. In the standardized approach, Basel III assigns a credit risk weight of 85 percent to SMEs (75 percent if considered retail). This weight can be lower only if the SME has a rating of A– or above; but, of course, the vast majority of SMEs in EMDEs are not rated. Thus there is little differentiation between SMEs when attaching risk weights, with insufficient consideration of firms' history of repayments or as potential subjects of credit. In contrast, the large corporations that are usually rated can potentially benefit from lower risk weights. For example, a corporate bond rated A– would enjoy a risk weight of 50 percent and a corporate bond rated AA– would benefit from a 20 percent risk weight.[10]

An important concern in this context is that the implementation of Basel III in EMDEs could generate a trade-off between financial stability and financial inclusion. While more empirical analysis is needed, evidence suggests that SMEs on the fringes of financial inclusion were the most affected by the introduction of Basel III in EMDEs.[11] That is, Basel III may have a negative effect on financial inclusion, a major challenge in many EMDEs.[12]

What to Do?

The heart of the problems outlined above lies in the fact that the Basel standards (Basel III and its predecessor, Basel II) do not calibrate risks appropriately for EMDEs, as these risk weights have mostly been calibrated for advanced economies. Appropriate risk calibration may reduce the trade-off between financial stability and financial inclusion significantly. In this regard, there are some feasible actions for policymakers, both at the country level and within the BCBS.

RECOMMENDATION FOR POLICYMAKERS. The determination of risk weights should be a process driven by data. Rather than gold-plating, banking regulators in EMDEs should maximize the use of available data in their countries to improve the calibration of risk weights. Credit registries provide a

---

10. BCBS (2017).
11. Based on firm-level data for a sample of EMDEs, the analysis by Fisera, Horvath, and Melecki (2019) shows that SMEs that had a bank account but not a credit loan before the implementation of Basel III could have been the ones most adversely affected by the introduction of the accord.
12. There is also the issue that different versions of the Basel standards have changed the risk weights attached to SMEs, creating regulatory uncertainty.

wealth of information, including loan-level data covering practically every loan in the financial system. Utilizing these databases could allow regulators to determine risk weights for credit exposures that better reflect the particular risk characteristics in their economies than Basel III risk weights. Credit registries and/or credit bureaus operate in many EMDEs, making this a viable alternative for a large number of countries.[13]

In countries where loan-level data are not available, improving data collection and implementing reforms to promote the establishment of credit registries should be pursued as a medium-term goal. However, country-specific calibration of credit risk weights may not be necessary. Establishing regional or subregional agreements among countries with similar financial structures and risk characteristics could be sufficient. This approach would not only help improve credit risk weights in countries without adequate mechanisms for data collection, it would also allow for relevant country comparisons.

An important clarification is that utilizing data from credit registries does not imply that risk weights will decrease for SMEs or any other risk category. Rather, if the distortions created by gold-plating were eliminated and credit risk weights were better aligned with the risk structure of the economy, the implementation of (adjusted) Basel III recommendations would be more effective in containing excessive risk-taking behavior and ensuring financial stability without unduly penalizing critical sectors such as SMEs.

What if, under the alternative calibration, risk weights for SMEs should increase? That would imply that additional government policies, such as credit guarantees or other risk-mitigating schemes, were needed to support SMEs and other socially desirable sectors. Appropriate calibration of risk weighs combined with additional policies would minimize the trade-off between financial stability and financial inclusion.

RECOMMENDATIONS FOR THE BCBS. The committee should support country/regional calibration of credit risk weights based on information from public credit registries and credit bureaus with extensive loan-level databases. It would be important for the committee to recognize that there is large variation in SMEs' track records on loan repayments. Having just a couple

---

13. See World Bank, *Public Credit Registry Coverage (% of Adults)—World* (database, n.d.), at https://data.worldbank.org/indicator/IC.CRD.PUBL.ZS?locations=1W.

of buckets for attaching risk weights for SMEs does not contribute to financial stability and hurts financial inclusion. Since the vast majority of SMEs lack ratings from external credit rating agencies, credit registries can provide more granularity for assessing SMEs' credit risk.

Being able to count on support from the BCBS is essential for EMDEs. To improve their integration into the international financial system, these countries are making efforts to comply with international standards and regulations. Thus it is hard for EMDEs, especially the least developed, to be perceived as unilaterally diverging from the standards. The seal of approval from the BCBS is therefore a must.

The recommendations in this chapter are consistent with the principle of proportionality advocated by the BCBS, whereby countries should adopt and adapt Basel III according to their circumstances. For example, the committee recommends that countries should delay implementation of Basel III until they have an adequate supervisory capacity in place. Likewise, the committee is flexible with the risk weight of some instruments, such as government paper. Notwithstanding, it remains silent regarding calibration of credit risk weights in the standardized approach using alternative methods like the one advanced here. A plausible reason is that an alternative method could give rise to a plethora of credit risk weights schemes that could defy the concept of standardization advocated by the committee. This issue, however, could be resolved by calibrating risk weights on a regional or subregional basis, as proposed above.

Basel III and SDG 8: Supporting Infrastructure Finance in EMDEs

The Problem

Infrastructure is widely acknowledged as a cornerstone of economic growth, yet EMDES suffer from a large infrastructure deficit.[14] Moreover, data from the Global Infrastructure Hub (2023b) reveal a concerning trend: while private investment in infrastructure has been increasing in advanced economies, it has mostly stagnated in EMDEs in recent years.

The landscape of infrastructure funding has also evolved. Although loans, particularly from international banks, remain the primary funding

---

14. The global infrastructure investment cumulative gap was estimated to reach $15 trillion between 2021 and 2040 (G20, 2021).

source, their importance has decreased globally as banks have shown less dynamism in this area. In advanced economies, bond finance, through the issuance of long-maturity instruments, has compensated for the sluggishness in bank funding. This, however, has not been the case in EMDEs, resulting in an overall significant decline in funding for infrastructure projects.

While not the only factors, some Basel III recommendations have implications for bank funding of infrastructure, notably liquidity requirements and the so-called output floor limiting banks' use of their internal risk assessment models in the computation of capital requirements.

THE NEW LIQUIDITY REQUIREMENTS. Liquidity requirements were incorporated into the Basel III framework in acknowledgment of the inadequacy of existing regulation during the global financial crisis to prevent the substantial liquidity problems faced by banks in advanced economies. A key issue was the large proportion of banks' long-term assets financed with short-term funding (wholesale funding), which proved highly volatile during periods of severe bank stress. In response, the BCBS introduced the Net Stable Funding Ratio (NSFR) as part of Basel III's liquidity recommendations.[15] The NSFR aims to enhance the alignment between the maturities of banks' assets and liabilities.[16] Thus, assets with a maturity of more than a year need to be matched with funding with a maturity of more than a year.

While not requiring exact matching, the regulation induces banks to align longer-term assets, such as infrastructure finance, with correspondingly longer-term funding, which tends to be more expensive. Thus, by increasing the cost of infrastructure finance, the NSFR creates incentives for banks to reduce their exposure to such loans, or even abandon them, in favor of shorter-term assets or to shorten the maturity of their infrastructure loans. Moreover, the regulation could have a disproportionate impact on those domestic banks in EMDEs that lack easy access to medium- and long-term funding, thus further constraining the availability of infrastructure finance sources.[17]

---

15. In addition to the NSFR, Basel III includes the liquidity coverage ratio (LCR) requiring banks to hold sufficient liquid assets to sustain them for thirty days during times of stress.
16. BIS (2014).
17. See Garcia-Kilroy and Rudolph (2017) for additional discussion of these issues.

THE OUTPUT FLOOR. A second regulatory addition in Basel III that affects banks' decisions to finance infrastructure projects is the imposition of constraints on the use of IRB models.[18] The BCBS introduced the output floor in Basel III in response to evidence of significant disparities in the estimation of risk-weighted assets among banks holding similar portfolios and operating in comparable financial settings. This regulatory addition limits banks' use of internal models by stipulating that their calculation of risk-weighted assets using IRB models cannot, in the aggregate, be less than 72.5 percent of the estimate using the standardized approach.[19]

Increased use of the standardized approach poses challenges for infrastructure finance. Most important, the Basel framework does not recognize infrastructure finance as a distinct asset class. Therefore the standardized approach does not provide specific risk weights for calculating capital requirements pertaining to infrastructure finance. Instead, the risk weights typically used for infrastructure loans reflect the credit risk of the borrowing entity. The problem is that in EMDEs, the project finance entity involved is often a new entity especially created for a particular infrastructure project, lacking a credit history and therefore not rated by credit rating agencies.[20] In such cases, the standardized approach assigns very high risk weights to banks' exposures to project finance: 130 percent during the construction phase and 100 percent during the operational phase. The higher weights during the construction phase are intended to account for the greater risk associated with the early stages of the project (e.g., because of lack of collateralizable assets).[21]

However, data from Moody's analyzed by the Global Infrastructure Hub (2023b) show that the actual default rates for infrastructure debt have been consistently lower than for noninfrastructure debt. Also, default rates for infrastructure debt converge over time to those of investment-grade corporate debt (although with differences across geographic regions).[22] Because of the nature of their operations and the diversification

---

18. In those jurisdictions where use of the IRB approach is allowed (most advanced economies and some emerging markets), large banks are the usual users of the approach.

19. BCBS (2017).

20. These project finance entities are created to facilitate the collaboration of the public and private sector to develop infrastructure projects.

21. BCBS (2017). In the infrequent cases (at least in EMDEs) in which the project finance entity uses external ratings that are allowed for the computation of regulatory capital, project finance can have the same weights as corporate finance.

22. Global Infrastructure Hub (2023b).

FIGURE 7.2. **Infrastructure and Other Project Finance Debt Performance by Region, 1983–2018: Ultimate Recovery Rate (Percent)**

Region	Infrastructure Loans (83%)	All Projects Finance (78%)
Africa	100	67
Middle East	100	82
Eastern Europe	96	98
Asia	87	78
Western Europe	82	77
North America	82	79
Oceania	80	79
Latin America	76	77

Source: Kelhoffer (2020).

of their portfolios, banks can assume the higher risk at the beginning of the infrastructure projects—a feat that is not possible for most other financial institutions. Without banks' participation, it is hard to envision significant reductions in EMDEs' large infrastructure gap.

Moreover, data from Moody's, presented in figure 7.2, show that ultimate recovery rates—namely, funds recovered from an outstanding loan following a default—are higher for infrastructure debt than for noninfrastructure debt in most regions.[23]

In a nutshell, the existing Basel III framework of risk weights is not suitable for infrastructure finance owing to its unique characteristics. The risk profile of corporate and general project finance does not align with the actual risks associated with infrastructure financing. Facing higher

23. Kelhoffer (2020).

capital requirements, banks have an incentive to shift away from infrastructure finance and toward less expensive assets, such as projects by large, highly rated corporates.[24]

What to Do?

The effect of Basel III on bank-based infrastructure finance is a significant concern for many EMDEs because of the limited availability of alternative market-based funding sources and the substantial infrastructure gap. Recommendations for addressing this issue align with those advanced for improving SMEs' finance, focusing on better reflecting banks' risks in countries' regulatory framework. Each recommendation relates to specific concerns.

ADJUST THE NSFR. Ideally, the NSFR could be adjusted. Rather than concentrating on maturity mismatches that penalize long-term bank assets, the NSFR could directly constrain banks' reliance on volatile short-term sources of funding; after all, the problem identified by the BCBS was the rapid loss of liquidity in wholesale funding. Similarly, the output floor could be modified to allow banks to leverage their expertise in assessing the risk characteristics of infrastructure lending. Enhanced supervision of banks' use of internal models could also mitigate the problem of inconsistent use of these models.

However, amending Basel III regulations on liquidity requirements and the output floor would prove exceedingly challenging. There is no appetite for further modifications to Basel III. Reaching agreement on the latest accord took years of negotiations and numerous rounds of deliberations. Undoubtedly, on an overall basis, Basel III represents a significant improvement in regulatory standards compared to its predecessors, but it is important to recognize that it required the upheaval of a global financial crisis to galvanize consensus for reform.

What about improving and enhancing the utilization of credit-risk mitigation instruments, such as guarantees offered by the World Bank and multilateral development banks (MDBs)? While Basel III allows for the

---

24. Banks especially move toward corporate assets with shorter-term maturities to reduce the liquidity constraint imposed by the NSFR ratio, as discussed above.

Although the BCBS has set January 1, 2028, as the deadline for compliance with the output floor (BCBS, n.d.), banks do react to expected changes in regulation by adjusting their portfolio in anticipation of the changes.

reduction of capital charges through the use of such instruments,[25] it requires compliance with the *legal certainty* condition to qualify for these reductions. This condition demands that all legal documentation be binding for all parties involved, legally enforceable in all relevant jurisdictions, and continuously upheld. However, these requirements are extremely hard to meet in infrastructure finance owing to the intricate nature of contracts, where legal obligations are defined for various categories of performance outcomes and risk categories.[26] For instance, although governments and multilateral development banks are willing to provide guarantees for political risks, these risk-specific guarantees often fail to meet Basel III's legal certainty conditions, thereby not resulting in lower capital requirements. Efforts by the private sector to develop market solutions compliant with regulatory requirements have begun but are still in early stages and require substantial cooperation between governments and the private sector. This collaboration is necessary but will likely take considerable time to fully materialize.

ESTABLISH INFRASTRUCTURE AS AN ASSET CLASS. In this context, intensifying efforts to establish infrastructure as an asset class is the correct approach for at least two important reasons. First, it would facilitate the participation of institutional investors in the financing of infrastructure projects since these investors typically prefer standardized assets. The mobilization of private savings managed by institutional investors for infrastructure financing has been a goal of the G20 since 2017, when the Argentinian presidency proposed a "Roadmap to Infrastructure as an Asset Class"[27]; after all, by 2023, total assets under management by institutional investors had reached close to $100 trillion. However, as discussed above, because of the complex nature of infrastructure projects, institutional investors can complement but not substitute for the role of banks, which are pivotal in structuring and in financing the initial stages of such projects.

Second, establishing infrastructure as an asset class would facilitate an amendment to Basel III without significantly affecting the overall

---

25. BCBS (2023), paragraph 22.3, even states: "No transaction in which credit-risk mitigation (CRM) techniques are used shall receive a higher capital requirement than an otherwise identical transaction where such techniques are not used."
26. See Global Infrastructure Hub (2023a).
27. G20 (2018).

framework, thereby minimizing controversy. Designating infrastructure as a clearly distinguishable asset class would naturally warrant the inclusion of an additional risk category in Basel III's capital requirements, without necessitating a reopening of discussions on the entire framework.

What is needed to establish infrastructure as an asset class? The most important requirements are standardization of key project characteristics and collection of comprehensive data on the characteristics and performance of infrastructure projects globally.

Standardization is needed in various aspects of infrastructure development, including greater standardization of contracts and required documents in the bidding and procurement phases of projects, as well as standardization of financial funding contracts involving similar analyses of cash flows and risks. This would enhance comparability between projects and facilitate the issuance of securities backed by infrastructure projects. Unfortunately, progress in this area has been slow, and a major push is needed. The G20 has established an annual G20 Infrastructure Working Group to propose recommendations. An important recommendation put forth in 2023 is the establishment of consistent and comparable taxonomies that include infrastructure definitions and classifications.[28] Although explicitly defining the type of assets considered to be infrastructure may seem basic and straightforward, challenges arise because of the evolving infrastructure landscape with the emergence of new forms of infrastructure over time. Examples include nontraditional types of infrastructure such as digital infrastructure or circular infrastructure (e.g., fuel derived from waste).

Detailed data are indispensable for investors' assessments of the expected risk-return profiles of projects. Significant strides in data collection have been made since the establishment of the G20 Global Infrastructure Hub, but more efforts are needed to fill large information gaps in many countries. Importantly, the lack of a clear taxonomy of infrastructure impedes adequate collection of data by national authorities. Moreover, enhancing transparency by publicly sharing country-level and project-level data on defaults and recovery rates from loans provided by multilateral development banks for infrastructure projects could significantly contribute to supporting investors' risk assessments. Presently, these data are housed in

28. G20 (2024).

the Global Emerging Markets (GEMs) Risk Database,[29] but only a report with summary statistics is available, despite repeated calls for open access to this information.[30] Promptly resolving standardization issues and closing data gaps requires a clear timeline for actions and procedures to achieve well-specified goals and the involvement of multilateral organizations to support necessary countries' reforms in these areas. It would be advisable to consider empowering an institution like the World Bank to lead this task.

Concluding Remarks

Basel III has undeniably improved banking regulation and contributed to financial stability worldwide. However, implementation of the framework has not been free of unintended consequences, some of which may potentially constrain progress toward achieving several SDGs. This chapter has highlighted how Basel III may discourage bank lending to SMEs (impacting SDG 10) and hinder banks' pivotal role in infrastructure finance (impacting SDG 8). While reopening discussions on the accord would be challenging, a significant part of addressing these issues lies in implementing initiatives that focus precisely on Basel III's core objective: accurate risk assessment.[31]

For SMEs, calibrating risk weights for the calculation of capital requirements using the large databases on loan performance collected by local credit registries offers a data-driven approach. This would allow EMDE regulators to tailor risk assessments to their economy's specific characteristics rather than relying solely on Basel III risk weights, which have largely been calibrated for advanced economies. Support from the BCBS is essential in realizing this recommendation.

Similarly, maximizing data usage is vital for assessing the unique risk profiles of infrastructure projects, which differ significantly from those of

---

29. Initially established in 2009 by the European Investment Bank (EIB) and the International Finance Corporation (IFC), GEMs has since grown to encompass twenty-five MDBs and finance institutions. See the website at https://www.gemsriskdatabase.org/.

30. See Mathiasen (2023) for a review of the issues involved in the publication of GEMs databases.

31. The optimal solution would imply changes in the regulatory framework. But there is reform fatigue. Although the Basel III framework was first published in 2010, more than seven years elapsed before it was finalized, after protracted and difficult negotiations among regulators from major advanced economies.

corporate and other project finance endeavors. This underscores the importance of establishing infrastructure as an asset class with its own specific risk categories for calculating capital requirements. Additionally, it necessitates the development of market solutions that allow credit risk mitigation instruments, such as guarantees from MDBs, to result in reductions of capital requirements.

The path to implementing these recommendations might be long and challenging, but it is achievable. Greater involvement from key multilateral organizations, with the World Bank taking a larger role in spearheading pivotal initiatives, such as the establishment of infrastructure as an asset class, could help accelerate progress. It is crucial to emphasize that these solutions hold the potential to ensure financial stability while fostering inclusive growth.

REFERENCES

BCBS (Basel Committee on Banking Supervision). 2023. *CRE: Calculation of RWA for Credit Risk; CRE22: Standardised Approach: Credit Risk Mitigation.* January.

———. 2017. *Basel III: Finalizing Post Crisis Reforms.* December.

———. 2010. *Basel III: A Global Regulatory Framework for More Resilient Banks and Banking Systems.* December.

———. n.d. "Basel III Transitional Arrangements, 2017–2028." Graph. https://www.bis.org/bcbs/basel3/b3_trans_arr_1728.pdf.

Beck, Thorsten, and Liliana Rojas-Suarez. 2019. *Making Basel III Work for Emerging Markets and Developing Economies.* Washington, DC: Center for Global Development.

BIS (Bank for International Settlements). 2022a. *Basel III Monitoring Report.* February 21. https://www.bis.org/bcbs/publ/d531.htm.

———. 2022b. *High-Level Considerations on Proportionality.* July. https://www.bis.org/bcbs/publ/d534.pdf.

———. 2014. "The Net Stable Funding Ratio." October. https://www.bis.org/bcbs/publ/d295.pdf.

———. 2011. *Basel III: A Global Regulatory Framework for More Resilient Banks and Banking Systems—Revised Version June 2011.*

Fisera, Boris, Roman Horvath, and Martin Melecki. 2019. *Basel III Implementation and SME Financing: Evidence from Emerging Markets and Developing Economies.* Policy Research Working Paper 9069. New York: World Bank, December.

G20. 2024. "The Second G20 Infrastructure Working Group (IWG) Meeting Concludes Successfully in Visakhapatnam." Press release, May 2.

———. 2021. *2021 G20 Infrastructure Investors Dialogue: Financing Sustainable Infrastructure for the Recovery.* October.

———. 2018. "Roadmap to Infrastructure as an Asset Class."

Garcia-Kilroy, Catiana, and Heinz Rudolph. 2017. *Private Financing of Public Infrastructure through PPPs in Latin America and the Caribbean.* Washington, DC: World Bank Group.

Global Infrastructure Hub. 2023a. "Banks Are Critical for Closing Infrastructure Deficits, but Banking Regulations Are Not Supportive." Washington, DC: World Bank, Global Infrastructure Hub, June 23.

———. 2023b. *Infrastructure Monitor 2023: Global Trends in Private Investment in Infrastructure.* Washington, DC: World Bank, Global Infrastructure Hub.

Gruenberg, Martin K. 2023. Remarks. Peterson Institute for International Economics, Washington, DC, June 22.

Kelhoffer, K. 2020. "Examining Infrastructure as an Asset Class." Moody's Analytics.

Mathiasen, Karen. 2023. *Mining for GEMs.* Washington, DC: Center for Global Development, August.

EIGHT

Stewarding a Resilient Future

Why Insurance Matters

EKHOSUEHI IYAHEN

Insurance is a cornerstone of the global financial system. It plays a multi-faceted role in mitigating risks, strengthening household and business resilience, facilitating the flow of capital, and promoting economic stability. The annual premium volume of nearly $7 trillion generated by insurers worldwide reflects their scale of impact, translating into annual contributions of between $5 and $5.5 trillion toward global financial resilience through insurance claims and benefits payouts.[1] Only governments make larger payouts to individual, business, and community resilience.[2] The global

---

Much of this chapter draws on, adapts from, and synthesizes material from existing sources, as indicated throughout the text. In the process of drafting, ChatGPT was used as an editorial assistant to help paraphrase some passages and insights. Prior to publication of this chapter, the author and editors reviewed and substantially revised all such text outputs for factual accuracy, clarity, and consistency of voice with the rest of the chapter.

1. Aizpun, Xing, and Lechner (2022); Schanz (2022).
2. Schanz (2022).

insurance industry also manages more than $35 trillion of assets, nearly a third of all global assets under management.[3]

Insurers assign a value to risk to capture both the expected occurrence and financial consequences of specific potential outcomes. Doing so can encourage behaviors that mitigate risk and help safeguard lives, livelihoods, and assets.[4]

Despite the functions and potency of insurance as a tool for sustainable development, its full potential contributions to the UN's 17 Sustainable Development Goals (SDGs) have not been fully realized. The SDGs outline an integrated approach to promoting peace and prosperity for people and the planet, but the formal framework has an uneven emphasis on insurance-focused issues. As examples, *insurance* itself is mentioned in only one of the 169 SDG targets, *risk* is mentioned in only three SDG targets and in seven of the 231 latest "unique indicators," and *resilience* (or "resilient") is mentioned in two of the seventeen overarching goals and eight targets, but in none of the indicators.

Too often, insurance is perceived either as a luxury reserved for affluent households or as burdened by challenges such as limited scalability, owing to insufficient awareness.[5] When government engagement is limited to setting targets or employing rudimentary tools such as premium subsidies and compulsory product offerings, insurance gets overlooked in the development policy landscape.[6] As a result, broader risk management techniques and principles have not featured as a central pillar in the work of development institutions despite the growing consensus that developing insurance markets and risk management capacities could lead to dramatically better development outcomes.[7]

History is rife with numerous examples of the insurance sector's core capabilities driving monumental social and economic transformations. These instances range from marine insurance enabling European colonial ventures into the wider world in the fifteenth century to more recent social, economic, and industrial disruptions during which economic and policy leaders leveraged insurance-related solutions to address deep structural challenges.[8]

---

3. Statista (2024b); PricewaterhouseCoopers (2023).
4. UN Climate Change High-Level Champions, the UN Race to Resilience, the Adrienne Arsht-Rockefeller Foundation Resilience Center, and Marsh McLennan (2022).
5. Lin Chiew (2021).
6. Ibid.
7. Holliday, Remizova, and Stewart (2021).
8. Draper (n.d.); Douglas (2021).

In the 1890s, the insurance industry established the Underwriters Laboratory to test the fire safety of electrical appliances.⁹ In the early 1900s, the insurance sector advocated for fire hydrants and local fire stations.¹⁰

Governments have played major roles, too. In the nineteenth century, Germany's first chancellor, Otto von Bismarck, prioritized insurance systems as a pivotal component of his reconstruction plans and policy reforms, as did Prime Ministers David Lloyd George and Winston Churchill in early twentieth-century Britain, President Franklin Delano Roosevelt in the post–Great Depression United States, and Prime Minister Ichirō Hatoyama in postwar Japan.¹¹ Many of these efforts have become entrenched as centerpieces of long-term national governance systems.

Growing Protection Gaps

Insufficient progress on the SDGs underscores the growing urgency to consider how insurance can help societies respond to the challenges the world is facing.¹² In 2022 the UN's Human Development Index for the first time in its thirty-two-year history registered a global decline two years in a row. Under the title *Uncertain Times, Unsettled Lives: Shaping Our Future in a Transforming World*, the operative report argued that "layers of uncertainty are stacking up and interacting to unsettle [people's] lives in unprecedented ways."¹³ The same report championed insurance (inclusive of social protection) and innovation to equip societies for the changing conditions of a precarious global environment. Expanded social insurance schemes can help bolster food security, encourage risk-taking and investment, and promote other forms of policy progress, helping households and communities prepare for uncertainty and minimize vulnerability.¹⁴

---

9. UN Climate Change High-Level Champions et al. (2022).
10. Ibid.
11. On Bismarck's use of insurance systems in reforms, see Bauernschuster, Driva, and Hornung (2017). In Britain, the Beveridge Report, published in 1942, established the basis for postwar social policy, including the passing of the National Health Service (NHS) Act in 1946 and the subsequent NHS formation in 1948. On President Roosevelt's use of insurance schemes in rebuilding the U.S. economy after the Great Depression, see Little (2023). On Prime Minister Hatoyama's similar efforts in postwar Japan, see Ikegami (2014) and the Japan Health Policy NOW website (https://japanhpn.org/en/section-1-2/).
12. United Nations (2023).
13. United Nations Development Programme (2022), iii.
14. Bowen et al. (2020).

As the world contends with increasingly frequent and more lethal disasters and shocks, the cost of these events has generally been shared across governments, businesses, and individuals, as well as by insurers, in varying proportions, depending on the country and its level of development. In general, higher-income countries have a larger proportion of disaster costs covered by insurance and the public sector, with less risk retained by individuals.[15] The opposite is true in lower-income countries, where vulnerable populations shoulder more of the cost of these shocks and draw on their savings or credit to cope.[16] The implication is significant underinvestment in development and a consistent drag on gains across the SDGs, with many populations caught in persistent poverty traps or escalating humanitarian appeals.

Consider the case of Nigeria, where a 2018 study found that fewer than 2 percent of adults are insured, barely 10 percent of salaried employees have insurance coverage, and the National Health Insurance Scheme serves only 1 percent of the population.[17] Many individuals rely on familial or social networks to manage risks.[18] Absent insurance, individuals may forgo consumption or tap savings, which undermines resilience over time.[19] Meanwhile, limited-scale premium pools and short-term liability structures constrain insurers' capacity to play a part in capital market development.[20]

At the other end of the spectrum, the cost of UK public insurance—broadly defined to include pensions, public welfare systems, and health care insurance—was more than £520 billion in 2022, or nearly half of public spending.[21] This is separate from government insurance–related facilities to support domestic or commercial risks, manage government contingent liabilities, and pay for related expenditures by local government. Private life and nonlife insurance industry premiums were estimated to add up to more than £290 billion in 2022.[22] Collectively, these public and private expenditures represented more than a third of the UK's GDP.[23]

Despite these differences in local context, the COVID-19 crisis and heightened awareness of climate change have revealed both the vulnerability

---

15. Linnerooth-Bayer et al. (2009).
16. Ibid.
17. Hougaard et al. (2018).
18. Ibid.
19. Ibid.
20. Ibid.
21. Chantrill (2024).
22. Statista (2024a).
23. Statista (2024b).

of our global society to systemic risks and the pressing need for improved protection systems.[24] The urgency only grows because the overall value of unprotected risk exposure continues to rise steadily. A recent report from Swiss Re Institute researchers estimated that in 2022, the global protection gap—defined as the difference between insured and uninsured losses—set a record high of $1.8 trillion, up from $1.5 trillion in 2018.[25] Protection gaps are a pervasive issue across all countries, spanning emerging, developing, and developed economies. Again, however, in emerging and developing nations, the repercussions of uninsured risks, when realized, can be even more severe and enduring because of limited personal or state resources to mitigate losses.

The Swiss Re research report also estimated protection gaps across several dimensions of risk highly relevant to the SDGs.[26] It found that, in 2022, 60 percent of global insurable crop production remained unprotected against natural disasters and accidents. This crop protection gap of $113 billion poses a considerable threat to global food security and to farm income fluctuations. Meanwhile, only 24 percent of natural catastrophe exposures are currently covered by insurance globally, leaving a protection gap of $368 billion in premium equivalent in 2022.[27] The global mortality protection gap, meaning the insurance required to cover families' financial needs when an income earner dies, was estimated at $406 billion.[28] A related estimate by the Geneva Association put the global pension gap at around $41 trillion.[29]

Several different factors drive the respective protection gaps, but collectively they draw attention to the need for the insurance industry to address consumer needs and develop new risk-financing and risk-mitigation products and services.[30] Governmental intervention is also important.[31] Even if it is not viable or appropriate to fully insure all economic losses resulting from

---

24. Centeno et al. (2014); Noordhoek, Marcoux, and Schanz (2022).
25. Aggarwal et al. (2023).
26. Ibid.
27. Ibid.
28. Ibid.
29. The Geneva Association's projections stem from calculations made using a 60 percent wage replacement ratio, Richard Marin's (2013) work on pension deficits, and an OECD evaluation of pay-as-you-go pension financing. The $41 trillion figure is from Schanz (2018). This pension gap represents the difference between the present value of the annual lifetime income required to maintain a reasonable standard of living and the actual retirement savings and the present value of pay-as-you-go contributions over a forty-year time frame.
30. As previously argued in Ariss and Iyahen (2022).
31. Ibid.

disasters, there is a threshold beyond which individuals, households, and businesses purchase inadequate insurance, prompting a need for policymakers to do their part.[32]

Strengthening Risk Management Capabilities: Understanding and Managing Risks

In light of the heightened risks and uncertainties in the context of the vast environmental, social, and economic policy shifts occurring in the world, it is important to understand the mechanisms behind risk absorption, the impact of insurance, and strategies for enhancing resilience and driving stable gains toward sustainable development.[33] Doing so requires attention to how risk is understood and managed.

In 2020, colleagues at the Insurance Development Forum (IDF), which I lead as secretary general, published a framework logic titled *The Development Impact of Risk Analytics*.[34] In this framework, *risk insight* forms the cornerstone of risk prevention and resilience. The essential ingredients for promoting this form of insight are largely available: scientific knowledge, advanced computing capabilities, satellite and ground data, indigenous wisdom, and interdisciplinary methodologies.[35] Transitioning from managing disasters to managing risks is an imperative for sustainable development.[36] But the world remains trapped in a recurring cycle of disaster–response–reconstruction because of systemic barriers that limit the availability of risk insight to vulnerable communities.[37]

Decision-making about risk presents problems that require judgment and compromise, especially as comprehension of the nature of risk continues to evolve.[38] The 2019 UN *Global Assessment Report on Disaster Risk Reduction* cautions of the impending threat from "cascading and systemic risks, largely driven by climate change."[39] As Moody and coauthors at the

---

32. Schanz (2018).
33. Aggarwal et al. (2023).
34. Moody et al. (2020).
35. Ibid.
36. Ibid.
37. Ibid.
38. Ibid.
39. UNDRR (2019), iii.

IDF point out, such systemic risks create an imperative for ambitious collective action spanning domains, scales, and sectors to deepen our understanding of risk, fortify resilience, and foster sustainable, regenerative development.[40]

Positive public-private collaborations led by the insurance industry point to opportunities to drive progress in deepening global risk understanding and analytics capabilities. Examples include the Global Risk Modelling Alliance (GRMA, see box 8.1), Resilient Planet Data Hub, and the Global Resilience Index Initiative (GRII), among others.

Investing in Loss Prevention

Loss prevention forms another crucial element of resilience strategies for sustainable development. Researchers at Swiss Re have estimated the net benefit-to-cost ratios from preemptive measures to mitigate natural catastrophe losses to range from 2:1 to 10:1, and sometimes higher.[41] However,

---

Box 8.1. Global Risk Modelling Alliance: Helping Vulnerable Countries Access Risk-Related Insights

The Global Risk Modelling Alliance (GRMA) was launched in June 2022 by the Insurance Development Forum (IDF) and the Vulnerable Twenty (V20) Group of Ministers of Finance of the Climate Vulnerable Forum, with backing from the government of Germany. The alliance serves as a global public resource, drawing on private sector capabilities to enhance access to climate risk data and analytics among countries most vulnerable to climate change. It thereby aims to facilitate investment in resilience measures and risk transfer mechanisms to safeguard vulnerable populations and foster economic development.

Under the program, participating countries receive access to open-source technology and data standards, tailored for public sector stakeholders, in addition to grant financing to help governments address any model and data gaps. A technical assistance team with public and private sector expertise also works with countries to support implementation efforts.

Sources: Global Risk Modelling Alliance (https://grma.global/about-the-alliance/); UN Climate Change High-Level Champions et al. (2022).

---

40. Moody et al. (2020).
41. Aggarwal et al. (2023).

the macroeconomic return on prevention is found to be higher in lower-income countries, where insurance penetration rates are also lower.[42] Substantial investment gaps persist, owing to insufficient financing and challenges related to risk reduction.[43]

Extending Risk Protection

The Swiss Re researchers also emphasize that, on top of individual-level benefits, shifting risk to insurance markets improves macroeconomic resilience by enabling faster recovery after a shock event and by promoting secondary network effects.[44] Collaboration among governments, regulators, insurers, and businesses is key to increasing insurance uptake.[45] Government entities can use tax and regulatory frameworks to promote insurance take-up.[46] Product innovations can also help, such as when advances in data analytics extend insurance coverage to previously underserved risk segments.[47] Products may range from comprehensive policies covering multiple risks to integrated insurance packages bundled with other purchases.[48] The adoption of microinsurance and other novel distribution channels can further expand access to coverage.[49]

Innovative public-private partnerships are increasingly seeking to facilitate the insurability of risks that are traditionally challenging to cover. Such partnerships may include regional entities such as the African Risk Capacity (box 8.2) and global partnerships such as the IDF.

Rowan Douglas, chair of the IDF Operating Committee, has argued that "insurance is not the silver bullet for climate resilience (which is the product of many factors), but it is a necessary component."[50] He asserts that vulnerable populations can partake of the collective benefit of insurance as a communal asset, pointing out that risks can be distributed among public, private, and mutual systems through premiums, taxation, and hybrid

42. Ibid.
43. Ibid.
44. Ibid.
45. Ibid.
46. Ibid.
47. Ibid.
48. Ibid.
49. Ibid.
50. Douglas (2021).

Box 8.2. Pooling Climate-Related Disaster Risks Across African Governments

A vast continent spanning diverse geographies on both sides of the equator, Africa is home to an incredibly wide range of localized climate patterns. Because agriculture provides the largest share of economic activity on the continent, most African countries' local development paths are uniquely susceptible to the consequences of severe weather events.

To help address this challenge, the African Risk Capacity Limited (ARC Ltd.) was established in 2014 as a hybrid mutual insurer and financial arm of the African Risk Capacity Group. ARC offers parametric insurance services to African Union (AU) member states and farmer organizations, consolidating disaster-related risk across Africa and transferring it to global markets. Its membership consists of African governments that have adopted a policy agreement in a given year, along with capital contributors. ARC aims to shift climate-related disaster risks away from governments and populations, enhancing the continent's ability to address disasters, promote food security, and bolster overall resilience. Current maximum coverage for a country is $30 million per season. It allocates financing to support pre-approved contingency plans, ensuring rapid and predictable responses to disasters.

ARC was established with a commercial mandate as a Class 2 mutual insurance company, originally funded with seed capital. The organization receives funding from a wide range of donor entities, with the aim of eventual full ownership by African sovereign states. It operates out of Bermuda until a comparable legal and regulatory framework can be established in an AU member state, conducting commercial insurance activities in compliance with national regulations for parametric weather insurance. ARC continues to pursue new products to meet its African member states' needs.

Source: African Risk Capacity Ltd. (https://www.arc.int/arc-limited).

approaches. Douglas further observes that costs, payouts, and incentives can be structured to promote affordability, signal risk, foster resilience, and encourage broader solidarity.[51] It is for these reasons that businesses and governments should take further steps to assess and formally manage their potential risks and liabilities where needed.[52]

Today's societies face a broad spectrum of industrial and environmental shocks along with significant economic, industrial, and social transformations. New risks and dislocation are being generated as sectors retreat,

51. Ibid.
52. Ibid.

regions decline, and long-established occupational skills become outmoded.[53] This situation draws attention to the importance of social protection systems that would encompass both government and business.[54] It is becoming increasingly urgent to proactively research, design, and prepare insurance systems before major disasters and dislocations occur. This approach is much more effective than delivering unprepared responses in emergency contexts. Public, private, and mutual-cooperative expertise and capital should be applied to develop the optimum levels of alignment, incentives, and risk sharing at local, regional, and global scales and across time scales and generations.[55]

Focus on Climate: Social Protection for Sectors and Economies in Transition

Despite the advantages of insurance, significant protection gaps persist, particularly in emerging markets where insurance penetration rates remain low compared to more established markets.[56] But as Douglas has also argued, the insurance industry has unique capabilities, expertise, financial resources, and influence that can help inform optimal pathways for diverse industries and regions amid the challenges posed by climate change.[57] (See, for example, box 8.3 regarding "loss and damage.") The sector has a distinctive ability to integrate disparate risks into a holistic perspective, evaluate their community- and asset-level impacts, and articulate the micro- and macro-scale consequences.[58] Equipped with this information, insurance underwriting and investment strategies can jointly influence the direction, magnitude, and distribution of capital allocations to facilitate a net zero transition that adheres to sustainable risk parameters.[59]

Investment policies by insurers as asset owners will be important, too, and this will be amplified by the unique role of risk underwriters. Underwriting coverage can affect the operational standards of public, corporate,

---

53. CISL (2021).
54. Douglas (2021).
55. CISL (2021).
56. Aggarwal et al. (2023).
57. Douglas (2021).
58. Ibid.
59. Ibid.

Box 8.3. Climate Change and Loss and Damage

In international climate policy debates, "loss and damage" considerations mainly focus on strategies to assist developing nations facing heightened vulnerability to the detrimental consequences of climate change.* According to Byrnes and Surmiski (2019), a broader definition of loss and damage relates to the adverse economic and noneconomic impacts of climate change on both human communities and the environment. But as Plichta and Poole (2023) describe, the loss and damage issue has proved politically delicate when it comes to global public financing debates, largely because of the long-standing reluctance of developed nations to assume legal obligations for compensating climate-vulnerable states.

The outcomes of COP27 and COP28 were pivotal in this regard, generating a breakthrough consensus on establishing a new, dedicated funding instrument to support developing countries that are most susceptible to the adverse impacts of climate change. The fund is designed to incorporate a "mosaic" of approaches both within and outside the UN Framework Convention on Climate Change.[†]

Plichta and Poole have summarized some of the constraints regarding the extent and efficacy of pre-arranged financing instruments such as insurance in addressing loss and damage. For example, pre-arranged financing entails tools and strategies that aim to ensure funds are available to manage sudden shocks, and sometimes to execute preparedness measures. Existing pre-arranged instruments are typically used more for crisis planning and readiness rather than for mitigation, adaptation, and restorative measures that could address both preventable and unavoidable losses and damages.[‡]

While insurance is not the single answer to the issue of loss and damage, it is clear that insurance thinking and capabilities will be needed to address elements of loss and damage. In December 2022 the OECD issued a report offering a framework for governments to manage the risks of losses and damages, with a focus on how emerging markets and developing countries could improve capacities to navigate the financial implications of climate-related risk.[§] The recommendations include clear pointers for how insurance-related thinking and capabilities can be practically applied. These processes range from identifying and evaluating climate-related risks and financial implications for governments to applying strategies to minimize financial losses arising from climate risks. They may include targeted efforts to promote affordable insurance options to protect vulnerable groups through regulatory measures and by leveraging international reinsurance markets.

*Grantham Research Institute (2022).
†Plichta and Poole (2023).
‡Ibid.
§OECD (2022).

or governmental entities by either speeding up or stopping their activities.[60] Businesses may be unable to operate without insurance owing to statutory, legal, regulatory, or financial obligations and unprotected contingent liabilities.[61] These capabilities are powerful levers in helping the global community navigate the whole economy transition to low-carbon energy systems and support individual companies on their own transition pathways. In this respect, risk-informed capital management can align systematically with approaches that prioritize human security and well-being.[62]

Considered from another angle, global resilience can be achieved only if investments in infrastructure, residences, and other tangible assets integrate physical climate risk into their design, accounting, and pricing.[63] Otherwise, urban development along coastlines and rivers, for example, will only intensify risk, leading to the loss of millions of livelihoods and potentially lives, in addition to billions of dollars' worth of depleted assets.[64] Through its functions as influential investor, underwriter, and risk manager, the insurance sector can play a leadership role in promoting relevant risk-aware rating systems, pricing mechanisms, and economic frameworks across related finance, infrastructure, and government sectors.[65]

Boosting Resilience through Insurance: Recommendations

A central message of this chapter is that public policy, regulation, and market actors collectively are central to advancing the risk management and insurance instruments needed to promote resilient and sustainable development. As Noordhoek and colleagues (2022) emphasize, coming up with precise, accurate assessments of insurance's contributions to economic and societal well-being remains challenging. Nonetheless, the IDF and the Geneva Association have recently published recommendations key to elevating insurance rates and minimizing protection gaps, with the goal of better aligning insurance provisions with the SDGs in the context of the uncertainties

60. Ibid.
61. Ibid.
62. Ibid.
63. Ibid.
64. Ibid.
65. Ibid.

associated with navigating climate change, pandemics, cybersecurity, and other risks.[66] Key recommendations include the following:[67]

For governments and policymakers:

- Adopt a comprehensive approach to risk management, including national-level disaster risk management, and foster collaboration with insurance regulators and the insurance sector.
- Provide regulatory authorities with clear mandates for insurance market development and allocate appropriate resources to the formulation, implementation, and enforcement of insurance laws and regulations.
- Update tax and subsidy incentives to foster sustainable insurance purchasing behavior.
- Remove undue market-access barriers for insurers and reinsurers to promote competition, innovation, and global risk diversification.
- Elevate financial literacy across all levels of society, including in core school curricula where appropriate.

For regulators:

- Embrace expanded mandates for insurance market development as a key complement to traditional roles of policyholder protection and financial stability maintenance.[68]
- Adopt a comprehensive approach to insurance market development that caters to the needs of both low-income and middle-class populations.
- Proactively educate policymakers about both the economic and the social value of insurance.
- Pursue active dialogue with the insurance industry to enhance national insurance markets through such opportunities as promoting technology and data analytics for consumer needs and enabling digital or other distribution methods to serve remote customers cost-effectively.

66. Noordhoek, Marcoux, and Schanz (2022).
67. Ibid.
68. An example of this is the International Association of Insurance Supervisors' (2023) call to action regarding protection gaps.

- Support collaborative programs to enhance financial literacy and risk awareness.

For insurers:

- Focus on meeting the insurance needs of specific market segments and offer straightforward, economical products to meet those needs.
- Educate policymakers and government officials about insurance's role in protecting society, enabling economic development, and enhancing resilience.
- Engage with regulators in constructive, transparent dialogues to address market issues and explore potential solutions.
- Play an active role in increasing financial literacy and raising risk awareness.

These recommendations offer basic stepping stones toward a better long-term approach to risk management and enhanced resilience in societies around the world. Resilient insurance and reinsurance markets buttress societal resilience by safeguarding lives, livelihoods, and assets. Increased efforts to foster collaborative, multistakeholder approaches to insurance market development can help promote long-term sustainable development for communities that need it most.

REFERENCES

Aggarwal, R., C. Banerjee, L. Bevere, et al. 2023. *Restoring Resilience: The Need to Reload Shock-Absorbing Capacity.* Swiss Re Institute, June 21.

Aris, J., and E. Iyahen. 2022. "Foreword." In *Insurance Development in Emerging Markets: The Role of Public Policy and Regulation*, ed. D. Noordhoek, B. Marcoux, and K.-U. Schanz. Geneva Association, June.

Aizpun, F. C., Li Xing, and R. Lechner. 2022. *World Insurance: Inflation Risks Front and Centre.* Sigma 4/2022. Swiss Re Institute, July.

Bauernschuster, S., A. Driva, and E. Hornung. 2017. "Bismarck's Health Insurance and the Mortality Decline." IZA.org, December 23.

Bowen, T., C. Del Ninno, C. Andrews, et al. 2020. *Adaptive Social Protection: Building Resilience to Shocks.* Washington, DC: World Bank Group.

Byrnes, R., and S. Surminski. 2019. "Addressing the Impacts of Climate Change through an Effective Warsaw International Mechanism on Loss and Damage." Grantham Research Institute, October 16.

Centeno, M. A., M. Nag, T. S. Patterson, et al. 2014. "The Emergence of Global Systemic Risk." *Annual Review of Sociology* 41:65–85.

Chantrill, C., comp. "Multiyear Download of UK Government Spending." Database. UKPublicSpending.co. https://www.ukpublicspending.co.uk/download_multi_year (last accessed May 2024).

CISL (University of Cambridge Institute for Sustainability Leadership). 2021. *Risk Sharing in the Climate Emergency: Financial Regulation for a Resilient, Net Zero, Just Transition.* November.

Douglas, R. 2021. "The Insurance Development Forum after 5 Years: Renewed Vision and Growing Ambition toward Stewardship of a Resilient Climate Transition." Insurance Development Forum, January 21.

Draper, N. n.d. "Lloyd's, Marine Insurance and Slavery." London: Lloyd's.

Grantham Research Institute. 2022. "What Is Climate Change 'Loss and Damage'?" October 28.

Holliday, Susan, Inna Remizova, and Fiona Stewart. 2021. *Developing Insurance Markets: The Insurance Sector's Contribution to the Sustainable Development Goals (SDGs).* World Bank Report 36353. Washington, DC: World Bank Group, June.

Hougaard, Christine, Albert van der Linden, Baraka Msulwa, et al. 2018. *The Role of Insurance in Inclusive Growth: Nigeria Diagnostic.* CENFRI.org, December.

Ikegami, N., ed. 2014. *Universal Health Coverage for Inclusive and Sustainable Development: Lessons from Japan.* World Bank Study 91163. Washington, DC: World Bank Group.

International Association of Insurance Supervisors. 2023. *A Call to Action: The Role of Insurance Supervisors in Addressing Natural Catastrophe Protection Gaps.* November.

Lin Chiew, H. 2021. *Insurance and the Sustainable Development Goals: Why It Matters and How Data Can Help.* Access to Insurance Initiative (A2ii) Policy Note. March.

Linnerooth-Bayer, Joanne, Koko Warner, Christoph Bals, et al. 2009. "Insurance, Developing Countries and Climate Change." *Geneva Papers on Risk and Insurance: Issues and Practice* 34 (3): 381–400.

Little, B. 2023. "Why Social Security Was the Cornerstone of FDR's New Deal." History.com, April 11.

Marin, R. A. 2013. *Global Pension Crisis: Unfunded Liabilities and How We Can Fill the Gap.* Wiley.

Moody, N., S. Fraser, K. Miles, and J. Schneider. 2020. *The Development Impact of Risk Analytics.* Insurance Development Forum.

Noordhoek, D., B. Marcoux, and K. U. Schanz. 2022. *Insurance Development in Emerging Markets: The Role of Public Policy and Regulation.* Geneva Association, June.

OECD (Organization for Economic Cooperation and Development). 2022. *Building Financial Resilience to Climate Impacts: A Framework for Governments to Manage the Risks of Losses and Damages.* Paris: OECD Publishing, December 8.

Plichta, M., and L. Poole. 2023. *The State of Pre-arranged Financing for Disasters 2023.* London: Centre for Disaster Protection.

PricewaterhouseCoopers. 2023. "One in Six Asset and Wealth Management Companies Will Be Swallowed Up or Fall by the Wayside in the Next Five Years: PwC Global Asset & Wealth Management Survey." Press release, June 27.

Schanz, K.-U. 2022. *The Role of Insurance in Promoting Social Sustainability.* Geneva Association, November.

———. 2018. *Understanding and Addressing Global Insurance Protection Gaps.* Geneva Association, April.

Statista. 2024a. "Insurance Industry in the United Kingdom: Statistics & Facts." January 9.

———. 2024b. "Assets of Global Insurance Companies." February 6.

———. 2024c. "Gross Domestic Product of the United Kingdom from 1948 to 2023." February 19.

United Nations. 2023. *The Sustainable Development Goals Report 2023: Special Edition.* July 10.

UN Climate Change High-Level Champions, the UN Race to Resilience, the Adrienne Arsht-Rockefeller Foundation Resilience Center, and Marsh McLennan. 2022. *Fulfilling a Legacy of Societal Risk Management.* Marsh McLennan, November 11.

UNDRR (United Nations Office for Disaster Risk Reduction). 2019. *Global Assessment Report on Disaster Risk Reduction.* Geneva.

United Nations Development Programme. 2022. *Human Development Report 2021/2022: Uncertain Times, Unsettled Lives: Shaping Our Future in a Transforming World.* September 8.

PART III

Policymakers and Regulators

NINE

Global Sustainability Reporting Standards

On the Threshold of a New Era of Internationally Coherent Regulation?

RICHARD SAMANS

After more than two decades of voluntary, market-led development, corporate sustainability reporting has reached a critical juncture. National regulators and international accounting authorities have begun to act in the coordinated fashion necessary to ensure the comparability and quality of nonfinancial information reported by companies. Their actions over the next few years have the potential to drive the routine

---

Much of the first half of this chapter is drawn and updated from R. Samans and J. Nelson, "Corporate Reporting and Accounting," in *Sustainable Enterprise Value Creation: Implementing Stakeholder Capitalism through Full ESG Integration* (Palgrave Macmillan, 2022). Microsoft Copilot was used as an editorial assistant to help paraphrase relevant passages from Samans and Nelson and also to help paraphrase insights in box 9.1 and at the end of the second major section, "Key Challenges in the Years Ahead," from Financial Stability Board, *Progress Report on Climate-Related Disclosures: 2023 Report* (Basel, October 2023). Prior to publication of this chapter, the author reviewed and substantially revised all such text outputs for factual accuracy, clarity, and consistency of voice with the rest of the chapter.

internalization of social and environmental externalities in the capital allocation of firms and financial markets, both within and across jurisdictions. In addition, the rise of mandatory sustainability reporting has the potential to increase corporate transparency and accountability to stakeholders. These outcomes have long been the holy grail of the private sector reform sought by activists and many economists and policymakers.

Notwithstanding the recent progress toward mandatory mainstream reporting of sustainability considerations by companies, this journey continues to face considerable challenges. Notable among them is the risk that some national regulators will decide to go their own way and thereby replicate the fragmentation that characterized the competing private voluntary standards their actions were meant to replace. All stakeholders, not least the business community, will need to remain engaged in this process during the next few crucial years in order to avoid such an outcome.

A Rapidly Evolving Landscape

Over the past twenty years, corporate sustainability reporting has expanded substantially. A 2017 study found that about three quarters of the top one hundred companies in each of forty-nine different countries published corporate responsibility or sustainability reports, nearly four times more than the roughly 20 percent that did so in 2001–2002.[1] Worldwide, the average reporting rate is more than 60 percent across all industrial sectors. Almost half of the reporting companies seek external verification for at least some of the relevant data.[2]

Such reporting is now common practice for large and publicly traded companies. Many are now seeking to integrate these factors into their core strategy, governance, and reporting procedures. A survey of four hundred CEOs, CFOs, and other high-ranking executives and senior accounting professionals from large companies in over fifty countries found that the great majority believe that financial and nonfinancial data ought to be combined more systematically to enhance risk management, decision-making, and trust.[3] However, only 24 percent expressed confidence that current sustainability reporting practices are adequate for investors' information needs.

---

1. KPMG (2017).
2. Ibid.
3. AICPA, IIRC, and Black Sun PLC (2018).

Moreover, 84 percent of the investors surveyed in the same exercise reported that they often exclude nonfinancial information in their decisions because of a lack of comparable information across companies and the limited external assurance of such information.[4]

Accordingly, despite all the progress that has been made, the field of nonfinancial reporting remains disjointed, generating information of limited value to capital providers and society more generally.[5] However, the pace of change is accelerating. More corporations, investors, accountants, and governments are recognizing that well-governed companies and properly functioning financial markets require integrated reporting of financial and sustainability performance.

Following are signs of this growing consensus.

BUSINESSES. In 2020, the International Business Council (IBC) of the World Economic Forum (WEF), comprising around 120 of the globe's most significant companies, established a consistent set of metrics and disclosures of sustainable value creation for mainstream reports.[6] The purpose of this exercise was to demonstrate, in a more credible and comparable manner, the shared societal value they generated and the related contribution to progress toward achieving the UN's Sustainable Development Goals (SDGs). They also wanted to encourage regulators and accounting authorities to take steps of their own to enhance the coherence and quality of corporate reporting around the world. With the support of the four biggest accounting firms, they identified and committed to report against twenty-one common metrics and disclosures applicable to all industries, derived from existing standards.[7] In parallel, the number of companies using the Sustainability Accounting Standards Board (SASB) standards in their reporting, many of which are U.S.-based, rose from roughly five hundred to twenty-five hundred between 2020 and 2023.[8] At the same time, several sector-specific coalitions established sustainability reporting and performance expectations for their member companies. Examples include the International Council on Mining and Metals, the Consumer Goods Forum, and the Responsible Business Alliance.

4. Ibid.
5. For an in-depth discussion on progress and persisting fragmentation, see ACCA and CDSB (2016).
6. WEF IBC (2020).
7. Ibid.
8. SASB (n.d.).

INVESTORS. The UN-endorsed Principles for Responsible Investment were established in 2006.[9] Since then, over three thousand institutional investors and service providers have joined the initiative, including five hundred asset owners accounting for $90 trillion in assets under management (AUM).[10] A recent survey of such asset owners found that nearly all, 95 percent, are already integrating sustainable investing into their portfolios or considering doing so, and more than half (57 percent) foresee a future in which they allocate funds only to third-party investment managers who adopt formal ESG strategies.[11] As for individual investors, 81 percent of those responding to a global survey indicated a desire to match their consumer spending behaviors with their values, and 39 percent reported already having sustainable investments in their portfolios. A majority (58 percent) predicted that it would become standard practice within a decade.[12]

ACCOUNTANTS. The International Federation of Accountants (IFAC) represents nearly three million accountants in 130 countries and jurisdictions. It sees "a significant opportunity to enhance trust in companies and confidence in markets by including information in corporate reporting . . . derived from the financial statements (i.e., 'non-GAAP' or 'non-IFRS' measures), other 'Key Performance Indicators' connected to financial performance, and broader information related to value creation, sustainability or environmental, social, and governance factors."[13] It believes that "integrated reporting, bringing together the relevant information about a company, provides a holistic picture of performance and provides insights on an organization's ability to create sustainable value over time. . . . Integrated reporting supports 'integrated management thinking'—which fosters organizational decision-making and change focused on broader, longer term value creation." Similarly, Accountancy Europe, representing about one million accountants from thirty-five countries, states that "inclusion of a core set of global metrics for [non-financial information] in mainstream reports and in a connected way with financial information would respond to

---

9. For the UN Principles of Responsible Investing, see "About the PRI" at https://www.unpri.org/about-us/about-the-pri.
10. Saa (2020).
11. Morgan Stanley Institute for Sustainable Investing (2020).
12. UBS (2018).
13. IFAC (2019). For information on IFAC's representation, see the "About" web page at https://www.linkedin.com/company/ifac/.

stakeholders' concerns that these issues that are often material to business resilience are not reported with the same discipline and rigour as financial information. An approach to interconnected standards setting for corporate reporting is therefore needed that will standardise the qualitative characteristics of information and disclosure principles for mainstream reports, connecting nonfinancial information with financial reporting."[14]

STOCK EXCHANGES. Stock exchanges have been an important driver of increased sustainability reporting. In a global survey of fifty-seven stock and derivatives exchanges, 84 percent reported either encouraging or mandating disclosure on sustainability or ESG factors.[15] Nearly one-third recommended or required companies to incorporate such disclosures in their annual reports. However, a majority reported that interest on the part of investors was not high, with only 18 percent considering it "extensive." Only six exchanges (19 percent) included the recommendations of the Task Force on Climate-Related Financial Disclosures (TCFD) in their guidelines, although over half indicated an intention to do so.[16]

REGULATORS. The interest of regulators in mainstream ESG disclosure is also on the rise. By 2016 the number of mandatory ESG and sustainability reporting requirements around the world was 248, a significant increase from thirty-five in 2006. By 2020 the count had risen to about 350.[17] While many of these requirements focus on a specific sector or issue, some have a broader scope. Examples include the EU's 2014 Non-Financial Reporting Directive, the related 2016 UK regulations, and Japan's 2014 Stewardship Code and Corporate Governance Code. In particular, the EU and the State of California have enacted requirements for the disclosure of sustainability and climate change for large firms doing business in their jurisdictions, and these requirements are scheduled to be phased in beginning in 2024 and 2026, respectively.

Intergovernmental regulatory bodies have become more active in this area as well. The Financial Stability Board's (FSB's) industry-led TCFD

---

14. Accountancy Europe (2019), 9. For information on the organization's representation, see Accountancy Europe (n.d.).
15. WFE (2019), 13–15.
16. Ibid.
17. GRI and USB (2020), 17.

published recommendations in 2017 that prompted over one hundred governments and financial regulators involved in the Network for Greening the Financial System group to urge "all companies issuing public debt or equity as well as financial sector institutions to disclose in line with" such recommendations.[18] Many regulators are taking steps to enforce these disclosures. Similarly, the International Organization of Securities Commissions (IOSCO), which oversees more than 95 percent of the world's securities markets across approximately 130 jurisdictions, in February 2020 decided to form a Task Force on Sustainable Finance.[19] The goal was to enhance the consistency and investor value of corporate sustainability-related disclosures, including by preventing duplicative and incoherent efforts among regulators and other organizations.[20] In 2021, the organization declared its priorities and vision for the creation of an International Sustainability Standards Board (ISSB) under the IFRS Foundation. Also in 2021, the U.S. Securities and Exchange Commission (SEC) initiated a public consultation on approaches to facilitate the disclosure of consistent, comparable, and dependable climate change information, following a recommendation from the ESG Subcommittee of its Asset Management Advisory Committee.[21] The SEC's final rule, issued in March 2024, requires climate disclosures in annual reports and registration statements for large filers beginning with reports for the year ending December 31, 2025.[22]

INTERNATIONAL ACCOUNTING AUTHORITIES. In response to calls by IOSCO and others for more uniform corporate sustainability reporting, in 2020 the Board of Trustees of the IFRS Foundation, which oversees the International Accounting Standards Board's (IASB's) financial reporting standards, implemented in over 140 countries and jurisdictions, initiated a formal consultation process to assess its potential entry into this field.[23] Its constitution was subsequently amended in April 2021, granting it authority to create the ISSB as a counterpart to the IASB. The foundation then

---

18. NGFS (2019), 3. The Financial Stability Board was created by the G20 following the global financial crisis and comprises the financial regulators of G20 countries, including those of major developing countries in every region.
19. IOSCO (2020).
20. See IOSCO (2021a, 2021b).
21. Lee (2021).
22. SEC (2024).
23. IFRS (2021a).

convened an informal group of voluntary standard setters to support the technical preparations for such a board.[24]

Thus there has been growing agreement among these *market actors*—not solely environmental, human rights, or development advocates—on the importance of mainstreaming sustainability reporting, in the sense of formally integrating sustainability reporting into annual reports and other key communications to capital providers and linking it to financial reporting. International accounting authorities and national securities regulators have finally begun to address this challenge by establishing a globally consistent baseline reporting standard through the IFRS Foundation.

The obstacles likely to be encountered along the way should not be underestimated. For example, the sustainability and ESG corporate reporting ecosystem encompasses multiple different actors and interests (e.g., rating agencies, disclosure frameworks, sustainability stock and bond indices, advocacy initiatives, proprietary service providers) as well as multiple tools and frameworks within each distinct functional layer of the ecosystem.[25] Moreover, it has many audiences, which often require different information (e.g., investors, NGOs, governments, the public). Indeed, investors themselves are a diverse group, including active, passive, quantitative, value, engagement, and other styles of asset management, each with somewhat different information needs and preferences. Finally, there often are important differences in how individual industrial sectors view the relevance or materiality of information; for example, some sustainability issues are inherently more relevant or material for extractive industries that interact extensively with governments and remote communities than others that are more significant for B2C (business-to-consumer) firms than B2B (business-to-business) enterprises.

In the absence of a central international authority to prescribe a harmonized core or baseline set of metrics and disclosures, numerous frameworks and mandates have surfaced over time, sowing considerable confusion and resulting in expensive inefficiencies. The Reporting Exchange, a free online platform created by the World Business Council for Sustainable Development, has charted the international mosaic of reporting requirements and tools. It displays information on ESG- and

24. IFRS (2021b).
25. See, e.g., ACCA and CDSB (2016) and WEF (2019).

SDG-linked resources and reporting mandates for more than seventy countries.[26]

The European Commission has sought to lead the charge with respect to the mainstreaming of consistent sustainability reporting by companies. In early 2020, it launched an initiative to provide detailed guidance on how publicly traded companies with more than five hundred workers should report in a comparable and comprehensive manner on environmental, social, and employee topics, human rights, and bribery and corruption. In 2020, it explained its reasoning as follows:

> "1. There is inadequate publicly available information about how non-financial issues, and sustainability issues in particular, impact companies, and about how companies themselves impact society and the environment. In particular:
>   a. Reported non-financial information is not sufficiently comparable or reliable.
>   b. Companies do not report all non-financial information that users think is necessary, and many companies report information that users do not think is relevant.
>   c. Some companies from which investors and other users want non-financial information do not report such information.
>   d. It is hard for investors and other users to find non-financial information even when it is reported; and
> 2. Companies incur unnecessary and avoidable costs related to reporting non-financial information. Companies face uncertainty and complexity when deciding what non-financial information to report, and how and where to report such information. . . . Market pressures on their own have not proven to be sufficient to ensure that companies report the non-financial information that users say they need. The market is characterised by a number of overlapping and sometimes inconsistent private non-financial reporting frameworks and standards, and companies face significant challenges in deciding whether and to what extent they should use these different frameworks and standards."[27]

---

26. ESG Book (n.d.).
27. DG FISMA (2020).

The EU's initiative, which was later expanded to address a larger universe of companies, including those not listed,[28] instilled a sense of urgency in the business sector and other participants in the sustainability reporting sphere. Big corporations and investors tend to favor the development of a unified international system for sustainability reporting, given that their operations and supply chains often span many jurisdictions. For this reason, many have been encouraging international accounting authorities and regulators to establish a universally accepted baseline international standard as soon as possible based on (but not necessarily limited by) the best practices of existing private voluntary standards.

Such an approach would mirror the evolution of financial accounting standards in the twentieth century, which resulted from a process of iterative collaboration among businesses, investors, accounting bodies, and governments. Starting with railroads and heavy industry, which needed to raise capital from public markets, to large industrial companies requiring improved data to oversee intricate and far-flung operations, to institutional investors seeking increased transparency about the performance of their portfolio companies, to individual investors aiming to safeguard themselves against the risks of asymmetric information (e.g., misrepresentation or self-dealing by large firms and their top managers and investors), financial accounting and disclosure practices grew out of the practical learnings of companies and their accountants in navigating market demands. These innovations were eventually distilled into best practices, with many ultimately being codified initially as private standards set by the accounting community (the American Institute of Certified Public Accountants Accounting Principles Board) and later as formal standards under the quasi-public independent authority of the Financial Accounting Foundation and its two similarly independent and public-private standards boards, the Financial Accounting Standards Board and the Governmental Accounting Standards Board, whose decisions have been recognized as authoritative by the U.S. securities regulator, the SEC, since 1973.

The previous two decades can be viewed as a "market discovery" phase for sustainability reporting, akin to the development of more organized financial reporting initially within the private sector in the late nineteenth century and much of the twentieth. Multiple fundamentally complementary sustainability reporting structures have been developed and trialed in the market in recent years. Their best features can form the building blocks of

---

28. European Commission (2021); Accountancy Europe (n.d.).

the systemically coherent mandatory solution that international accounting authorities and securities regulators are beginning to develop.

The strategy the IFRS Foundation and IOSCO are pursuing for their entry into this domain tracks the vision initially framed by the accounting profession sector and a group of influential voluntary standard setters in the 2019 Accountancy Europe Cogito series paper and the 2020 Joint Declaration of the "Group of 5" leading voluntary standard setters, respectively.[29] IOSCO and the IFRS Foundation consulted extensively with these private standard setters and the TCFD in establishing the ISSB. Indeed, in order to achieve a running start, in 2022 the ISSB integrated much of the staff and intellectual property of two of them—the Climate Disclosure Standards Board and the Value Reporting Foundation.

In March 2022 the new board published two proposals ("exposure drafts") for public consultation, Draft IFRS S1, General Requirements for Disclosure of Sustainability-related Financial Information, and Draft IFRS S2, Climate-related Disclosures. More than 1,400 comment letters on these exposure drafts were submitted during the consultation period, from all over the world and from a wide range of stakeholder groups.[30] The feedback prompted the ISSB to revise the standards and include some transitional measures. In the first year that companies apply these ISSB standards, they do not need to:

"1. provide disclosures about sustainability-related risks and opportunities beyond climate-related information;
2. provide annual sustainability-related disclosures at the same time as the related financial statements;
3. provide comparative information;
4. disclose information about Scope 3 greenhouse gas (GHG) emissions; and
5. use the Green House Gas Protocol to measure emissions, if they are currently using a different approach."[31]

In addition, companies that report solely on climate-related risks and opportunities in the first year have a slightly easier path in their second year, when they do not need to present comparative information about sustainability-related risks and opportunities beyond climate issues.[32]

29. Accountancy Europe (2019); CDP, CDSB, GRI, IIRC, and SASB (2020).
30. IFRS (2023a).
31. FSB (2023).
32. Ibid.

In June 2023, the final versions of IFRS S1 and IFRS S2 were published, alongside the ISSB's Bases for Conclusions, Accompanying Guidance, Effects Analysis, Project Summary, and Feedback Statement. These will apply to annual reporting periods beginning on or after January 1, 2024 (i.e., to the 2024 annual reports by companies).

IOSCO has endorsed IFRS S1 and IFRS S2.[33] The organization has urged its 130-member jurisdictions, which account for more than 95 percent of global financial market activity, to consider how they could adopt, implement, or be guided by these standards.[34]

Thus, more than three decades after the 1992 UN Conference on Environment and Development in Rio de Janeiro, which framed a global agenda for the pursuit of sustainable development, the world finally has its first official international standard for the disclosure of sustainability-related information by companies. This is an important milestone on the journey toward greater corporate transparency and accountability and the systematic internalization of social and environmental externalities in the operations and capital allocation of companies and investors, as implied by the SDGs.

Key Challenges in the Years Ahead

Nevertheless, several major challenges remain regarding the role of corporate reporting in advancing progress on sustainable development.[35] These will be important for the international community to address as it seeks to accelerate progress on the SDGs in the run-up to 2030 and begins to craft the post-2030 Agenda for Sustainable Development. Such challenges relate to the following:

- the ultimate breadth of jurisdictional adoption and substantive scope of the ISSB standards;
- the interoperability of these global standards with those in specific jurisdictions having a different substantive scope, in particular those requiring reporting not only of the impact of sustainability factors on enterprise value creation (financial materiality) but also

---

33. IOSCO (2023).
34. FSB (2023), IOSCO (2023).
35. Part of this section is drawn or adapted directly from FSB (2023).

of the company's sustainability impact on society, or so-called double materiality;
- the fitness for purpose of both these types of reporting in terms of generating reliable, decision-useful information to guide strategic decision-making by boards, management teams, and investment committees (as opposed to creating unnecessary complexity and detail that produce a perfunctory, check-the-box compliance mentality); and
- the need for capacity building for small and medium-size enterprises (SMEs) and other related issues, especially in developing countries.

Breadth and Interoperability of Jurisdictional Adoption

Many jurisdictions have indicated that they plan to adopt the first two ISSB standards. As of October 2023, seventeen out of twenty-four government members of the FSB stated that they had established or were putting in place structures and processes to bring them into compliance with local regulatory requirements.[36] At the December 2023 UN COP28 climate change negotiations in Dubai, the ISSB announced that "regulators and standard setters from ASEAN, Brazil, Brunei, Canada, the European Union, Germany, Ghana, Hong Kong, Japan, Kenya, Mauritius, Mexico, Myanmar, Nigeria, the Philippines, Singapore, Turkey, the United Kingdom, Uruguay and Vietnam have . . . welcomed the work of the ISSB," in addition to hundreds of industry, investor, accounting, and civil society organizations.[37] Moreover, the CDP (formerly the Carbon Disclosure Project), a member of the Climate Disclosure Standards Board (CDSB) and sponsor of the world's largest environmental disclosure platform, announced the year before at COP27 that it would incorporate IFRS S2 into its annual questionnaires issued to companies on behalf of 680 financial institutions with over $130 trillion in assets.[38]

---

36. For country-specific details in this regard, see FSB (2023).
37. For a full list, see IFRS (2023c).
38. The CDP is a not-for-profit charity that runs a global disclosure system supporting investors, companies, cities, states, and regions to manage their environmental impacts. It was established in 2000 as a platform issuing questionnaires to companies about their climate impact for the benefit and use of institutional investors (https://www.cdp.net/en/info/about-us/). Since then, the CDP has broadened its scope to incorporate disclosures on deforestation and water security while also expanding its reach to support cities, states, and regions. See also CDP (2022).

Despite the progress that is being made, a significant number of jurisdictions have expressed reluctance to adopt the standards in full, at least for the foreseeable future, owing to concerns about the readiness of their business communities and the perceived rigor of the standards. Accordingly, the actual breadth and depth of the global uptake of these new standards may prove to be slower and more uneven than many had hoped, other things being equal.

Among first-mover jurisdictions are the EU, Singapore, Canada, the UK, and California,[39] the last of which looks poised to set the pace in the large U.S. market in light of the significant political disagreement and likely litigation on this issue at the federal level and the large number of U.S. and foreign firms doing business in the state.[40] The EU's Corporate Sustainability Reporting Directive (CSRD) includes a requirement for more than 50,000 large and listed companies based in the EU (but also certain third-country companies based outside the EU with undertakings in the EU) to report sustainability-related information under European Sustainability Reporting Standards (ESRS), the EU sustainability reporting framework.[41] The final ESRS was adopted on July 31, 2023, and states:

"Companies will have to start reporting under ESRS according to the following timetable:
- Companies previously subject to the Non-Financial Reporting Directive (NFRD) (large, listed companies, large banks and large insurance undertakings—all if they have more than 500 employees), as well as large non-EU listed companies with more than 500 employees: financial year 2024, with first sustainability statement published in 2025.
- Other large companies, including other large non-EU listed companies: financial year 2025, with first sustainability statement published in 2026.
- Listed SMEs, including non-EU listed SMEs: financial year 2026, with first sustainability statements published in 2027. However,

---

39. For an overview of California's new requirements (which will affect an estimated three quarters of Fortune 500 firms, among others), see AFREF, Public Citizen, and Sierra Club (2023).
40. The State of California initiative is also being challenged by some parts of the U.S. business community. See, e.g., Mindock (2024).
41. European Parliament (2022).

listed SMEs may decide to opt out of the reporting requirements for a further two years. The last possible date for a listed SME to start reporting is financial year 2028, with first sustainability statement published in 2029."[42]

These EU developments illustrate both the promise and challenge facing corporate sustainability reporting in the years ahead. The early action of such a large jurisdiction will certainly accelerate the mainstreaming of such reporting by companies, particularly larger ones and those with global operations. However, the European directive has moved ahead of the international process in a number of key respects and will likely have a certain extraterritorial effect on non-EU companies having important operations in the EU. Their home jurisdictions ultimately may choose not to regulate in the same way as the EU, potentially creating conflicting disclosure requirements and additional complexity for companies operating in both jurisdictions (and others).

The first and most fundamental potential source of discontinuity is the EU's use of the "double materiality" concept. Unlike the ISSB standards, which are focused on aspects of sustainability deemed financially relevant to a firm's performance, the EU is requiring companies also to report on the firm's material impact on society and the environment, and to do so irrespective of the extent to which such effects have or are likely to have a significant bearing on the firm's financial performance and prospects. The EU is not alone in preferring this wider scope of reporting; however, such an approach creates challenges for the international coherence of corporate reporting and the complexity of compliance for companies that operate across jurisdictions.

The EU and the ISSB have been working to mitigate this risk by seeking to make their standards interoperable in the sense of having the ISSB global baseline standard serve as a foundational "building block" of the more expansive European reporting requirements. The stated goal is to ensure that companies using the global ISSB standard will not have to redo or substantially adapt that aspect of their reporting in their EU filings; rather, they would focus on supplementing it with reporting on the additional topics and scope of materiality mandated by the EU. However, this remains a work in progress, and the jury is still out on how seamless the modularity of ISSB

---

42. European Commission (2023).

and ESRS standards will be. Indeed, there remains a risk that companies will feel compelled to choose between the two, in effect creating two global baseline standards and thereby defeating the original purpose of shifting from the "alphabet soup" of initialisms of competing voluntary standards to a coherent global framework of official ones.

In the case of climate-related reporting, this challenge is made somewhat easier by the reliance of both the ISSB and the ESRS standards on the pioneering and mutually reinforcing work of the TCFD, CDSB, and SASB (box 9.1). These voluntary standards initiatives have facilitated the quality and comparability of corporate climate reporting for many years. Nevertheless, questions persist about the data collection methodologies and the quality and thoroughness of such disclosure and its actual impact on company strategy, capital allocation, and operational decision-making.[43]

Substantive Scope of Reporting Requirements

Another potential source of incongruity among national regulatory requirements and between them and the global baseline standard being created by international accounting authorities relates to the scope of the sustainability topics they cover. One of the most important contributions of the EU's initiative has been to create some of the first officially mandated topical requirements for corporate sustainability reporting beyond climate change. The ESRS includes twelve standards covering a range of sustainability topics, as summarized in table 9.1.

Here again, the quest for global consistency and comparability of reporting is facilitated by the EU's reliance on the earlier work of voluntary standard setters, in this case that of the Global Reporting Initiative (GRI).[44] GRI standards are used by over 10,000 companies and other organizations in more than one hundred countries, and the European Commission has acknowledged that "from the beginning of the development of draft ESRS by EFRAG, the GRI served as an important reference point, and many of the reporting requirements in ESRS were inspired by the GRI standards,"[45] which in turn drew from other relevant frameworks, such as the UN Guiding Principles on Business and Human Rights.[46]

---

43. See, e.g., EY (2023).
44. See GRI (2024).
45. European Commission (2021).
46. See OHCHR (2011) and Business and Human Rights Resource Centre (n.d.).

Box 9.1. The Status of Climate Change Reporting as of 2023

The 2023 Status Report of the Task Force on Climate-Related Financial Disclosures used artificial intelligence (AI) to assess how alignment with its eleven recommended disclosures evolved across more than 1,350 large public companies from 2020 through 2022. The same publication examined 2022 reports from a broader global sample of around 3,100 diverse companies and presented results from a survey on climate-related reporting practices across leading global asset managers and asset owners. Key findings include the following:

- TCFD-aligned disclosure is expanding. Over half (58 percent) of surveyed public companies aligned with at least five recommendations in 2022, a significant increase from 18 percent in 2020.

- However, only 4 percent of firms aligned with all eleven TCFD recommendations.

- Disclosure of climate-related risks increased by 26 percent between 2020 and 2022, whereas reporting on board oversight and targets increased by twenty-five and twenty-four percentage points, respectively.

- Climate information was four times more likely to be disclosed in sustainability and annual reports than in financial filings.

- The most frequently disclosed TCFD recommendation was reporting of metrics relating to climate-related risks or opportunities (71 percent of companies). At the same time, 66 percent of companies reported on greenhouse gas (GHG) emissions and climate-related targets, compared to only 42 percent in 2020.

- By contrast, a mere 11 percent of the sample disclosed information pertaining to resilience under different climate-related scenarios.

- European companies averaged 7.2 out of the eleven recommended disclosures, whereas Middle Eastern and African firms disclosed 3.8 recommendations on average.

- Larger companies were more likely than smaller companies to disclose TCFD-aligned information, reporting on average 6.7 recommendations in 2022 compared to 3.9 in 2020. Climate-related targets (85 percent) and metrics (83 percent) were the areas most reported by larger companies.

- Asset managers and owners referenced insufficient availability of information from investee companies as the biggest challenge to climate-related reporting. Public companies posed the biggest problem for asset managers (62 percent), as did private investments for asset owners (84 percent).

Sources: FSB (2023); TCFD (2023).

Table 9.1. Topics Covered by European Sustainability Reporting Standards (ESRS)

Group	Number	Subject
Cross-cutting	ESRS 1	General requirements
Cross-cutting	ESRS 2	General disclosures
Environment	ESRS E1	Climate
Environment	ESRS E2	Pollution
Environment	ESRS E3	Water and marine resources
Environment	ESRS E4	Biodiversity and ecosystems
Environment	ESRS E5	Resource use and the circular economy
Social	ESRS S1	Own workforce
Social	ESRS S2	Workers in the value chain
Social	ESRS S3	Affected communities
Social	ESRS S4	Consumers and end users
Governance	ESRS G1	Business conduct

Source: European Commission (2023).

In addition, two other voluntary multistakeholder sustainability standards initiatives are seeking to lay the foundation for the rapid creation of high-quality, globally coherent official standards on the topics of biodiversity and inequality: the Task Force on Nature-Related Financial Disclosures (TNFD) and the Task Force on Inequality and Social-Related Financial Disclosures (TISFD), respectively.[47] The TNFD is further along, having issued its recommended standard in September 2023, whereas the TISFD was formed in mid-2023 from a merger of two related initiatives.[48] Both efforts seek to track the basic architecture of the TCFD framework, which was organized around the four topics of governance, strategy, risk management, and metrics and targets.

These two initiatives are timely. Now that the ISSB has completed work on its general-purpose and climate-specific standards, it is considering the next sustainability topics on which to develop standards,[49] and some jurisdictions are already engaged in standard setting on ESG topics beyond climate change. This expanded scope is important for three reasons. First, the public interest is at stake. Progress is lagging badly on nearly all of the 17 SDGs,

---

47. TNFD (n.d.); TIFD (n.d.a).
48. TIFD (n.d.b).
49. ISSB (2024) and IFRS (2024a).

which were universally adopted by governments in 2015. The private sector has a critical role to play in the achievement of these goals. Second, many companies are interested in the internal benchmarking and public reporting of wider SDG progress on a credible and comparable basis. Such reporting was an explicit rationale invoked by WEF International Business Council CEOs in creating their common metrics in 2020. Third, absent a structured and internationally coordinated effort to create high-quality reporting standards across much of the ground covered by the SDGs, low-quality and inconsistent reporting on such matters is likely to result. This will frustrate the internalization of social and environmental externalities by companies and the greater corporate transparency that leaders have promised in multiple multilateral declarations, complicating efficient resource allocation by firms, investors, and governments and undermining public accountability.

Relevance for Decision-Making

However, achieving comprehensiveness and consistency in corporate sustainability reporting is only half the battle. Ensuring its effectiveness in terms of influencing board, C-suite, and investor thinking and decision-making is an equally important and difficult challenge, one that is sometimes referred to as the connectivity of financial and sustainability reporting.

To this end, the IFRS Foundation has stated that one of its priorities for the foreseeable future will be to facilitate dialogue and outright cooperation between the IASB and ISSB on such matters. According to a 2023 report of the FSB,

> The outcome of this project could be narrow-scope amendments to IFRS Accounting Standards, limited new application guidance, new illustrative examples, or further educational materials. One of the related challenges will be to determine the precise boundary between this project and the requirements of the new ISSB Standards. The feedback the IASB has received so far is quite mixed. Some stakeholders hold the view that the existing accounting requirements are principles-based and thus already address any climate-related risks sufficiently. Others disagree with this view and are requesting a review of all existing accounting standards with a view to explicitly addressing climate-related risks.[50]

50. FSB (2023), 11.

Capacity Building and Other Challenges

Based on a survey of its member jurisdictions, the FSB identified a number of other salient challenges for the future of corporate sustainability reporting, including the following:[51]

ADOPTION BY EMDEs AND SMEs AND PROPORTIONALITY. The ISSB standards are likely to present a greater implementation challenge in emerging markets and developing economies (EMDEs) and for smaller firms more generally. Member jurisdictions suggested a range of possible strategies in response, for example applying a sense of proportionality in reporting requirements based on firm size and offering transitional or phase-in periods to enable the gradual introduction of certain disclosure requirements for smaller firms.

CAPACITY BUILDING. Knowledge gaps exist among various stakeholders. Efforts to provide technical and regulatory information and advice along with initiatives to strengthen ESG-related technical abilities among both regulators and market participants will be needed to ensure firms are prepared for the new disclosure requirements. In addition, there is much work to be done in refining methods to quantify the impact of climate-related risks in companies' financial statements.

DATA AVAILABILITY, DATA QUALITY, AND TRUSTWORTHINESS. Data scarcity and subpar data quality are likely to present challenges in the early stages. There is also a risk that companies will cherry-pick the most positive or easily available information or otherwise engage in "greenwashing." Third-party assurance of climate-related and other sustainability information is critical; however, it also requires considerable further development and application among firms.

CHALLENGES IN PROVIDING VARIOUS METRICS, SUCH AS SCOPE 3 GHG EMISSIONS AND SCENARIO ANALYSIS. Some metrics require further refinement to facilitate broader and more consistent application. The calculation and reporting of Scope 3 GHG emissions in particular are likely to benefit from

---

51. Ibid. Material in the next four paragraphs is paraphrased from this source (FSB 2003).

additional assistance and guidance.[52] A number of jurisdictions emphasized the importance of ensuring consistency between the requirements of IFRS S2 and the GHG Protocol Corporate Accounting and Reporting Standard.[53]

Implications for the Post-2030 Development Framework

Thus the strength and coherence of official standards governing private sector conduct are important new issues to be prioritized in a post-2030 (i.e., post-SDG) sustainable development framework. So too is the considerable increase in capacity-building assistance for SMEs and developing countries that the spread of such standards implies. These topics received very limited attention in the MDGs and SDGs.

Across the business, investor, and accounting communities, private sector actors have a pivotal role to play in sustaining the momentum and ensuring the ultimate success of each aspect of this process: standard setting, standards adoption (by both jurisdictions and firms), and capacity building.[54] These actors wield considerable influence, especially when they push in the same direction, and they would benefit enormously from the efficiencies that improved international coordination of norms, tools, and capacity building would bring in a post-2030 development framework that prioritized them. These actors are most familiar with current market conditions, opportunities, and challenges. They are also well positioned, by virtue of their role in the development of voluntary standards over many years in cooperation with NGOs, to ensure the robust involvement of civil society and academic experts in key aspects of sustainability, supported, where necessary, by development assistance institutions. This influential community is likely to retain a critical role in shaping how societies evaluate the adequacy of regulators' efforts.

---

52. From the EPA's website, "Scope 3 emissions are the result of activities from assets not owned or controlled by the reporting organization, but that the organization indirectly affects in its value chain. An organization's value chain consists of both its upstream and downstream activities" (https://www.epa.gov/climateleadership/scope-3-inventory-guidance#:~:text=Scope%203%20emissions%20are%20the,its%20upstream%20and%20downstream%20activities).
53. FSB (2023), 28–29.
54. As discussed in Samans and Nelson (2022).

Board chairs and CEOs have substantial convening and agenda-setting power.[55] With a certain amount of collective attention and action, they could help to ensure that the most relevant international organizations, governments, and industry and civil society organizations maintain the necessary political and material backing for the realization of a high-quality, truly interoperable international system of corporate sustainability reporting standards that incentivizes the routine internalization of social and environmental externalities in corporate and investor decision-making.

The next few years are likely to prove decisive in this regard. With so much at stake, the private sector should engage proactively with governments and civil society partners to:

- encourage political authorities in various jurisdictions, and particularly first-mover jurisdictions such as the EU and California, to ensure that their standards are designed to achieve building-block modularity and interoperability with the international baseline that is being developed by the ISSB;
- ensure the fitness for purpose of market-based tools and methods on which implementation of official standards relies, such as the Greenhouse Gas Protocol, which recently embarked on a technical review and potential refreshment of its widely used framework[56]; and
- expand capacity building for SMEs and developing country firms that otherwise might struggle to compete fairly with larger and more experienced and better-resourced firms with respect to sustainability management and reporting.[57] Even larger firms have begun expressing qualms about the sheer volume of work that will be required to comply with ESRS, which has published a list of over 1,100 data points corresponding to its framework.[58]

Finally, business leaders wishing to strengthen the sustainable value creation performance of their own firms while helping to accelerate broader

---

55. Ibid.
56. Greenhouse Gas Protocol (n.d.).
57. A significant new initiative in this regard is the ESG Exchange.
58. See, e.g., Michel (2023).

progress toward achieving the SDGs should do more than express support for and await the results of the construction of this new, harmonized corporate sustainability reporting ecosystem. They should act swiftly to put into practice their own firm's approach to integrated reporting by applying a pragmatic, best-practice combination of the most relevant mandatory and voluntary standards in their annual report in a manner their board determines best enhances the shared value created by their firm. This is especially the case for the social dimension of sustainability reporting (e.g., respect for labor standards and other human rights, payment of a fair living wage, and other workplace practices that bear on worker safety, health, agency, and productivity). These aspects have thus far received less attention from regulators and accounting authorities than environmental issues despite their central importance to both business and societal value creation. Such a proactive posture will help ensure that their firm's disclosures keep pace with a rapidly changing business and corporate governance context in which employees, board members, and investors are increasingly interested in benchmarking firm performance and strategy on a full range of sustainability considerations.

In particular, the ISSB and GRI standards appear to provide a sound basis for any firm seeking to satisfy respectively the financially material and societal impact dimensions of its disclosure. National regulators should make a point of building on these frameworks by incorporating or cross-referencing them in their requirements in the interests of reducing business complexity and enhancing the overall consistency and thus effectiveness of sustainability reporting.

Accordingly, there is no need for company management teams and boards to hold off until the international sustainability standards regulatory landscape is fully developed. Higher performance, lower risk, and more satisfied investors and other stakeholders are in store for firms that take immediate action along these lines. They can do so by utilizing the internationally accepted frameworks that are already available and by actively encouraging regulators to progress rapidly in the direction of a more complete and consistent international system of mandatory sustainability reporting requirements that serves to internalize social and environmental externalities in investment decisions at scale across the world economy, as implied by the SDGs, to which all governments have agreed.

At the same time, economic policymakers and development institutions should recognize that improving the accountability and facilitation of the private sector's contribution to progress on sustainable development merits much greater emphasis in both current policy and the post-2030 framework. The SDGs set specific objectives with respect to the overall economic, social, and environmental progress humanity seeks. But a sharper focus on implementation is clearly required in the years ahead, particularly in the private sector, where most of the corresponding changes in behaviors and priorities must ultimately occur. It follows that the norms, policies, and metrics of private sector governance and conduct, including but not limited to those pertaining to sustainability disclosure, ought to become far more central to the way humanity organizes and encourages progress on sustainable development in the years to come.

REFERENCES

Accountancy Europe. 2019. "Interconnected Standard Setting for Corporate Reporting." Cogito series. Brussels: European Commission, December.

———. n.d. "Covenant of Companies for Climate and Energy." Brussels: European Commission.

ACCA (Association of Chartered Certified Accountants) and CDSB (Climate Disclosure Standards Board). 2016. *Mapping the Sustainability Reporting Landscape: Lost in the Right Direction*. London.

AFREF (Americans for Financial Reform Education Fund), Public Citizen, and Sierra Club. 2023. *How Might California's New Climate Disclosure Laws Impact Federal Rulemaking?* October.

AICPA (Association of International Certified Professional Accountants), IIRC (International Integrated Reporting Council), and Black Sun PLC. 2018. *Purpose beyond Profit: The Value of Value—Board Level Insights*. London and Durham, NC.

Business and Human Rights Resource Centre. n.d. "UN Guiding Principles on Business and Human Rights."

CDP (Carbon Disclosure Project). 2022. "CDP to Incorporate ISSB Climate-Related Disclosure Standard into Global Environmental Disclosure Platform." November 8.

CDP, CDSB (Climate Disclosure Standards Board), GRI (Global Reporting Initiative), IIRC (International Integrated Reporting Council), and SASB (Sustainability Accounting Standards Board). 2020. "Statement of Intent to Work Together Towards Comprehensive Corporate Reporting." IFRS.

DG FISMA (Directorate-General for Financial Stability, Financial Services and Capital Markets Union). 2020. *Revision of the Non-Financial Reporting Directive: Inception Impact Assessment*. Brussels: European Commission.

EY. 2023. *Global Climate Risk Barometer 2023: How Will Understanding Climate Risk Move You from Ambition to Action?* London: Ernst & Young Global Ltd.

ESG Book. n.d. "The Reporting Exchange."
ESG Exchange. n.d. "Global Exchange for How to Deliver Decision-Useful Sustainability Information."
European Commission. 2023. "Questions and Answers on the Adoption of European Sustainability Reporting Standards." Press release, July 31.
———. 2021. "Questions and Answers: Corporate Sustainability Reporting Directive Proposal." Press release, April 21.
European Parliament. 2022. "Sustainable Economy: Parliament Adopts New Reporting Rules for Multinationals." Press release, November 10.
FSB (Financial Stability Board). 2023. *Progress Report on Climate-Related Disclosures: 2023 Report.* Basel, October.
Greenhouse Gas Protocol. n.d. "GHG Protocol Corporate Suite of Standards and Guidance Update Process."
GRI (Global Reporting Initiative). 2024. *Full Set of GRI Standards.*
GRI and USB (University of Stellenbosch Business School). 2020. *Carrots and Sticks: Sustainability Reporting Policy—Global Trends in Disclosure as the ESG Agenda Goes Mainstream.* Amsterdam and Cape Town.
IFAC (International Federation of Accountants). 2019. "Enhancing Corporate Reporting."
IFRS (International Financial Reporting Standards). 2024a. "Climate-Related and Other Uncertainties in the Financial Statements." April.
———. 2024b. "Management Commentary." March.
———. 2023a. *Feedback Statement: IFRS Sustainability Disclosure Standards.* London.
———. 2023b. "IASB and Joint FASB-IASB Update September 2023." September.
———. 2023c. "ISSB at COP28: Close to 400 Organisations from 64 Jurisdictions, Including Associations Gathering over 10,000 Member Companies and Investors, Join Multilateral and Market Authorities to Commit to Advance the ISSB Climate Global Baseline." Press release, December 4.
———. 2021a. *IFRS Foundation Trustees' Feedback Statement on the Consultation Paper on Sustainability Reporting.* London.
———. 2021b. "IFRS Trustees Announce Working Group to Accelerate Convergence in Global Sustainability Reporting Standards Focused on Enterprise Value." Press release, March 22.
IOSCO (International Organization of Securities Commissions). 2023. "IOSCO Endorses the ISSB's Sustainability-related Financial Disclosures Standards." Press release, July 25.
———. 2021a. "IOSCO Elaborates on Its Vision and Expectations for the IFRS Foundation's Work towards a Global Baseline of Investor-Focussed Sustainability Standards to Improve the Global Consistency, Comparability and Reliability of Sustainability Reporting." Press release, June 28.

———. 2021b. "IOSCO Sees an Urgent Need for Globally Consistent, Comparable, and Reliable Sustainability Disclosure Standards and Announces Its Priorities and Vision for a Sustainability Standards Board Under the IFRS Foundation." Press release, February 24.
———. 2020. "IOSCO Steps Up Its Efforts to Address Issues around Sustainability and Climate Change." Press release, April 14.
ISSB (International Sustainability Standards Board). 2024. "ISSB Consultation on Agenda Priorities." April.
KPMG. 2017. *The Road Ahead: The KPMG Survey of Corporate Responsibility Reporting 2017.* Zürich: KPMG International.
Lee, A. H. 2021. "Public Input Welcomed on Climate Change Disclosures." Washington, DC: SEC, March 15.
Michel, M. 2023. "Sustainability Directors Concerned about Volume of ESRS Data Points." CSO Futures, November 9.
Mindock, C. 2024. "California's Landmark Climate Disclosure Laws Challenged by Business Groups." Reuters, January 30.
Morgan Stanley Institute for Sustainable Investing. 2020. "Sustainable Signals: Asset Owners See Sustainability as Core to the Future of Investing." Press release, May 27.
NGFS (Network for Greening the Financial System). 2019. *A Call for Action: Climate Change as a Source of Financial Risk.* Paris.
OHCHR (Office of the United Nations High Commissioner for Human Rights). 2011. *The UN Guiding Principles on Business and Human Rights: An Introduction.* Geneva.
Saa, L. 2020. "PRI Welcomes 500th Asset Owner Signatory." UNPRI.org, January 27.
Samans, R., and J. Nelson. 2022. "Corporate Reporting and Accounting." In *Sustainable Enterprise Value Creation: Implementing Stakeholder Capitalism through Full ESG Integration.* Geneva: Palgrave Macmillan.
SASB (Sustainability Accounting Standards Board). n.d. "Global Use of SASB Standards." San Francisco.
TCFD (Task Force on Climate-Related Financial Disclosures). 2023. *Task Force on Climate-Related Financial Disclosures: 2023 Status Report.* October.
TIFD (Task Force on Inequality-Related Financial Disclosures). n.d.a. "Inequality Is a Systemic Risk." https://thetifd.org/.
———. n.d.b. "Joint Statement on Convergence Between TIFD and TSFD."
TNFD (Task Force on Nature-Related Financial Disclosures). n.d. "About." https://tnfd.global/.
UBS (Union Bank of Switzerland). 2018. "Return on Values: Most Investors Expect Better Performance, Bigger Impact." *UBS Investor Watch*, vol. 2, September 19.

SEC (United States Securities and Exchange Commission). 2024. "The Enhancement and Standardization of Climate-Related Disclosures for Investors." Washington, DC.

WEF (World Economic Forum). 2019. "ESG Ecosystem Map." Cologny, CH.

WEF IBC (World Economic Forum International Business Council). 2020. *Toward Common Metrics and Consistent Reporting of Sustainable Value Creation.* Geneva.

WFE (World Federation of Exchanges). 2019. *WFE Sustainability Survey April 2019: Exchanges Advancing Sustainable Finance.* London.

TEN

Assurance and Its Contribution to Sustainable Development

TOM SEIDENSTEIN AND WARREN MAROUN

The last two decades have seen different types of integrated and sustainability reporting becoming a norm rather than an exception.[1] More than 90 percent of the world's largest companies are now engaged in at least some form of extra-financial or sustainability reporting. At least 60 percent recognize explicitly the risks posed by climate change to their business models.[2] An increasing number of asset managers are incorporating social and environmental issues into investment decisions. Like their investees, both asset managers and owners are reporting more frequently

---

1. Different types of reporting on more than just financial information have emerged over the last thirty years. Examples include triple bottom line, corporate social responsibility (CSR), environmental, social, and governance (ESG) factors, sustainability, and integrated reports. A review of their differences and similarities is beyond the scope of this chapter, which, for brevity, refers collectively to "sustainability reports" and "sustainability reporting."
2. KPMG (2020, 2022).

on social and environmental matters as part of their primary communications with clients and beneficiaries.³

To date, most large corporations have reported on environmental, social, and governance (ESG) measures voluntarily, but this is changing. Policymakers are increasingly mandating ESG reporting requirements with the goal of generating the same level of trust in sustainability reporting as stakeholders have in financial statements. Accurate, complete, and reliable ESG information should help enable capital markets to function efficiently and support increased accountability for organizations' financial and extra-financial performance.⁴

For this reason, there has been growing cohesion behind a few leading and globally applicable reporting standards. For example, the Task Force on Climate-Related Financial Disclosures (TCFD) released its recommendations in 2017. As of November 2023, almost five thousand organizations were using these recommendations, which form the basis for minimum reporting requirements under consideration by the U.S. Securities and Exchange Commission (SEC).⁵ During 2022, the EU approved the Corporate Sustainability Reporting Directive (CSRD).⁶ This requires a wide range of sustainability disclosures according to European Sustainability Reporting Standards (ESRSs), drafted by the European Financial Reporting Advisory Group. At the international level, the Global Reporting Initiative published updates to its standards during 2021 to promote ease of application and even more relevant and reliable sustainability reporting. In the same year, the International Sustainability Standards Board (ISSB) was formed. It published its first two standards during 2023 as part of an ongoing effort to develop a "comprehensive global baseline of sustainability disclosures."⁷

Reporting standards alone, however, are insufficient to support the goal of more sustainable and efficient capital allocations. Any trusted corporate

---

3. FSB (2022).
4. "Extra-financial" refers to the combination of environmental, social, and governance matters, including their interconnection with economic factors.
5. At the time of writing, the SEC had not reached a firm conclusion on sustainability reporting requirements in general. In March 2024, the SEC announced rules for enhancing and standardizing climate-related disclosures for investors. For the number of companies following the recommendations, see the web page at Task Force on Climate-Related Financial Disclosures | TCFD (fsb-tcfd.org).
6. See the European Commission's web page, "Corporate Sustainability Reporting."
7. See the IFRS website at https://www.ifrs.org/groups/international-sustainability-standards-board/.

reporting system must include external third-party assurance. In its simplest form, "assurance" means that an independent expert, exercising due care and skill, examines and reaches a conclusion on the appropriateness of information being reported to investors or other stakeholders.

In the world of financial reporting, assurance takes the form of financial statement audits. Independent audits by subject experts help address principal-agent issues and improve the quality of financial reporting. By reducing the risk that financial statements include material misstatements, audits bolster the confidence of capital market participants and other stakeholders in financial reporting. The same applies in the sustainability space, where leading institutions (such as the International Organization of Securities Commissions, the Financial Stability Board, and the ISSB) and academic research highlight the important role that assurance can play in ensuring the accuracy, completeness and reliability of organizations' sustainability reporting.[8] The International Auditing and Assurance Standards Board (IAASB) has responded by complementing the development of internationally comparable and accepted reporting standards with a timely and robust assurance solution.[9]

In addition to dealing with the audit of financial statements (an example of assurance), the IAASB has long written standards for assurance of nonfinancial information. Most notable is ISAE 3000, which can be used for a range of nonfinancial information, and ISAE 3410, which deals specifically with greenhouse gas statements.[10] In April 2021 the IAASB published guidance aimed at helping assurance providers apply these standards to sustainability reports. Research by the International Federation of Accountants (IFAC) shows that demand for assurance is growing globally,

---

8. IFAC (2023); Maroun (2019a); Zhou, Simnett, and Hoang (2019).

9. IAASB (2022). The IAASB is an independent and publicly accountable body that develops assurance principles and practices used in over 130 jurisdictions. The standard setter's activities are overseen by the Public Interest Oversight Board. The Consultative Advisory Group gives an important public interest perspective on the development of assurance standards. The International Federation of Accountants provides further supporting structures and process. For further details on the IAASB, see the website at https://www.iaasb.org/about_iaasb.

10. Information on the ISAE standards can be found in *International Standard on Assurance Engagements (ISAE) 3000 (Revised): Assurance Engagements Other than Audits or Reviews of Historical Financial Information* and *ISAE 3410 Assurance Engagements on Greenhouse Gas Statements*, which can be accessed at https://eis.international-standards.org/standards/iaasb/2020?section=MASTER_45.

and the IAASB's standards form the basis for the great majority of assurance practices today.[11]

Policymakers have, however, asked for more specificity. They have called for an assurance standard that directly addresses the various types of sustainability reporting emerging globally in the interest of ensuring sustainability reporting of comparable quality to financial reporting. In November 2024 the IAASB approved "ISSA 5000: General Requirements for Sustainability Assurance Engagements" (ISSA 5000).[12]

The remainder of this chapter examines the factors driving the development and some of the key features of ISSA 5000. These features, in our view, position ISSA 5000 well to serve as a global baseline for assuring sustainability information and contribute to the advancement of sustainability reporting and, more broadly, sustainable development. Our opinions are based on extensive engagement with the business community, regulators, policymakers, and sustainability experts. The starting point is the role played by sustainability reporting under a responsible capitalism ethos.

Why Sustainability Reporting Is Relevant to Responsible Capitalism

Sustainable development is not about reorganizing the global economy along political and ideological lines but an attempt to balance current economic considerations with the rights of current and future generations to satisfy their needs.[13] Sustainable development is at the heart of "responsible capitalism," or an approach to doing business according to which economic imperatives are pursued with due consideration for society and the environment. An organization still generates value for its investors, but this is done mindful of the interconnections among the economic, environmental, and social capitals on which the entity depends and how its activities have an impact on those capitals.

An assessment of how an entity creates, preserves, or erodes value for itself and its stakeholders is also relevant. Taking cognizance of the immediate needs of investors, in addition to the long-term goals of the

---

11. IFAC (2023).
12. ISSA 5000 (2024).
13. United Nations (1987); IODSA (2016).

organization and its other stakeholders, is not an exercise in political correctness but an economic imperative. A business cannot operate in isolation or by pursuing only short-term profit-taking for financial capital providers. A multifaceted approach to strategy development, risk assessment, and operations management is needed that recognizes economic aims and balances them with social and environmental objectives, some of which may be at odds with short-term increases in financial wealth. This is frequently referred to as "integrated thinking."[14]

Sustainability reporting is about communicating how an organization is working toward the realization of sustainable development.[15] Sustainability reporting provides the information necessary for investors and creditors to make more informed decisions than by merely relying on financial statements, which provide a one-dimensional view of an entity's position and performance. Other key stakeholders may also rely on sustainability reports, including, for example, employees, customers, suppliers, and nongovernmental organizations.

Sustainability reports need to include useful information. The reports provide a basis for governing bodies to interact with their investors, creditors, and other stakeholders. They allow organizations to be compared with peers according to economic, environmental, and social indicators. In keeping with the maxim that what is measured is managed, sustainability reporting can drive changes at the strategic, risk management, and operational levels as part of the process of postimplementation review and continuous improvement.[16] When prepared to the highest standards of care and skill, sustainability reports lower information asymmetry by explaining how an entity manages trade-offs among economic, environmental, and social factors; the full range of risks to which it is exposed; and the opportunities available for advancing its interests.[17] These principles apply irrespective of whether sustainability reporting is mandatory or voluntary.

A growing body of empirical evidence illustrates how firms that incorporate responsible capitalism or integrated thinking into their business models and report on the outcomes benefit from improved internal decision-making, lower costs of capital, and greater access to financial and other

14. IIRC (2021); IOSCO (2021); King and Atkins (2016).
15. IODSA (2016).
16. Guthrie, Manes-Rossi, and Rebecca (2017); McNally and Maroun (2018); Stubbs and Higgins (2014).
17. De Villiers, Hsiao, and Maroun (2020); IIRC (2020).

resources. When the valid interests of other stakeholders are taken into consideration, organizations realize gains from more stable supply chains, less regulatory intervention, and continuing support for their social license to operate.[18]

Why External Assurance Is a Necessary Complement to Sustainability Reporting

The world is accustomed to the role of external audits in financial reporting. Audits of financial statements have been used for over a century to reassure market participants that income statements and balance sheets are fit for purpose. The same rationale applies to an even greater extent to sustainability reporting in light of the inherently complex, diverse, and discretionary nature of the content of these documents. Sustainability reports prepared by management may be biased, lack specificity, obscure important information, or omit key details. This is especially the case when applicable guidelines or regulations are not sufficiently mature, leading to significant variations in the nature and extent of disclosures. Assurance can play an important role in addressing these problems.

An expert exercising due care and skill and operating according to the highest ethical standards performs appropriate fieldwork to conclude whether the sustainability information supplied to capital markets is free of material misstatements. Without external assurance, investors, creditors, and other stakeholders have no practical means of determining whether sustainability information is credible. For example, it is difficult (or impossible) to conclude that all applicable facts and circumstances have been incorporated into a sustainability report. The accuracy of disclosures remains in doubt. There is no guarantee that the events detailed in a sustainability report have occurred and pertain to that entity. Instead, stakeholders must operate on the good faith assumption that there is no disconnect between what is presented in sustainability reports and the underlying economic, environmental, and social reality.

In addition to providing a basis for stakeholders to rely on sustainability reports, assurance leads to improved compliance with laws and regulations

---

18. Baboukardos (2018); Barth et al. (2017); Churet and Eccles (2014); De Villiers, Hsiao, and Maroun (2020).

and more robust internal monitoring and control systems. Insights obtained during the course of assuring sustainability information can highlight risk areas, deficiencies in reporting systems, or inconsistencies between operational activities and strategic objectives. As a result, assurance helps those charged with an organization's governance to discharge their fiduciary duties and accept responsibility for external reporting to debt and equity providers or other stakeholders.[19] This may be especially relevant in jurisdictions where institutional structures, governance systems, and investor protection mechanisms are less advanced relative to those of global leaders.

As a result, the EU, the International Organization of Securities Commissions (IOSCO), the Financial Stability Board (FSB), and the ISSB are just some of the leading institutions iterating the importance of external assurance for ensuring the integrity of the extra-financial information, which is becoming increasingly important for capital markets, regulators, and other parties. All these organizations have highlighted the need for the IAASB to act in response to growing demands for reliable and consistent sustainability reporting.

ISSA 5000 should be seen both as the IAASB's response to these calls and as the best possibility for providing a globally standardized basis for assurance. The standard builds on widely used and tested practices and principles and has been developed independently in the public interest. ISSA 5000 taps into a long history of appointing an independent external expert to attest to the fair presentation of reported information or its preparation according to specified criteria.

Why Building on Tried-and-Tested Principles Makes Sense

The development of ISSA 5000 was not a greenfield project. The standard capitalizes on tried-and-tested principles from the audit of financial statements and other types of assurance engagements. There are three reasons for this:

- First, the IAASB wanted to ensure that the standard could be understood by the people responsible for overseeing the preparation of sustainability reports and those assuring the documents.

19. Farooq and De Villiers (2017); Maroun (2019).

To do this, principles that have been well established over the past fifty years (and that are at the core of most engagements dealing with sustainability assurance) form the foundation of ISSA 5000.[20] Additional guidance is provided to inform the application of assurance principles in a sustainability reporting context.

- Second, speed to market is critical. Sustainability reporting is advancing at an unprecedented rate, as are related regulations. At the time of writing, some two-thirds of the world's largest companies use some type of third-party assurance for their sustainability reports. The demand for sustainability reports to be externally assured is growing rapidly in North and South America, Europe, Asia, Oceania, and sub-Saharan Africa.[21] Capital markets are best served by having a well-designed standard available as soon as possible for guiding the assurance of sustainability reports. If that standard leads to high-quality assurance engagements performed consistently irrespective of industry or jurisdiction, the benefits from enhanced comparability, certainty, and accountability would be substantial.
- Finally, companies have already been using various standards to have certain parts of their sustainability reports assured, including ISAE 3000, AA1000AS, and other jurisdiction-specific publications.[22] Engaging an external expert to assure sustainability information can often lead to reduced financing costs, more accurate analyst forecasts, improvements in disclosure quality, and governing bodies better equipped to discharge their monitoring and control functions.[23] Rather than rethinking assurance, ISSA 5000 incorporates the approach to risk assessment and response that underpins existing assurance practice and has been confirmed empirically to add value for organizations and their investors.

---

20. These include, for example, the requirements to identify and assess risks that could result in information being materially misstated, the use of different types of test procedures to respond to those risks, and the application of professional judgment, skepticism, and the highest standard of ethics throughout an assurance engagement.

21. IFAC (2023).

22. IFAC (2023). ISAE 3000, produced by the IAASB, and AA1000AS, produced by AccountAbility, are used internationally by both reporting entities in both developed and emerging economies. Per recent surveys by IFAC, the former is more frequently used by assurance providers than the latter.

23. Maroun (2022); Wang, Zhou, and Wang (2019); Zhou, Simnett, and Hoang (2019).

Why Adaptability Matters in a Maturing Environment without Undermining Quality

Sustainability assurance poses practical challenges for organizations and their assurance providers, especially in the initial years of implementation.[24] The criteria according to which sustainability reports are prepared are still in development. The systems, processes, and internal controls necessary for high-quality reporting are not yet in place in every organization. Considerable variations in the nature, timing, and extent of what companies are expected to report will have implications for how assurance engagements are conducted. Therefore, ISSA 5000 is designed to be flexible.

The standard must cater to the assurance of specific or multiple parts of a sustainability report. Disclosures may be based on one or more reporting guidelines, codes of best practice, or regulations, complemented by internally developed criteria. A mix of qualitative and quantitative information will be encountered covering past and prospective performance. The objective of reducing information asymmetry by issuing credible sustainability reports cannot be compromised by having an assurance model that can be applied only rigidly. ISSA 5000 draws on lessons learned from financial statement audits and from extensive experience with other types of assurance engagements to offer a principles-based approach to assurance. The standard is an overarching one that outlines the essential elements of high-quality sustainability assurance and equips practitioners to develop context-specific methods for tackling the great variety of information found in sustainability reports.

Another reason for flexibility is the need to develop capacity to undertake sustainability assurance. In most jurisdictions, the assurance of sustainability reports is voluntary. The identity of the assurance providers, minimum training and experience requirements, regulatory restrictions, and professional backgrounds are not yet set. It follows that ISSA 5000 cannot be aimed only at those who have been auditing financial statements. The standard is designed to be used by any practitioner suitably trained in assurance techniques, sustainability reporting, and the fundamentals of professional behavior, including ethics. Developing a practitioner-neutral standard is pragmatic given the dynamic nature of the assurance market. It also aligns with the axiomatic stance that markets benefit from competition.

---

24. Maroun and Atkins (2015), 56; Simnett and Huggins (2015).

Flexibility and adaptability do not require quality to be compromised. To contribute to accountability, ISSA 5000 must enable the type of fieldwork necessary for ensuring that sustainability information is free from material misstatement. The standard stresses the importance of professional judgment and skepticism. This means that engagements are not performed according to a checklist logic but are context-specific. Multidisciplinary teams are required and must possess a sound understanding of the environment in which the client operates. Practitioners must have questioning minds and remain alert at all times to the facts and circumstances that might call into question the integrity of the sustainability information. Assurance providers must be satisfied that engagements are not being used to legitimize greenwashing or other forms of impression management but have a rational purpose grounded in a commitment to advancing sustainable development.

Why Different Levels of Assurance Exist and Make Sense in the Maturing Environment

An ISSA 5000 engagement can provide two levels of assurance: limited and reasonable. Based on differences in the nature and extent of the work performed, the first yields a lower level of assurance or "comfort" than the second. When a reasonable assurance engagement is conducted, the practitioner's conclusion takes a positive or direct form. The practitioner states whether the sustainability information has been prepared according to applicable criteria or provides a fair presentation of the facts and circumstances. In a limited assurance engagement, the conclusion takes a negative or indirect form. The assurance report concludes that nothing has come to the practitioner's attention that casts doubt on the fact that the sustainability information is fairly presented or has been prepared according to the applicable framework. While the difference may seem subtle, it reflects the fact that limited assurance engagements are based on less stringent risk assessment and testing than is the case for a reasonable assurance engagement. As a result, the conclusion in a limited assurance engagement is stated with less confidence than in a reasonable assurance engagement.

Financial statement audits are an example of a reasonable assurance engagement. Engagements on sustainability information can be conducted using an approach to risk assessment and the performance of fieldwork that also culminates in a reasonable assurance engagement. Providing the same level of assurance on financial and extra-financial information can promote confidence, signal the importance of sustainability reporting, and avoid uncertainty about the assurance provider's work effort.

Not all organizations may, however, be in a position to support reasonable assurance engagements because of cost and capacity constraints (including the availability of assurance providers), technical challenges, and the maturity of their reporting systems. For example, there may be insufficient expertise or capacity to meet the demand for reasonable assurance in some areas. As a result, certain policymakers and regulators may require organizations to have their sustainability reporting subject to limited assurance, with a planned transition to reasonable assurance.[25] ISSA 5000 addresses these situations. The standard provides a robust pathway from limited to reasonable assurance and differentiates clearly between the two to accommodate organizations operating according to different industry and regulatory requirements in the numerous jurisdictions where, it is hoped, ISSA 5000 will be adopted.

Dealing with reasonable and limited assurance also accords organizations the opportunity to develop the accounting and management infrastructure necessary for improving the scope and quality of sustainability reporting over time. In the initial years of reporting, having an independent expert provide limited assurance on sustainability reports under ISSA 5000 can provide important insights for management and governing bodies to expand the scope of their organizations' reporting and develop the accounting infrastructure necessary for supporting reasonable assurance engagements.

Concluding Remarks

In November 2024, the IAASB formally approved ISSA 5000. Shortly after the standard's publication, IOSCO issued a strong statement of support for it and encouraged its use throughout the world. Major emerging economies such as Brazil and Turkey have already publicly committed to its use.[26] The

---

25. This is currently the case in the EU, which, under CSRD, will begin with limited assurance as the mandatory requirement before considering a reasonable assurance requirement. See PwC (2023).

26. See, e.g., Silveira (2024) and Kamu Gözetimi (2023).

EU is also actively considering the use of the standard for its limited assurance regulatory requirements, which will take effect in 2026.[27] The speed at which the standard has been developed and considered for adoption reflects the urgent need for a global baseline for the assurance of sustainability information. Ensuring consistent performance of high-quality assurance engagements grounded in technically rigorous practice and sound ethical requirements promotes an improved understanding of assurance, reduces the costs of assurance solutions, and avoids fragmenting the assurance and broader governance space.

While developing ISSA 5000, the IAASB was mindful of the fact that sustainability reporting and related assurance engagements are still in a developmental stage. As a result, the proposed standard is principles based. It is deliberately confined to dealing with the core features of high-quality sustainability assurance. This avoids the risk of inadvertently constraining reporting and assurance practices or developing an assurance solution that can be operationalized only by a limited number of service providers. Catering to both limited and reasonable assurance engagements also gives organizations the time to familiarize themselves with new reporting requirements, design suitable accounting systems, and implement appropriate internal controls aligned with best governance practices.

Pragmatism must not, however, be misunderstood as compromising on quality. ISSA 5000 builds on well-established principles and practices to ensure that stakeholders can place confidence in the assurance provider's conclusions. The standard iterates the critical roles of ethics, sound quality management, professional expertise, and professional judgment when performing an assurance engagement. This is especially important as sustainability reporting grows in prominence and becomes more susceptible to the risk of being used to mislead investors and other stakeholders.

The practitioner is expected to conduct each engagement diligently and with a questioning mind, irrespective of professional background. The aim is not just to collect sufficient appropriate evidence to conclude on the applicable sustainability information but to ensure that assurance engagements form an integral part of the broader system of checks and balances on which effective corporate governance and efficient capital markets depend. When conducted to the highest technical, ethical, and quality standards, ISSA 5000 engagements can reduce information

---

27. Bassi (2024).

asymmetry, promote accountability along extra-financial lines, and enable those charged with governance to monitor and direct their organizations more effectively. As a result, sustainability assurance should not be dismissed as a compliance exercise or passing trend but should be understood as an integral part of the capital market and governance machinery that advances sustainable development.

REFERENCES

Baboukardos, D. 2018. "The Valuation Relevance of Environmental Performance Revisited: The Moderating Role of Environmental Provisions." *British Accounting Review* 50 (1): 32–47.

Barth, M. E., et al. 2017. "The Economic Consequences Associated with Integrated Report Quality: Capital Market and Real Effects." *Accounting, Organizations and Society* 62:43–64.

Bassi, U. 2024. "Request for the Adoption of Non-binding Assurance Guidelines and for a Technical Advice for the Development of EU Specific Add-ons and Carve-outs (If Applicable) to be Included in the Delegated Act Adopting Limited Assurance Sustainability Standards Based on the Final Version of ISSA 5000." Letter. European Commision, March 7.

Churet, C., and R. G. Eccles. 2014. "Integrated Reporting, Quality of Management, and Financial Performance." *Journal of Applied Corporate Finance* 26 (1): 56–64.

De Villiers, C., P.-C. K. Hsiao, and W. Maroun. 2020. *The Routledge Handbook of Integrated Reporting*. Abingdon, Oxon: Routledge.

Farooq, M. B., and C. De Villiers. 2017. "The Market for Sustainability Assurance Services: A Comprehensive Literature Review and Future Avenues for Research." *Pacific Accounting Review* 29 (1): 79–106.

FSB (Financial Stability Board). 2022. *Task Force on Climate-Related Financial Disclosures: 2022 Status Report*. Basel.

Guthrie, J., F. Manes-Rossi, and L. Orelli Rebecca. 2017. "Integrated Reporting and Integrated Thinking in Italian Public Sector Organisations." *Meditari Accountancy Research* 25 (4): 553–73.

IAASB (International Auditing and Assurance Standards Board). 2022. *IAASB 2021 Public Report: Spearheading Change to Enhance Confidence in Audits and Assurance*. New York, July 18.

IFAC (International Federation of Accountants). 2023. *The State of Play: Sustainability Disclosure & Assurance 2019–2021 Trend Analysis*. New York.

IIRC (International Integrated Reporting Council). 2020. *Integrated Thinking & Strategy: State of Play Report*. IFRS Foundation.

IODSA (Institute of Directors in South Africa). 2016. *King IV Report on Corporate Governance in South Africa*. Lexis Nexus South Africa, Johannesburg.

IOSCO (International Organization of Securities Commissions). 2021. *Report on Sustainability-Related Issuer Disclosures*. Madrid.

Kamu Gözetimi. 2023. "Kamu Gözetimi Kurumu Başkanı Sayın Dr. Hasan Özçelik'in COP28 Konferans Mesajı." Press release, May 12.

King, M., and J. Atkins. 2016. *The Chief Value Officer: Accountants Can Save the Planet*. Abingdon, Oxon: Greenleaf.

KPMG. 2022. *Big Shifts, Small Steps: Survey of Sustainability Reporting 2022*. KPMG International.

———. 2020. *The Time Has Come: The KPMG Survey of Sustainability Reporting 2020*. KPMG International.

Maroun, W. 2022. "Corporate Governance and the Use of External Assurance for Integrated Reports." *Corporate Governance: An International Review* 30 (1).

———. 2019a. "Does External Assurance Contribute to Higher Quality Integrated Reports?" *Journal of Accounting and Public Policy* 38 (4): 1066–70.

———. 2019b. "Exploring the Rationale for Integrated Report Assurance." *Accounting, Auditing & Accountability Journal* 32 (6): 1826–54.

Maroun, W., and J. Atkins. 2015. *The Challenges of Assuring Integrated Reports: Views from the South African Auditing Community*. Association of Chartered Certified Accountants, November.

McNally, M.-A., and W. Maroun. 2018. "It Is Not Always Bad News: Illustrating the Potential of Integrated Reporting Using a Case Study in the Eco-tourism Industry." *Accounting, Auditing & Accountability Journal* 31 (5): 1319–48.

PwC. 2023. "European Union Corporate Sustainability Reporting Directive (CSRD)." *Viewpoint* (blog).

Silveira, P. G. 2024. "Sustainability Reporting around the World." *Enhesa*, April 16.

Simnett, R., and A. L. Huggins. 2015. "Integrated Reporting and Assurance: Where Can Research Add Value?" *Sustainability Accounting, Management and Policy Journal* 6 (1): 29–53.

Stubbs, W., and C. Higgins. 2014. "Integrated Reporting and Internal Mechanisms of Change." *Accounting, Auditing & Accountability Journal* 27 (7): 1068–89.

Task Force on Climate-Related Financial Disclosures. n.d. "Climate Change Presents Financial Risk to the Global Economy. Task Force on Climate-Related Financial Disclosures | TCFD (fsb-tcfd.org)."

United Nations. 1987. *Report of the World Commission on Environment and Development: Our Common Future* (Brundtland Report). World Commission on Environment and Development.

SEC (United States Securities and Exchange Commission). 2024. "SEC Adopts Rules to Enhance and Standardize Climate-Related Disclosures for Investors." Press release, March 6.

Wang, R., S. Zhou, and T. Wang. 2019. "Corporate Governance, Integrated Reporting and the Use of Credibility-Enhancing Mechanisms on Integrated Reports. *European Accounting Review* 29 (4): 1–33.

Zhou, S., R. Simnett, and H. Hoang. 2019. "Evaluating Combined Assurance as a New Credibility Enhancement Technique." *Auditing: A Journal of Practice & Theory* 38 (2): 235–59.

ELEVEN

The Institutionalization of Corporate Contributions to the SDGs in India

KATSUO MATSUMOTO

In India, private companies have played a vital role in social development. In particular, the 2013 amendment to the Companies Act, which made corporate social responsibility (CSR) activities mandatory for companies that meet certain size, revenue, or profit thresholds, has led to formal consideration of social development issues by large businesses. This world-first mandate requiring affected companies to invest 2 percent of net profits in CSR activities has institutionalized corporate contributions that were previously voluntary and, in so doing, has given a real boost to the efforts to achieve CSR.

Mandatory CSR and Increased Scale of Expenditure

The amount allocated to CSR activities has been on the rise, with actual spending reaching approximately Rs. 263 billion (U.S. $3.2 billion) in FY2021, up from approximately Rs. 100 billion ($1.2 billion) in

FY2014.[1] Its volume is equivalent to the net disbursement amount for development projects financed by the World Bank, which has been a major international development financier for India.

From a religious and cultural perspective, philanthropy, including donations by merchants to temples and schools, has been practiced in India since before the country's independence. The theory of trusteeship that Mahatma Gandhi championed during the independence movement—namely, that wealth is legitimate if used for the benefit of the poor—fit these efforts to mandate corporate philanthropy. After independence, employee welfare and the reduction of external diseconomies also came within the ambit of corporate social contributions, in line with the development of human rights and environmental legislation covering corporate activities.

Background to CSR Institutionalization

From the 1990s onward, when economic liberalization was in full swing, the progress of corporate multinationalization and the entry of foreign companies also led to the international standardization of CSR, which included ISO (International Organization for Standardization) audit principles. One example is that the Securities and Exchange Board of India, established in 1992, imposed guidelines for CSR on listed companies. This trend has led to a gradual shift in corporate CSR from a philanthropic to a multistakeholder approach.[2]

Even before the 2013 revision of the Companies Act, the Indian government had been pursuing policies to strengthen CSR. This emphasis was mainly attributable to the huge domestic demand for development activities, a demand that could not be met by public investment alone, and to a commitment to achieving international development outcomes such as the Millennium Development Goals (MDGs). Following the inclusion of the "inclusive development" concept in the Eleventh Five-Year Plan in 2007, the Ministry of Corporate Affairs in 2009 issued Corporate Governance Voluntary Guidelines to strengthen corporate governance. This was a first step toward mainstreaming the concept of business responsibilities. In 2011 the government endorsed the United Nations Guiding Principles on Business and

---

1. India's National CSR Portal, housed in the Ministry of Corporate Affairs, is located at https://www.csr.gov.in/.
2. Gatti et al. (2019).

Human Rights and issued National Voluntary Guidelines on the Social, Environmental and Economic Responsibilities of Businesses. These guidelines are based on a set of nine principles that offer Indian businesses an understanding of and an approach to inculcating responsible business conduct.

Indian industrial society has also envisaged a national movement for mainstreaming CSR for sustained inclusiveness as part of a social development agenda. Even before the CSR mandate, the Confederation of Indian Industry (CII) had been stepping up its efforts and constituted the CII National Committee on Corporate Social Responsibility & Community Development in 2001. This committee developed CSR guidelines and promotes the sharing of CSR experiences and best practices.

In line with recent government policy, the CII established the CII Foundation in 2011, a trust to lead industry involvement in CSR to strengthen its work in social development. The CII Foundation has been engaging with member companies in implementing and managing CSR projects. For example, some member companies had opposed the amendment of the Companies Act because of the added financial and human resource burdens and because penalties were recommended for non-achievement. However, these opinions did not become mainstream owing to an ongoing series of CII initiatives.

Target Companies and Use of Expenditure

Under the revised Companies Act, companies that meet one of the following criteria are required to implement CSR activities: having net assets of at least Rs. 5 billion ($60 million), having annual sales of at least Rs. 10 billion ($120 million), or having a net income of at least Rs. 50 million ($0.6 million). Companies that meet any of these criteria must allocate 2 percent of their average pre-tax profits for the preceding three years to CSR activities. The same applies to local subsidiaries of foreign companies. Around 20,000 companies have a CSR program covered by the Companies Act, approximately four times the number of companies listed on the Bombay Stock Exchange, implying that CSR goes well beyond listed companies to include a substantial number of privately held corporations.[3]

3. Khan (2022).

The amendment to the law also clarifies the activities covered by CSR. According to the revised law, twelve activities are eligible for spending, including eradicating hunger, poverty, and malnutrition, promoting health care, making available safe drinking water, promoting education, ensuring environmental sustainability, developing slum areas, and managing disasters. These mandated CSR activities should take place outside the company's business. In other words, some activities under the multistakeholder CSR guidelines that occur as part of regular business operations, such as ensuring employee welfare and reducing carbon dioxide emissions, are not eligible in terms of the expenditure targets mandated by law.

Since the CSR mandate become widespread, the law has been amended with the aim of strengthening CSR efforts: in 2019, the requirement to contribute unspent CSR budgets to a government-designated fund and penalties for violating companies were introduced, and in 2021, companies with average spending obligations of Rs. 100 million ($1.2 million) or more in the past three years were required to submit an impact assessment report of CSR projects above a certain amount.[4] Thus, through policy implementation and corporate responses, the institutionalization, standardization, and transparency of CSR activities that directly contribute to social development have been strengthened in India.

Case Studies of CSR Activities

On-site, company CSR activities are varied. Even before the CSR mandate went into effect, conglomerates such as Tata and Birla had established their own foundations and traditionally practiced social development as CSR activities. Tata has been very thorough in its efforts, holding approximately 70 percent of the Tata Group's total shares in its Tata Trusts.[5] It allocates billions of rupees each year to various social development projects, including health care, education, vocational training, and basic infrastructure. In the health care field, the foundation works with more than 150 local nonprofit organizations (NPOs) to provide services tailored to local needs. In terms of size and impact, its activities are comparable to those of the major bilateral foreign aid agencies in India.

4. KPMG (2021).
5. See the "Investors / Group Companies" web page at Tata.com.

Dalmia Cement, the fourth largest cement company in terms of sales, has made its commitment to climate change issues clear. In 2016 the company announced its participation in RE100, an international initiative for the use of renewable energy.[6] The company is the third Indian company to join the initiative, following Infosys and Tata Motors. Dalmia Cement has thirteen cement plants in nine states in India and owns an approximately 80 MW power plant that uses biogas and wind power for in-house power generation. The company is particularly enthusiastic about clean energy projects, and, through its subsidiary, the Dalmia Bharat Foundation, it has installed solar lanterns, mainly in nonelectrified villages near the plant. The company's CSR activities now cover a total of 1,200 villages in eleven states.

State Bank of India, the largest commercial bank in India, is working through its CSR activities to improve the living standards of the country's poor communities in a variety of areas, including health care, education, vocational training, implementation of livelihood improvement programs, preservation of traditional buildings, and livelihood support for women and the elderly. Its major achievements include health awareness programs for 11,000 households by 2020; repair of thirty-eight public schools and installation of computer classes; educational improvement curricula for about 500 elementary school students; vocational training for about 100,000 young people; electrification projects in 121 villages; the planting of more than 10,000 trees; and the introduction of waste disposal systems in fourteen villages. The company has made efforts to measure the effectiveness of the project. For example, the academic performance of children before and after the educational improvement curriculum program was instituted was measured. It was reported that there was an improvement of 20 percent in Hindi and 30 percent in math.

With production plants in Haryana and Gujarat and a nationwide sales network, Maruti Suzuki, which boasts a roughly 50 percent share of the Indian automobile market, has traditionally placed emphasis on CSR activities in three areas: the development of villages near its plants, road safety, and skills training of students. In each of these areas, the company clearly states its contribution to the relevant targets of the SDGs. About fifty staff members are directly in charge of CSR, and their activities are based on self-sufficiency. In other words, the staff members themselves

---

6. See the website of the RE100 group.

procure equipment and supervise on-site activities, and only when specialized knowledge is needed do they enlist the cooperation of outside personnel and local NPOs.

In the area of village development, the company focuses on supporting the expansion of public schools and health facilities for a total of twenty-six villages around its plant. In the area of road safety, the company operates seven driving technique training centers and nineteen road safety centers in five states in the country, providing driving technique instruction, teaching traffic etiquette, and analyzing accidents. As of 2021, the centers had provided training to approximately 3.4 million people over the preceding twenty years, including those who needed to renew their driver's license. In the area of skills training, the program is expanding facilities and providing lectures to thirty public industrial skills centers in a total of eleven states. A total of 10,000 students received skills training at these centers in 2019 alone.

Common Aspects

While CSR activities vary from company to company, these social projects have some common characteristics. In interviews conducted by the Japan International Cooperation Agency (JICA) in 2021 with seventeen Indian companies and forty-five Japanese companies, almost all respondents indicated that an important factor in selecting a CSR project site was proximity to the company or plant.[7] As for the types of projects in the area, they mainly included construction of hospitals and schools, in accordance with the requests of the local people. According to CSR statistics published annually by India's Ministry of Corporate Affairs, medical care and education are the two main fields and account for approximately 50 percent of total CSR expenditures.

The second factor in the choice of CSR activity is a link to the company's business. An automobile manufacturer may engage in traffic safety campaigns and driving instruction, while a hygiene product company may conduct educational activities for the health of village residents. These programs are designed to indirectly promote the company's activities, for example by improving the company's brand and introducing its products.

7. JICA (2021).

In the case of such programs, company employees are involved in the implementation because they are able to explain the company's products and services. For example, Maruti Suzuki assigns its own employees to teach safe driving based on their knowledge of vehicle performance.

A third factor is implementation capacity and cost-effectiveness. There are still not many companies that implement CSR projects on their own. According to the CSR statistics of the Ministry of Corporate Affairs for FY2014–FY2020 mentioned above, approximately 40 percent of all spending is outsourced to NPOs and other external organizations. If a company lacks the capacity to manage social development projects, or if it feels that a local philanthropy is effective, it outsources the projects to local NPOs or other organizations to maximize the benefit-cost ratio.

From the NPOs' point of view, outsourcing has increased fundraising opportunities and led to the expansion of their activities. In addition, the increased collaboration with companies has contributed to the sharing of technology and operational know-how, which in turn has contributed to the strengthening of the NPOs' capabilities.

Main Issues

The above three characteristics common to corporations' social programs also expose the main issues in CSR implementation. A first observation is that CSR projects are concentrated in states with a high business density, such as Maharashtra, Karnataka, Gujarat, Andhra Pradesh, Tamil Nadu, and Delhi.[8] As a result, social development projects under the CSR umbrella are scarce in areas such as the northeastern region, where companies are less likely to locate. In fact, CSR spending is not directly proportional to states with high poverty rates and other social needs.

For companies implementing their own CSR projects, the shortfall in internal human resources has become a critical constraint. The JICA survey identified a lack of human resources capable of understanding both corporate strategy and social issues in the field. It is a challenge to build a dedicated, capable CSR team. Some companies have found it difficult to assign staff to supervise and assess CSR activities because of their low HR capacity. This challenge applies even to large companies that are actively

8. CSRBOX (2022); KPMG (2020).

engaged in CSR activities. In a survey of 301 large companies, more than 50 percent said they preferred to execute their CSR projects through implementing agencies, including NPOs.[9]

However, it is not easy for companies to find suitable organizations to which they can outsource projects.[10] According to the JICA survey, about 50 percent of Japanese companies pointed to a lack of information on reliable NPOs, and about 40 percent cited a lack of capacity on the part of the NPOs to which they outsourced. Companies have accordingly looked for alternative ways to implement CSR activities. Some companies deliver a portion of their CSR budget to a government-designated fund and collaborate with government agencies. According to government statistics, 13 percent of companies transferred their CSR budgets directly to a government-designated fund (e.g., the Prime Ministers National Relief Fund) in FY2021.[11] In the survey mentioned above, almost 50 percent of 301 companies said they preferred government partnerships as a criterion for the initiation of CSR projects.[12]

Other challenges faced by Indian companies include difficulties in obtaining information on the development status of project sites and the risk of duplicating activities conducted by other agencies and companies.

Responses to Challenges

To address these challenges, the government and the private sector are working on measures and activities. For example, the government has periodically updated SDG indicators for each state and provided companies with information on the status of development in various regions, and it is implementing the Aspirational District Programme to encourage social development projects at the district level by using CSR budgets as well as public funds. This program, launched in 2018, aims to use specific indicators to select underdeveloped districts for focused budget allocation. It clarifies local development needs and facilitates CSR-eligible projects. In addition, the program aims to diversify the spending destinations of

---

9. CSRBOX (2023).
10. Ernst & Young LLP (2020).
11. See the National CSR Portal at https://www.crs.gov.in.
12. CSRBOX (2023).

CSR activities by providing information on states and districts where CSR projects are scarce.

In 2019 the Ministry of Corporate Affairs updated the Corporate Governance Voluntary Guidelines and released them as National Guidelines on Responsible Business Conduct to reveal alignments with international development goals, including the SDGs. The new guidelines aim to provide a framework for companies to fulfill CSR obligations in an inclusive and sustainable manner. The ministry publishes CSR statistics and surveys and conducts various activities to promote CSR, including offering a National CSR Award.

The private sector is also making efforts to strengthen the CSR "ecosystem," including through capacity building of CSR partner organizations such as NPOs. For example, Toyota Kirloskar Motor launched a training program called Social Academy of Learning in 2019 to build the capacity of NPO leaders. The program has multiple activities. In addition to the training program, there are pre- and post-assessments of the participating organizations through a third-party agency. Pre-assessment is designed to evaluate the current knowledge and practices of an organization to provide a specific training program. Post-assessment establishes the NPO's capability for future implementation of CSR projects or fundraising activities.

In the context of building the CSR ecosystem, a growing number of organizations provide CSR advisory services to companies. For example, Samhita, which opened an office in 2009 in Mumbai, has provided advisory services to hundreds of companies on its CSR activities, in addition to conducting research related to issues in CSR. Because of its access to a wide network of NPOs, Samhita also conducts matching activities between companies and NPOs. Especially after the CSR mandate went into effect, Samhita has increased its business volume significantly.

Role of Foreign Aid Agencies

What can international organizations and foreign aid agencies do to expand the CSR activities of private companies? The first action should be to provide information and data on development needs and local conditions. These organizations often conduct detailed surveys on project needs and are familiar with local conditions. They can therefore provide information and data that contribute to companies' design and selection of CSR projects. For the provision of information, activities such as holding regular seminars, publishing newsletters, and using the web are also appropriate.

Another role of foreign aid organizations is to facilitate the matching of companies and NPOs or to develop partnerships between companies and aid agencies. For example, the G20 Independent Experts Group's report on strengthening multilateral development banks recommended a special partnership window be established to mobilize CSR contributions for World Bank development projects.[13] This report was presented to the G20 finance ministers under India's presidency of the G20 and specifically responded to the challenge that companies experience in identifying cost-effective and impactful channels through which to spend their mandated CSR budgets.

Bilateral aid agencies can also support CSR activities implemented by multinational companies from their home countries. They can serve as a bridge to facilitate CSR by introducing competent NPOs and local authorities that they interact with in regular aid programs to companies. They can also provide information to home companies entering the Indian market. In particular, newcomers to the market may be unfamiliar with local conditions and appreciative of such advice. Thus support from bilateral foreign aid agencies can aid the smooth implementation and expansion of CSR activities.

In addition, international organizations and foreign aid agencies can help strengthen the capacity of companies' CSR teams. Insofar as the capacity of a company's CSR team may influence the effectiveness of the company's development projects, human resource development is useful. In this respect, the private sector should be regarded as an important development partner.

Policy Implications

What are the policy implications of making CSR mandatory, in addition to its contribution to development? The first is the realization of "stakeholder capitalism," which has been discussed mainly in relation to developed countries. A CSR mandate can correct the profit-first mentality and institutionalize corporate contributions to society. In this regard, India's efforts are more direct and practical than those of many developed countries.

---

13. G20 Independent Experts Group (2023).

The second implication is that mandatory CSR can generate significant financial resources for development projects. Mobilizing private sector funds for social projects is a useful complement in implementing government development policies, especially for developing countries that lack development budgets and rely on foreign aid agencies. Furthermore, foreign exchange risks can also be avoided by use of the CSR budget.

In India, there is still significant scope for increasing CSR expenditure since the share of companies actually meeting the legally required CSR budget is only 60 percent of the total. The remaining 40 percent of companies do not have proper mechanisms to spend the mandated CSR budget. Promoting mandatory spending is necessary, though it requires understanding and appropriate methods for companies. If CSR spending is strongly enforced, especially if the default is to fund government development projects, it will take on the character of an additional tax, and a backlash from companies can be expected.

The third policy implication is the effect of CSR activities in stimulating local domestic demand. The private sector has engaged in the construction of hospitals and schools and increasing the supply of goods continuously, and such expenses have the effect of increasing domestic demand. While this point has been made in past research, its specific economic impact is still not clear.[14] With CSR spending on the rise, its demand-side effects should be analyzed in the future.

India's CSR ecosystem is currently in the process of development. How it evolves will provide insights into the extent to which CSR can contribute to national development and the achievement of the SDGs. Further, it will provide learning on the division of roles between government and the private sector in development investment and the nature of the private sector's contribution to society in a liberal economy.

Final Remarks

According to the Sustainable Development Report 2023, India ranks 112 out of 166 countries in terms of achievement.[15] Thus it is imperative that the country continue its efforts to achieve the SDGs. In this context, there is no

---

14. Sharma et al. (2023).
15. Sachs et al. (2023).

doubt that CSR can play a significant role. Furthermore, in light of the country's population size, economic heft, and amount of carbon dioxide emissions as a percentage of the world's total, improvement of development indicators in India should also contribute to global security. We need to acknowledge that India's performance will directly affect the international achievement of the SDGs.

The institutionalization of corporate contributions in social development is an important part of the measures to achieve the SDGs in India. The success of institutionalization and the evolution of the CSR ecosystem as a result may also have a significant impact on the world's achievement of the SDGs. If India's efforts can show concrete results, the country could serve as a role model for other nations.

REFERENCES

CSRBOX. 2023. *India CSR Outlook Report 2023*. Bopal, Gujarat: CSRBOX, October.

———. 2022. *India CSR Outlook Report 2022*. Bopal, Gujarat: CSRBOX, November.

Ernst & Young LLP. 2020. *Corporate Social Responsibility in India: Re-engineering Compliance and Fraud Mitigation Strategies*.

G20 Independent Experts Group. 2023. *Strengthening Multilateral Development Banks: The Triple Agenda*. Washington, DC, and London: Center for Global Development, July 19.

Gatti, L., B. Vishwanath, P. Seele, and B. Cottier. 2019. "Are We Moving Beyond Voluntary CSR? Exploring Theoretical and Managerial Implications of Mandatory CSR Resulting from the New Indian Companies Act." *Journal of Business Ethics* 160:961–72.

JICA (Japan international Cooperation Agency). 2021. *Research Report on CSR Trend and Opportunities in India*. Tokyo: JICA.

Khan, F. 2022. "The Evolution of CSR Policies in India: From Philanthropy to Sustainable Development." Sigma Earth, July 25.

KPMG. 2021. *Implications of Companies (Corporate Social Responsibility Policy) Amendment Rules, 2021*. KPMG/In, January.

———. 2020. *India's CSR Reporting Survey 2019*. KPMG, February.

Sachs, J. D., G. Lafortune, G. Fuller, and E. Drumm. 2023 *Implementing the SDG Stimulus*. Sustainable Development Report 2023. New York: Sustainable Development Solutions Network; Dublin: Dublin University Press.

Sharma, E., and M. Sathish. 2022. "CSR Leads to Economic Growth or Not: An Evidence-Based Study to Link Corporate Social Responsibility (CSR) Activities of the Indian Banking Sector with Economic Growth of India." *Asian Journal of Business Ethics* 11 (1): 67–103.

TWELVE

The "Lobbying Gap" in the SDG Agenda

Aligning Corporate Political Engagement with Global Sustainable Development

ALBERTO ALEMANNO

Around the world, calls are growing for companies to take responsibility for their impact on the planet, employees, and the communities they depend on. Yet one area of impact is less discussed: their political footprint. This footprint includes all corporate political activities (CPAs), from corporate lobbying and political spending to other forms of corporate influence—including that exercised by trade associations and think tanks—aimed at influencing public policies.[1] Companies can fail in the exercise of their CPAs in two main ways, either by underinfluencing the causes they verbally support, such as climate policy action[2] and other of

---

1. For a generally accepted definition of lobbying, see OECD (2023): "lobbying as the oral or written communication with a public official to influence legislation, policies or administrative decisions."

2. Thus, for instance, although half of the S&P 100 companies in the United States have science-based targets, only 19 percent publicly supported the Inflation Reduction Act, the largest climate investment legislation in U.S. history. Ketu, Miller, and Ceres (2022).

the UN's Sustainable Development Goals (SDGs), or, more critically, by contributing to activities that inhibit or merely contradict these causes.[3] Thus, if on the one hand corporate political influence could potentially accelerate progress toward achieving the SDGs by 2030 by, for example, advocating for progressive legislation, on the other hand, CPAs are what undercut progress on numerous critical issues, ranging from reining in drug pricing (included in SDG 3) to taking action on climate change (SDG 13) and reducing the offshoring of assets (SDG 16).[4]

CPAs: From Transparency to Accountability

Despite being a significant factor in either protecting or harming the environment and society, CPAs are rarely discussed and fully internalized by corporations themselves. Instead, they remain concealed from both investors and members of the public, whether the latter are employees, consumers, or activists. Therefore, a company that pledges to reduce greenhouse gas emissions may actually be lobbying against stricter regulation of those emissions.[5] Similarly, drug companies may publicly support patient access to affordable drugs while funding industry associations that block low-price initiatives. Companies may publicly support LGBTQ+ issues while funding political candidates who oppose gay rights.[6] Many companies embrace smoking cessation while funding business trade associations, such as the American Chamber of Commerce, that have consistently lobbied against tobacco control measures. Most energy companies now recognize that burning fossil fuels is warming the planet, yet many continue to fund disinformation through communications and advocacy efforts that obscure industry's role in climate change and its harm to human health.[7]

---

3. Favotto and Kollman (2021).
4. On corporate political influence, Fred Krupp, president of the Environmental Defense Fund, stated, "CEOs . . . also need to unleash the most powerful tool they have to fight climate change: their political influence" (World Resources Institute, 2019).
   On corporations using CPAs to undercut progress, see, e.g., the case study by Boston Trust Walden (2019).
   A classic critique of the power of interest groups is T. J. Lowi's *The End of Liberalism: The Second Republic of the United States* (2019).
5. Lyon et al. (2018).
6. Leonhardt (2019).
7. Supran and Oreskes (2017).

The discrepancy between corporate lobbying and corporate commitment to purpose, values, or stakeholders is not necessarily intentional but is often caused by a lack of oversight, the existence of siloed organizations, or, more frequently, the involvement of industry associations.[8]

Indeed, despite the growing salience gained by undue, often misaligned corporate political influence, citizens, investors, governments, and the media still have no effective mechanisms to monitor the full scope and impact of CPA. Lobbying regulations requiring full disclosure of CPAs remain the exception, not the norm. Even where they exist—such as across OECD countries—they do not always accurately reflect whether, where, how much, and for what purposes a company invests in its impact.[9] Moreover, no mechanism assures disclosure of other, subtler forms of corporate political conduct, such as lobbying through trade associations, academic lobbying, or philanthropic donations.[10] Existing interventions essentially focus on making corporate lobbying transparent, which generally remains the tip of the iceberg.[11] Moreover, transparency captures the process, not the content, of corporate political influence and its requirements. This suggests that transparency alone is not enough: no company will give up its privileged access unless incentivized or forced to do so.[12] As a result, owing to the lack of a comprehensive regulatory framework (e.g., reporting mechanisms for both political and philanthropic spending), there is little clarity on which policies companies are investing in or failing to support through their influence efforts.

This is a cause of concern not only for nonprofits but also for investors, who are afraid that secret CPA strategies may disprove companies' public

---

8. Empirical research shows that corporate political behavior in the form of lobbying tends to be unaligned with corporate social responsibility whether through a lack of coordination or as an explicit strategy to misalign them. See, e.g., Favotto and Kollman (2021).

9. As of 2023, twenty-three out of thirty-eight OECD countries had lobbying regulations in place. Overall, regulating lobbying has proven difficult because of its complexity and sensitive nature. Many OECD countries rely on lobbyists' self-regulation instead. See OECD (2021). For a U.S. perspective on regulation of CPAs, see Drutman (2011). For an EU perspective, see European Court of Auditors, Special report 05/2024: EU Transparency Register.

10. On trade associations, see, e.g., B Team (n.d.). On academic lobbying, see, e.g., Koppl (2018), Lewis (2014), and McGarity and Wagner (2012). On philanthropic donations, see, e.g., Bertrand et al. (2020) and Jacobs (2023).

11. Traditional lobbying watchdogs are Transparency International, LobbyWatch, FinanceWatch, StateWatch, and Corporate Europe Observatory. As they all take a restrictive approach to lobbying, which they perceive as a form of corruption, not participation, they focus more on advocating for transparency than on aligning corporate political conduct with sustainability goals.

12. Preston and Post (2013 [1975]), 142–52.

statements, depart from climate science,[13] or involve the corporation in a public controversy as a result of the ensuing reputational damage.[14] In short, and in business-speak: CPAs are material activities for companies and their stakeholders, for society, and for the planet. This explains why more transparency on CPAs and internal governance is currently among the most popular ESG asks in shareholder meetings, alongside climate change resolutions.[15] As a result, a growing number of investors, employees, and third-party watchdogs now regularly scrutinize whether a company's political engagement is aligned with its declared commitments to purpose, values, and sustainability. Today's greater public awareness about the negative effects of corporate political power, both for market value and society, is set to create—as pioneered by the Corporate Sustainability Reporting Directive (CSRD, formerly the EU Non-Financial Reporting Directive)[16]—an unprecedented political demand for intervention. Yet no existing regulatory framework, not even the CSRD, requires companies to do so.

As such, a business case for aligning lobbying to global sustainable development might be emerging. But how to advance such a demand for greater corporate political accountability?

In the absence of legally mandated rules requiring full disclosure, it is up to the market—and partly to civil society—to collect corporate political data to inform the investor community and civil society, respectively. This explains the recent emergence of what Zinnbauer calls a "corporate political accountability ecosystem."[17] To maintain their license to operate, companies may be called upon to internalize not only their environmental and social impact but also the political footprint they leave behind through their lobbying and other CPAs. To protect themselves from risks associated with having misaligned statements, they may first disclose their policy

---

13. See Ketu and Rothstein (2024), 255.
14. InfluenceMap (2019).
15. See, e.g., Torres-Spelliscy (2021). While shareholder proposals are not binding, the proposals that are approved—or that fail but gather substantial support—generate public expectations that the company will address the subject matter of the proposal in the aftermath of the annual meeting. Thus "lobbying reviews" are often promised by the board in order to assuage shareholders' demand for greater public disclosure over corporate political expenditures. See, e.g., Climate Action 100+ (2023).
16. Article 29b(2)(c)(iv) of Directive (EU) 2022/2464 of the European Parliament and of the Council of 14 December 2022 amending Regulation (EU) No. 537/2014, Directive 2004/109/EC, Directive 2006/43/EC and Directive 2013/34/EU, as regards corporate sustainability reporting, OJ L 322, 16.12.2022, pp. 15–80.
17. Zinnbauer (2022).

positions on key proposals and publicly share how they communicate these positions. They may also state that they support evidence-based policies, and proactively lobby for such policies and against policies misaligned with evidence, such as those that weaken existing standards.

The Emergence of a Corporate Political Accountability Ecosystem

After being tacitly tolerated for a long time, self-serving corporate lobbying is being more closely examined today.[18]

Investors, employees, and customers are increasingly questioning the brands they invest in, work for, or consume, considering not only their environmental and social footprint but increasingly their political impact as well.

In response to this public and private demand and amid the imperatives of the sustainability movement, a growing universe of corporate political accountability initiatives has emerged and is rapidly evolving. Some of these initiatives are commercial in nature, such as ESG data and rating providers (e.g., Sustainalytics, S&P, Moody's, RepRisk, MSCI), while others are nonprofit. The latter include sustainability reporting standards (e.g., those promulgated by the Global Reporting Initiative [GRI] 415, the Corporate Disclosure Project [CDP]), and other guidance initiatives such as the OECD/UN Principles for Responsible Investment, the World Benchmarking Alliance, and the Erb Principles.[19]

As a result, a growing universe of initiatives encourages companies to disclose politically relevant information beyond what is legally required by lobbying regulations and transparency registers. This suggests that, when it comes to the realities of corporate lobbying, the market is ahead of the state. These initiatives tend to require companies to provide more detailed information about their corporate activities than is required by law in the United States, the EU, or other OECD countries.

Yet this information, although collected at the request of investors, often remains inaccessible to the majority of interested parties. In the sustainable finance and ESG space, since the methods used by the rating agencies are typically proprietary, they remain largely inaccessible and

---

18. See, e.g., Luyckx and Janssens (2016) and Murray (2022).
19. On the OECD/UN Principles for Responsible Investment, see Baumast (2013), on the World Benchmarking Alliance, see Urlings (2020); on the Erb Principles, see Erb Institute (2022) and Dolan (2023).

therefore difficult to compare.[20] Moreover, most initiatives tend to focus on CPAs either in specific policy areas (e.g., climate change), as seen in the Global Standard on Responsible Climate Lobbying,[21] or within specific industries (e.g., nutrition), as exemplified by the Access to Nutrition Initiative's Spotlight on Lobbying.[22] As a result, the current reporting and accountability ecosystem for corporate political activity is highly fragmented and uncoordinated.

Despite all these limitations, these initiatives and their underlying methods contribute to shaping and defining best practices concerning how companies are expected to engage politically today. As such, they act as de facto standard setters capable of normatively determining what "responsible" corporate political conduct entails. Hence the intuition that, if accurately identified and rigorously compared and assessed, these initiatives and underlying methods could better substantiate the emerging yet largely undefined concept of corporate political responsibility than what the existing literature offers.[23] That is what an applied research initiative, The Good Lobby Tracker—which I had the chance to design—has recently accomplished. Its main findings offer a more accurate, empirically driven understanding of the realities of responsible corporate political engagement.

Who Guards the Guardians of CPAs, and How?

The Good Lobby Tracker comprehensively assessed the major corporate political responsibility reporting initiatives, from sustainability frameworks to ESG ratings and other voluntary, noncommercial initiatives such as the OECD frameworks. Its immediate aim was first to unveil and then

---

20. On rating the rating agencies, see Escrig-Olmedo et al. (2019).
21. See the website at https://climate-lobbying.com. This builds on previous efforts, such as the Ceres Blueprint for Responsible Policy Engagement Benchmark. See Ketu and Rothstein (2024).
22. See Access to Nutrition Initiative (2021).
23. The term "corporate political responsibility" was advanced by Lyon et al. (2018) and further refined in Lyon (ed.) (2024). There is no commonly agreed-on definition of CPR, which remains normatively fuzzy, being largely undertheorized. The term is often used interchangeably with two other concepts, such as those of positive or ethical lobbying. For some literature on this concept, see Anastasiadis, Moon, and Humphries (2018), Bauer (2014), Hartwell and Devinney (2024), OECD (2022), Washington and Spierings (2021), and Zinnbauer (2022).

to examine different initiatives and evaluate their relative strengths, weaknesses, and ambition levels when it comes to CPAs. Ultimately, it asked whether and to what extent these voluntary initiatives contribute to making corporate political conduct more transparent, accountable, and responsible in today's policymaking.

A Taxonomy of Corporate Political Accountability Initiatives

Because of the variety and diversity of initiatives and standards covering CPAs, The Good Lobby Tracker identified and organized them into three groups. These can be seen as falling along a continuum from more formal and established frameworks to more aspirational, voluntary frameworks and standards:

1. ESG data and ratings providers that measure a company's exposure to environmental, social, and governance risks[24];
2. sustainability reporting standards, both voluntary and legally mandated; and
3. other standards that provide some guiding principles on CPAs.

Table 12.1 provides a taxonomy of the main CPA accountability initiatives

By gaining access to and reviewing the methods underpinning all major corporate political responsibility initiatives, The Good Lobby Tracker was able to identify more than thirty best practices. It organized them across eight different categories, each with its own relative weight (figure 12.1).

While most of these categories consist of process-related practices, or those having to do with disclosure requirements related to the process of CPAs, a few others are conduct-related as they venture into their content. Thus, for instance, under the latter (e.g., categories E and F), some initiatives intend to verify whether companies undertake proactive efforts to embrace "responsible" CPA practices. The latter can be inferred from adherence to self-imposed codes of conduct, such as the existence of escalation strategies for partnership termination if misalignment is identified between the company and its third-party lobbying partners, or the proactive publication of all lobbying positions. Responsible CPA practices can

---

24. While these risks may have financial implications, they typically are not covered by conventional financial reviews.

Table 12.1. Kinds of CPA Accountability Initiatives

ESG data and ratings providers	Sustainability reporting standards	Other initiatives
Bloomberg ESG & Climate Indices EcoVadis Fitch Solutions ESG Ratings FTSE4Good ISS Quality Score Moody's MSCI ESG Ratings Refinitiv ESG scores RepRisk ESG Issues S&P Global Corporate Sustainability Assessment Sustainalytics ESG Risk Rating	EFRAG ESRS G2 Business Conduct GRI 415 Public Policy ISSB IFRS S1 TCFD Recommendations	AccountAbility Lobbying Health Check B Lab Impact Assessment Methodology CDP Climate Change Scoring Methodology Erb Principles for Corporate Responsibility ICGN Guidance on Political Lobbying and Donations OECD Principles for Transparency and Integrity in Lobbying Positive Compass Responsible Lobbying Framework UN-PRI Investor Expectations on Corporate Climate Lobbying WBA Social Transformation Framework WEF Measuring Stakeholder Capitalism

Source: Alemanno, Zinnbauer, and Stewart (2023).

Note: Refinitiv has been renamed to LSEG (https://www.lseg.com/).

FIGURE 12.1. **Categories of Best Practices Derived from Questions Posed by the Main CPA Accountability Initiatives**

A	B	C	D
General disclosure of corporate political activities	Political contributions	Lobbying and advocacy activities	Influence via third parties
E	**F**	**G**	**H**
Disclosure of "lobbying and advocacy" policies and positions	Commitment to sustainable lobbying practices	Employees and internal policy	Governance standards

Source: Alemanno, Zinnbauer, and Stewart (2023).

also be inferred from positive impact goals, such as a public commitment to support the democratic process, respect for planetary boundaries, and efforts to equalize access to power.[25]

Rating the Raters of CPAs

After scoring every existing initiative against these emerging best practices, The Good Lobby Tracker rated each initiative to shed light on the quality and quantity of CPA data it had gathered.[26] Initiatives could receive a maximum score of 200 points.[27]

Trends in CPA Disclosure

The Good Lobby Tracker unveiled several structural trends in the nature and role of existing initiatives and their impact on CPAs.

---

25. On supporting the democratic process, see Erb Institute (2022). On respect for planetary boundaries, see Alemanno, Zinnbauer, and Stewart (2023). On efforts to equalize access to power, see Alemanno (2023).

26. The Good Lobby Tracker put together a checklist based on and inspired by the scope, strengths, and methods of each of the frameworks reviewed, and enriched by additional criteria developed by The Good Lobby that further contribute to raising the standards for corporate political engagement and improve the quality of the policy process. As such, it aspires to list all the qualities a reporting regulation or voluntary standard for corporate political transparency and accountability should include. Beyond informing regulatory action to better cover important CPAs, the tracker provides a guide for companies to improve their disclosure in response to expectations from investors and other stakeholders. See Alemanno, Zinnbauer, and Stewart. (2023).

27. The tracker is updated periodically to reflect changes in method and approach.

FIGURE 12.2. Ranking of Main Corporate Accountability Initiatives

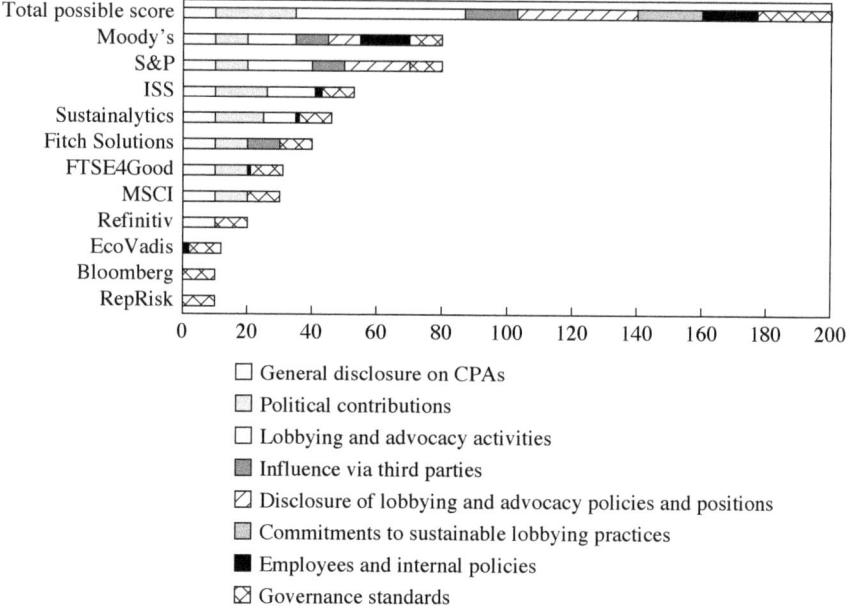

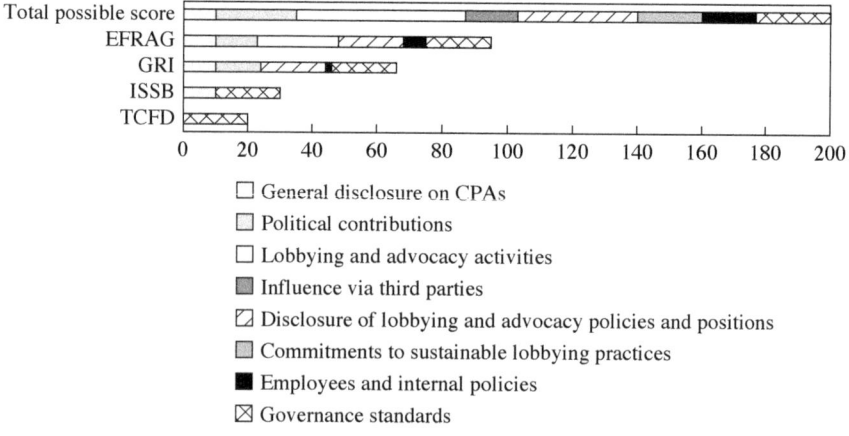

The "Lobbying Gap" in the SDG Agenda 237

FIGURE 12.2. (*Continued*)

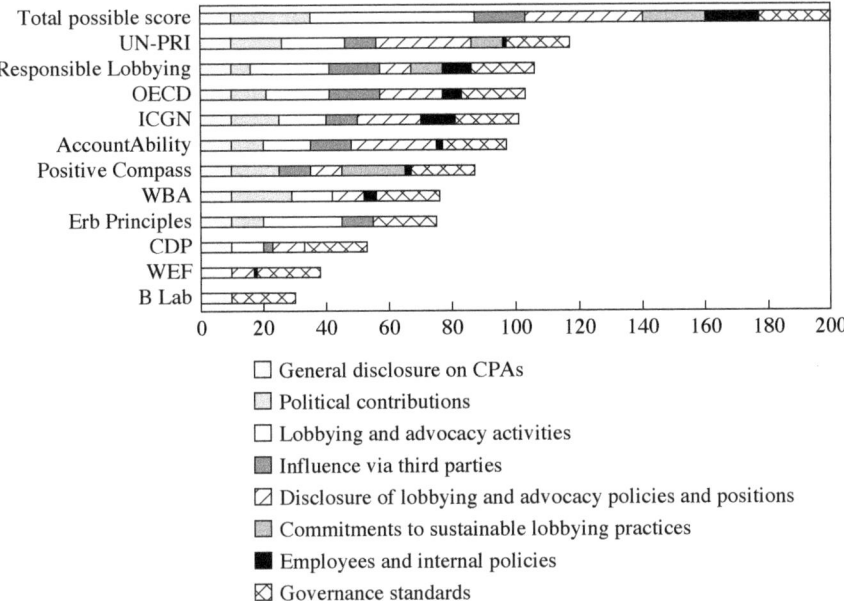

Source: Alemanno, Zinnbauer, and Stewart (2023).

First, corporate political activity is not consistently defined across ESG ratings, with few initiatives seeking to use more subtle forms of influence such as indirect lobbying, whether through industry associations or other third-party actors, including think tanks, charities, or academic interest groups.

Yet business associations are the primary vehicle for business lobbying and influencing in all major markets. They are among the largest lobbying spenders. In advanced countries such as the United States, they accounted for seven of the top ten lobbying spenders in 2023.[28] Given the well-documented impact of lobbying by third-party groups on core business issues, ranging from tax treatment to the regulatory environment, one might expect more consistent assessment of these indirect influence channels. As the influence of think tanks, trade associations, and in-kind sponsorship of academic research continues to grow, more consistent and granular scrutiny in this area is essential.

28. Massoglia (2023).

Second, though they are banned in some countries, corporate financial or in-kind contributions to political parties, candidates, and campaigns are essential for financing political competition in many others. However, these contributions can raise significant challenges to protecting the integrity and independence of policymakers and the political process, as well as to maintaining the integrity of businesses themselves.[29] Yet these standards do not consistently require identification of different types of financial contributions to political parties and elected officials, making it difficult to properly understand the extent of a company's financial involvement in politics. Furthermore, none of the existing initiatives allows companies to develop corporate policies prohibiting any form of political contributions, whether donations or in kind, which could result in problematic corporate donations continuing to be the norm in many countries. However, while corporate political donations are substantial and continue to grow, they are dwarfed by lobbying expenditures. This is especially true in the United States, where, for example, the U.S. pharmaceutical sector's lobbying between 1999 and 2018 was nearly four times larger than this industry's political contributions.[30]

Third, very few initiatives require companies to disclose their lobbying positions in their disclosure requirements. Yet the publication of the former may enable all stakeholders to understand the rationale and objectives of a company's lobbying demands. Such publication could allow anyone to track how well the company executes on these priorities, to identify misalignments with a company's mission and other commitments that may create reputational risks, and, ultimately, to hold accountable corporate leaders who depart from their public statements.

Fourth, of the twenty-six standards examined, only one addresses proactive efforts by companies to embrace sustainable lobbying practices. Such proactive efforts may be deduced from a company's observance of self-imposed codes of conduct and its progress toward positive impact goals. Thus, being politically accountable also increasingly means meeting expectations to respect planetary boundaries, support the functioning of

---

29. The U.S. political finance system epitomizes these issues: corporate donations are impactful and rising sharply in the context of ever more expensive political contests. The total value of these contributions quadrupled between 2010 and 2018. Gilens, Patterson, and Hanies (2021).
30. Wouters (2020).

democracy,[31] and often several sector-specific public policy aims, such as promoting healthy diets,[32] reducing plastic usage, and responsibly deploying artificial intelligence. These increasingly ambitious normative expectations are also in line with a similar shift to a more substantive notion of corporate sustainability.[33] They show that assessing responsible lobbying is possible, thus indicating that a normative understanding of what accountable—or, more specifically, positive—lobbying may be developing out of ambitious corporate reporting on these themes and voluntary standards. While a growing number of initiatives focus on operationalizing companies' commitment toward responsible or positive lobbying, they do not yet appear to have been integrated into the standards and frameworks examined. The best illustration comes from the proliferation of "corporate political engagement frameworks" in the climate space.[34]

In sum, despite having large data-gathering and analytical capacities, ESG standards providers typically fail to capture the diverse reality of corporate political engagement. They often ignore the full scope of corporate lobbying and political activity when it comes to sustainability standards. Finally, because much of the information collected by these voluntary initiatives remains proprietary in nature, its collection does not automatically translate into greater public accountability.

In light of their narrow scope, limited methodological sophistication, low granularity, and proprietary nature, none of the initiatives reviewed appears to contribute to their stated goals of increasing transparency and accountability in CPAs. Hence the urgent need for the development of mandatory standards for CPAs.

Toward Mandatory Standards for CPAs

If the existing corporate political accountability ecosystem falls short of providing the level of transparency and accountability required to prevent misuse of corporate political power, it nonetheless marks a shift away from

---

31. Winston, Doty, and Lyon (2022).
32. ATNI (2021).
33. Montiel (2008); Scherer and Palazzo (2011).
34. See, e.g., We Mean Business Coalition (2023).

an exclusive focus on the CPA process and toward greater attention to its underlying content. This speaks to today's mounting expectations regarding corporations' appropriate engagement level with some of the most pressing global challenges, such as climate change, nutrition, and global health. In the past, it was enough for a company to commit to respect specific overarching principles, and plan its CPAs accordingly. However, companies today are increasingly expected to proactively support public policy goals, such as a decarbonized economy or other SDG goals. Indeed, there is an increasing demand for them to be held accountable for how credibly they approach and achieve results in this regard. For instance, watchdog initiatives such as InfluenceMap, one of the leading platforms to track and score companies and industry groups on their climate policy engagement, and the Access to Nutrition Initiative (ATNI), a similar endeavor to hold the agrifood industry accountable for its nutrition marketing and manufacturing practices, play a crucial role in holding companies accountable for their corporate political alignment with public commitments, such as on net zero climate goals or the nutritional content of food.[35] Likewise, the recently established Social LobbyMap intends to evaluate corporate lobbying for alignment with human rights and labor standards.[36]

Because of these incipient expectations, new corporate political standards and assessment frameworks are likely to emerge to verify compliance with explicit substantive commitments. As those commitments tend to be announced publicly by CEOs and boards, one may reasonably expect them to be reflected in companies' policy efforts. As such, dedicated systems for gathering information on sustainable lobbying practices carry the potential to open new avenues for holding corporations to account. This may be the case when such commitments are not pursued in a credible manner or are actively undermined through corporations' political activities. Therefore, at a time of growing corporate commitments to public interest objectives, the emergence of a new generation of accountability channels appears to be a key development contributing to the substantive alignment of corporate political engagement with global sustainable development.

---

35. For information on the InfluenceMap, see the website at https://ca100.influencemap.org/. For information on ATNI, see the website at https://accesstonutrition.org/.
36. See the website at https://eirisfoundation.org/social-lobbymap/.

For this alignment to occur, however, corporate public commitments must continue to increase. Although voluntary in nature, they currently are more an exception than the norm. Moreover, as discussed earlier in the chapter, efforts to improve alignment will benefit from the existence of accountability watchdogs active within each specific industry. This is far from reality in today's civil society.

So the question is whether and how to require greater disclosure requirements and accountability reporting standards for both the process and the content of CPAs. This is a critical question at a time of intense political instability and heightened polarization, when businesses are being asked to take a stance on contentious political issues under the watchful eyes of consumers, employees, and shareholders.[37] There is indeed some fresh appetite for public scrutiny of corporate policy engagement, appetite also fed by media coverage tracking growing public exasperation with undue influence exercised in a variety of concealed forms, ranging from academic lobbying to astroturfing, or the practice of disguising the true financial backers of a statement in an effort to enhance credibility.[38]

Against this backdrop, there exists an incipient debate over whether corporations should remain legitimate participants in the political process or, as happened in the case of the tobacco industry, could be excluded owing to an irreconcilable conflict between the public policies pursued by the state and companies' bottom line.[39] While corporations pursue legitimate political concerns, goals, and interests, these must be legally balanced with other social interests in the democratic process.[40] However, they may also be subject to mandatory requirements constraining their ability to engage with the policy process.

As a growing number of companies express their intention to become more responsible in their CPAs amid an unprecedented level of corporate scrutiny driven by the sustainability movement, there is a unique opportunity to extend the substantive conceptual framework of sustainability to corporate political conduct.[41] Hence the prospect of turning the exercise

---

37. Murray (2022).
38. See, e.g., Kluger (2023).
39. Article 5(3) of the WHO Framework Convention on Tobacco Control (2003).
40. Preston and Post (2013 [1975]). For the opposing view, see, e.g., Relch (1998) ("respect the political process by staying out of it").
41. On corporate scrutiny driven by the sustainability movement, see Anastasiadis et al. (2018), Zinnbauer (2022), Washington and Spierings (2021), and OECD (2022).

of corporate political power into the ultimate form of sustainable business practice.

Because sustainability requires that the interests of different stakeholders in the company be duly considered, the exercise of corporate political power must also include how general societal and environmental concerns are addressed. Therefore, if companies intend to remain legitimate participants in the political process, they must become more transparent and accountable in how they organize their CPAs internally and how they exercise them externally. This means embedding CPAs into a corporate sustainability framework by mandating greater political disclosure and alignment of corporate political conduct with global sustainable development. This could represent the most systemically impactful intervention today. As political engagement and lobbying are now set to be included in the European Financial Reporting Advisory Group's remit for the EU's CSRD, the extension of sustainability-inspired obligations to the realm of corporate political conduct appears not only plausible but also urgently needed. This new generation of legal duties may redefine both the role and the practice of corporate political power, ahead of and beyond the 2030 SDG Agenda.

REFERENCES

Alemanno, A. 2023. "The Lobbying for Good Movement." *Stanford Social Innovation Review* 22 (1): 36–43.

Alemanno, A., D. Zinnbauer, and H. Stewart. 2023. *The Good Lobby Tracker Report*. Brussels: The Good Lobby, October.

Anastasiadis, S., J. Moon, and M. Humphreys. 2018. "Lobbying and the Responsible Firm: Agenda-setting for a Freshly Conceptualized Field." *Business Ethics* 27 (3): 207–21.

ATNI (Access to Nutrition Initiative). 2021. "Spotlight on Lobbying: Baseline Benchmark of Major Breast-Milk Substitute Manufacturers' Lobbying Policies, Management Systems and Disclosure." Utrecht: Access to Nutrition Foundation, May.

B Team. n.d. "Addressing Trade Association Misalignment on Climate Policy: Toolkit."

Bauer, T. 2014. "Responsible Lobbying: A Multidimensional Model." *Journal of Corporate Citizenship* 53:61–76.

Baumast, A. 2013. "Principles for Responsible Investment." In *Encyclopedia of Corporate Social Responsibility*, ed. S. O. Idowu, N. Capaldi, L. Zu, and A. D. Gupta. Berlin: Springer.

Bertrand, M., M. Bombardini, R. Fisman, and F. Trebbi. 2020. "Tax-Exempt Lobbying: Corporate Philanthropy as a Tool for Political Influence." *American Economic Review* 110 (7): 2065–102.

Boston Trust Walden. 2019. "Engaging on Corporate Public Policy Lobbying." London: PRI Association.

Climate Action 100+. 2023. "Investors Welcome Climate Lobbying Review from National Grid Following Engagement." Press release, June 30.

Dolan, E. 2023. "How—and When—Should Companies Engage in the Political Process?" *Harvard Business Review*, May 26.

Drutman, L. 2011. "A Better Way to Fix Lobbying." *Issues in Governance Studies* 40. Washington, DC: Brookings Institution, June.

Erb Institute. 2022. "The Erb Principles for Corporate Political Responsibility." Ann Arbor: University of Michigan, Erb Institute.

Escrig-Olmedo, E., M. Á. Fernández-Izquierdo, I. Ferrero-Ferrero, J. M. Rivera-Lirio, and M. J. Muñoz-Torres. 2019. "Rating the Raters: Evaluating How ESG Rating Agencies Integrate Sustainability Principles." *Sustainability* 11 (3): 915.

Favotto, A., and K. Kollman. 2021. "Mixing Business with Politics: Does Corporate Social Responsibility End Where Lobbying Transparency Begins?" *Regulation & Governance* 15 (2): 262–79.

Gilens, M., M. Patterson, and A. Hanies. 2021. "Campaign Finance Regulations and Public Policy." *American Political Science Review* 115 (3): 1074–81.

Hartwell, C. A., and T. M. Devinney. 2024. "The Demands of Populism on Business and the Creation of 'Corporate Political Obligations.'" *International Business Review* 33 (2, April): 102075.

InfluenceMap. 2019. *Asset Managers and Climate Change: How the Sector Performs on Portfolios, Engagement and Resolutions.* November.

Jacobs, R. 2023. "Lobbying's Secret Frontier: Corporate Philanthropy." *Chicago Booth Review*, August 21.

Ketu, Y., T. Miller, and Ceres. 2022. "How Companies Are—and Aren't—Leading on Climate Policy." Harvard Law School Forum on Corporate Governance, December 12.

Ketu, Y., and S. Rothstein. 2024. "Measuring Climate Policy Alignment: A Study of the Standard and Poor's 100." In *Corporate Political Responsibility*, ed. T. Lyon, chap. 9, 247–77. Cambridge: Cambridge University Press.

Kluger, J. 2023. "There Are More Fossil Fuel Lobbyists Than Ever at COP28." *Time*, December 5.

Koppl, R. 2018. *Expert Failure.* Cambridge: Cambridge University Press.

Leonhardt, D. 2019. "AT&T against Gay Rights, General Electric, Home Depot and Pfizer Too." *New York Times*, July 2.

Lewis, D. L. 2014. *Science for Sale: How the US Government Uses Powerful Corporations and Leading Universities to Support Government Policies, Silence Top Scientists, Jeopardize Our Health, and Protect Corporate Profits.* New York: Skyhorse.

Lowi, T. J. 1979. *The End of Liberalism: The Second Republic of the United States*, 2nd ed. New York: Norton.

Luyckx, J., and M. Janssens. 2016. "Discursive Legitimation of a Contested Actor over Time: The Multinational Corporation as a Historical Case (1964–2012)." *Organization Studies* 37 (11): 1595–619.

Lyon, T., et al. 2018. "CSR Needs CPR: Corporate Sustainability and Politics." *California Management Review* 60 (4): 5–24.

Lyon, T. (ed.). 2024. *Corporate Political Responsibility.* Cambridge: Cambridge University Press.

Massoglia, A. 2023. "'Dark Money' Groups Have Poured Billions into Federal Elections since the Supreme Court's 2020 Citizens United Decision." OpenSecrets.org, January 24.

McGarity, T., and W. Wagner. 2012. *Bending Science: How Special Interests Corrupt Public Health Research.* Cambridge, MA: Harvard University Press.

Montiel, I. 2008. "Corporate Social Responsibility and Corporate Sustainability: Separate Pasts, Common Futures." *Organization & Environment* 21 (3): 245–69.

Murray, S. 2022. "When Should Business Take a Stand?" *Financial Times*, March 9.

OECD (Organization for Economic Cooperation and Development). 2023. "Recommendation of the Council on the Principles for Transparency and Integrity in Lobbying." OECD/LEGAL/0379.

———. 2022. "Regulating Corporate Political Engagement: Trends, Challenges and the Role for Investors." OECD Public Governance Policy Papers 13. Paris: OECD Publishing.

———. 2021. *Lobbying in the 21st Century: Transparency, Integrity and Access.* Paris: OECD Publishing.

Preston, L. E., and J. E. Post. 2013 (1975). *Private Management and Public Policy: The Principle of Public Responsibility.* Stanford University Press.

Relch, R. B. 1998. "The New Meaning of Corporate Social Responsibility." *California Management Review* 40 (2): 8–17.

Scherer, A. G., and G. Palazzo. 2011. "The New Political Role of Business in a Globalized World: A Review of a New Perspective on CSR and Its Implications for the Firm, Governance, and Democracy." *Journal of Management Studies* 48:899–31.

Supran, G., and N. Oreskes. 2017. "Assessing ExxonMobil's Climate Change Communications (1977–2014)." *Environmental Research Letters* 12 (8).

Torres-Spelliscy, C. 2021. "More Shareholders Seek Transparency on Corporate Political Spending and Climate Change." New York University, Brennan Center for Justice, June 16.

Urlings, L. 2020. "Benchmarking for a Better World: Assessing Corporate Performance on the SDGs." In *Assessment of Responsible Innovation: Methods and Practices*, ed. E. Yaghmaei and I.V.D. Poel. London: Routledge.

Washington, P., and M. Spierings. 2021. "Under a Microscope: A New Era of Scrutiny for Corporate Political Activity." New York: Conference Board.

We Mean Business Coalition. 2023. "Climate Ambition to Advocacy: A Framework for Responsible Policy Engagement." New York, June.

WHO (World Health Organization). 2003. *WHO Framework Convention on Tobacco Control*. Geneva: WHO Press.

Winston, A., E. Doty, and T. Lyon. 2022. "The Importance of Corporate Political Responsibility." *MIT Sloan Management Review*, October 24.

World Resources Institute. 2019. "Major Environmental Groups Call on Businesses to Lead on Climate Policy." Press release, October 19.

Wouters, O. J. 2020. "Lobbying Expenditures and Campaign Contributions by the Pharmaceutical and Health Product Industry in the United States, 1999–2018." *JAMA Internal Medicine* 180 (5): 688–97.

Zinnbauer, D. 2022. *Corporate Political Responsibility: Mobilizing the Private Sector for Political Integrity*. International Institute for Democracy and Electoral Assistance. Stockholm: International IDEA.

THIRTEEN

How the Japanese Business Community Has Embraced Sustainability

ICHIRO SATO AND KEI ENDO

In 2019, a survey by the World Economic Forum found that Japanese adult citizens (along with those in the UK) had the lowest recognition of the UN's Sustainable Development Goals (SDGs) in the world, with only half having even heard of the SDGs.[1] The low SDG recognition by Japanese small companies was even more striking: in 2018, 84.2 percent of five hundred small and medium-size business owners said they had never heard of the SDGs.[2] By 2022, the situation had completely reversed: 95.0 percent of Japanese companies recognized the SDGs and 68.6 percent of large firms and 48.9 percent of small and medium-size enterprises (SMEs) had started or planned to start activities linked to the SDGs.[3]

---

1. World Economic Forum (2019).
2. Kanto Bureau of Economy, Trade and Industry and Japan Industrial Location Center (2018).
3. Teikoku Databank (2022).

What caused this turnaround? Answering this question is important because countries recognize they need to utilize the resources and capabilities of the private sector to meet their own SDGs. However, it is not easy for them to identify appropriate solutions. This chapter introduces the policies and initiatives applied in Japan, where top-down and bottom-up efforts created a closed loop through which business could embrace sustainability.

Several accounts of the rapid corporate uptake of the SDGs in Japan have been offered. For example, Dooley and Ueno reported that some companies might have found SDGs convenient for promoting their corporate image and "jumped onto the bandwagon," while others might have felt obliged to proclaim their solidarity owing to social pressure to advance the SDGs.[4] However, Davis and others point out that, behind the seemingly frivolous look of the recent interest in SDGs in Japan, there were concerted efforts by business and government to create a momentum to revitalize the country using the SDGs as a common reference point.[5]

Japan's approach is distinctive because the public policies and initiatives to promote the SDGs have influenced the thinking and behaviors of businesses and the general public not only in a top-down manner but also in a bottom-up manner. On the one hand, there have been SDG-related institutional developments through the setting of guiding principles such as Japan's Corporate Governance Code and Stewardship Code (a top-down approach), while on the other hand, Japan has raised public and business awareness and provided incentives through various policies and initiatives, such as education on the SDGs in schools, awareness raising through the mass media, and the establishment of awards related to the SDGs (a bottom-up approach). Another feature of Japan's SDG policy is the coupling of the SDGs with the revitalization of regional societies and economies. Although there is only anecdotal evidence as to the effectiveness of these initiatives and policies, the Japanese case may serve as a helpful reference from which other countries can learn how to promote and sustain business contributions to the SDGs. The remainder of this chapter reviews the salient features of Japan's approach.

---

4. Dooley and Ueno (2022).
5. Davis, Suzuki, and Sasaki (2023).

Raising Public Awareness of and Education about the SDGs

Shortly after the SDGs were adopted, a survey conducted by an advertising agency found that only 14.8 percent of the general public in Japan were aware of them.[6] By 2023, SDG awareness had risen to 91.6 percent of civic respondents.[7] This dramatic increase in the public recognition of the SDGs can be attributed to the intentional promotion of the SDGs by Japanese public sector agencies.

First, education on the SDGs was introduced for students in schools. This became one of the most potent awareness-raising activities in Japan. New government education guidelines, including education for sustainable development (ESD), were established for primary schools, junior high schools, and high schools in 2020, 2021, and 2022, respectively. These guidelines and the ESD policy provide the necessary knowledge of and skills related to the SDGs for all students to become central players in the future of sustainable development.[8] Based on the new guidelines, schools have developed original curricular material related to the SDGs that entails students choosing their own goals in relation to the SDGs and considering how they and their community can contribute to achieving them.[9] This focus on SDG education in schools has had a positive impact on SDG awareness directly by influencing students and indirectly by influencing parents through daily parent-child communication in the home.

A second channel that was used to raise SDG awareness was the mass media, including television, websites, social networking services, and newspapers. Following the issuance by the government of the revised edition of *SDGs Implementation Guiding Principles*, which emphasized awareness raising through mass media, a chorus of Japanese national and local media started strong awareness campaigns of the SDGs.[10] TV stations

---

6. Dentsu (2023).
7. Ibid.
8. Japanese National Commission for UNESCO (2021).
9. Board of Education of Koriyama City (2022); Tokyo Metropolitan Board of Education (2020). In workshops, students may learn and discuss how to contribute to climate change mitigation in daily life, or participate in raising living plants and animals to foster respect for life and the natural environment, or learn about and then practice recycling and reuse for environmental protection.
10. SDGs Promotion Headquarters of Japan (2019).

launched numerous special segments, programs, and variety shows related to the SDGs, and the number of special segments broadcast on TV in Tokyo and Osaka areas reached 493 in 2020, more than three times the 117 segments in 2019.[11] As a result, in 2023, 91.6 percent of survey respondents recognized the SDGs, and 63.5 percent said they had learned about the SDGs through TV.[12]

Although the awareness-raising efforts were designed for consumption by the general public and were not specifically directed toward businesses, they have had wide-ranging and profound impacts on businesses. Consumer businesses cannot succeed without support from consumers—the general public. Indeed, the Japanese people, who are now very conscious of the SDGs, feel loyalty to companies engaging in activities related to the SDGs, which means that companies can gain a business edge by promoting their SDG activities.[13] In addition, businesses in Japan face a labor shortage owing to the falling birth rate and an aging population. The labor force in Japan is expected to show a constant decline at a rate of approximately 500,000 people a year from 2022 to 2035.[14] Thus all Japanese companies are under pressure to attract and retain young employees—people are now aware of the SDGs and prefer to work for companies that contribute to worthy social causes as embedded in the SDGs.[15]

Knowledge Dissemination and Awareness-Raising Activities Targeted at Businesses

In addition to the awareness-raising campaigns designed for the general public, the government has targeted business awareness. To this end, government ministries and agencies have published guidance materials related to the SDGs and ESG principles for businesses.[16] For example, the Ministry

---

11. Dentsu (2021).
12. Dentsu (2023).
13. Ibid.
14. Fujita (2023).
15. Teikoku Databank (2022); Gakujo (2021); Nikkei BizGate (2022).
16. In this chapter, we use the terms SDGs and ESG (environment, social, and governance) principles or factors interchangeably as they conceptually cover similar issues in the business context, although the SDGs are standardized while ESG metrics are informal and vary across businesses.

of Economy, Industry and Trade (METI) and the Ministry of the Environment (MoE) each have published SDG guides for businesses. In addition, the Small and Medium Enterprise Agency published an SDG guide dedicated to SMEs, which often have limited resources to plan and implement initiatives related to the SDGs. These guides emphasize the benefits to business of adopting an SDG perspective as part of their risk avoidance and new business creation strategies. For example, companies may spotlight their commitment to the SDGs as a way to promote their corporate image, appeal to potential employees, and present themselves as attractive partners in creating new business opportunities. The government-produced guides also provide model procedures for companies to link the SDGs to their business practices and to provide relevant information to stakeholders.

Second, the government established awards for companies' good practices related to implementing ESG principles and the SDGs (e.g., the Japan SDGs Award, provided by the Ministry of Foreign Affairs, the ESG Finance Award, provided by the MoE, and the Regional Revitalization SDGs Financial Award, provided by the Cabinet Office). The Japan SDGs Award is especially prestigious because of its presenters and history; the award was established by the SDGs Promotion Headquarters in 2017, and prizes are presented to five to fifteen companies or organizations every year by the prime minister, the chief cabinet secretary, the foreign affairs minister, and the SDGs Promotion Headquarters. These awards have contributed to raising awareness about socially responsible businesses and also assist in business public relations efforts, which incentivizes companies to take action on the SDGs.

Third, another awareness-raising activity by the government is the dissemination of good practices through online platforms. The guidelines mentioned above include good practices, including award-winning companies' activities. Some online platforms also showcase what other companies are doing, primarily focusing on SMEs. For instance, METI hosts a website to disseminate the good practices of SMEs working on the SDGs.[17] The website explains the actions some SMEs took to fulfill the SDGs and what benefits they obtained, giving other SMEs ideas for taking on new SDG-related activities. To date the website has introduced twenty-three good practices by SMEs. In addition, most local governments provide

---

17. See METI (2024).

information on the good practices of SMEs in their regions on their official websites.

Apart from government activities, other public sector entities and industry associations have also played significant roles in raising the profile of the SDGs and ESG principles in the corporate world. The views and actions of the Government Pension Investment Fund (GPIF) of Japan, the world's largest pension fund, brought a sea change in the Japanese financial sector by spearheading ESG-conscious investing. The GPIF became a signatory to the UN's Principles for Responsible Investment (PRI) in 2015 and urged its asset managers to become PRI signatories.[18] The GPIF also required its asset managers to undertake and report their ESG engagement with investee companies, adopted nine ESG indices, and made investments worth 12.5 trillion yen (roughly U.S. $83 billion at the current exchange rate) tracking these indices as of March 2023.[19] A series of GPIF initiatives and actions shifted the mindset of Japanese institutional investors and investee companies alike toward embracing ESG investment. The Japan Business Federation, Keidanren, also played a significant role. Keidanren revised its Charter of Corporate Behavior in 2017, declaring its member companies' aspiration for achieving the SDGs through realizing Society 5.0.[20] Because of its strong political influence, Keidanren's full-fledged support for the SDGs had a strong impact on the views of Japanese companies, particularly the leading large companies, toward the SDGs.

All these initiatives help companies learn what to address and how to do it when considering implementing practices to advance the SDGs and ESG principles. Awareness raising directed at businesses has positive indirect impacts on the awareness of the general public and vice versa, since the companies usually publicize their SDG-related activities in their public relations campaigns. Therefore, the recent dramatic increase in the recognition of the SDGs in Japan could be attributed to the synergy of government awareness-raising activities directed at the general public and those directed at businesses, which effectively raises awareness in the whole of society.

18. Otsuka (2020).
19. GPIF (2023).
20. The term Society 5.0 was first officially used by the Japanese government in 2016. It refers to a future smart society wherein social challenges are resolved by the integrative application of innovative technologies (Cabinet of Japan, n.d.). The relationship between the SDGs and Society 5.0 is discussed in detail in Davis, Suzuki, and Sasaki (2023).

Targeted Direct Incentives

Beyond awareness raising, the national and local governments have provided direct incentives for companies to start and sustain SDG-related activities. One of the most straightforward approaches is the provision of financial incentives. Even before the mainstreaming of the SDGs, both central and local governments had offered a number of subsidies related to SDGs (e.g., the Agency for Natural Resources and Energy provides subsidies for energy savings, which cover part of the renewal costs for energy-saving equipment in industrial facilities; the City of Yokohama provides a subsidy for SMEs to cover part of their capital investment in energy savings, digital transformation, and productivity improvements). Recently, however, an increasing number of local governments have begun to provide SDG-dedicated subsidies, explicitly mentioning SDGs in the name of the subsidy programs. For instance, Arakawa City launched a subsidy for SMEs to develop new products and technologies that will contribute to realizing the SDGs, and Nagano Prefecture has launched a subsidy to assist SMEs in finding new marketing channels for their products that contribute to realizing the SDGs. However, subsidies are not available to everyone; many SDG-dedicated subsidies require obtaining local government registration or certification on SDG alignment, as explained below. Furthermore, the subsidies tend to be small (most subsidies are up to 3 million yen, or approximately $20,000) and are often targeted at SMEs.[21] The Japanese government and other public sector agencies also provide incentives for private companies to promote SDG-related business overseas. For example, the Japan International Cooperation Agency (JICA) collaborates with and supports Japanese companies that are expanding their businesses in developing countries when such businesses can significantly contribute to achieving the SDGs there.[22]

In addition, local governments in Japan have also started incentivizing SDG-related activities by introducing preferential treatment in public works and procurement bidding. There are two mechanisms in the preferential treatment system. One introduces SDG-related perspectives on the

---

21. Based on data retrieved from subsidy databases (J-Net 21, "Information on Support for SMEs," https://j-net21.smrj.go.jp/snavi/; and Hojyokin Portal, "Searchable Database for Subsidies and Grants," https://hojyokin-portal.jp/). Subsidies that included the term "SDG" in their title were extracted and examined.

22. JICA (2023), 50–52.

activity into the scoring criteria. The other gives bonus points to companies with a track record of SDG registration or certification. For example, Kyoto City gives additional points to bidders for some public works projects if they demonstrate SDG-related merits in their proposal, such as records of employing disabled persons or female engineers, or a certification of environmental management. As other examples, Saitama Prefecture and Yokohama City give additional points to bidders for some public procurement projects if the bidders have registration or certification documentation of their contributions to the SDGs (box 13.1).

Box 13.1. Examples of Initiatives by Local Governments to Promote the SDGs

1. Yokohama City's SDGs Certification System

Yokohama City was one of the first local governments to establish a certification scheme for companies contributing to achieving the SDGs. The Yokohama City SDGs Certification System was established in 2020. Applications for certification that are submitted by companies are evaluated by Yokohama SDGs Design Center, an NPO operating in association with the public-private partnership between Yokohama City and private companies.* There are three categories of certification: Supreme, Superior, and Standard. Among the benefits of certification, certified companies are given additional points (three, two, and one point(s) for Supreme, Superior, and Standard certification, respectively) in bidding on public projects by Yokohama City. Certified SMEs based in Yokohama City are eligible to apply to a special loan program dedicated to the SDGs in which part of the credit guarantee fee is subsidized by the city.[†]

2. Society 5.0 Maizuru Version for SDGs

The City of Maizuru in Kyoto Prefecture has implemented a project called Society 5.0 Maizuru Version for SDGs. This project aims to realize a smart community in a rural setting through the introduction of smart technologies, in partnership with technology companies. The project helps introduce smart agriculture and fisheries, attracts remote workers from cities by providing coworking spaces, experiments with Mobility as a Service (MaaS) through a combination of public transport and private ride sharing, disseminates cashless payments for the convenience of citizens and tourists, strengthens the renewable electricity supply and energy saving, and monitors natural disasters using a network of sensors, cameras, and AI technologies.[‡] The project was selected as a Local Government SDGs Model Project, and the City of Maizuru was designated an SDGs Future City by the Government of Japan in 2019.[§]

*City of Yokohama (2022).
[†]City of Yokohama (2024).
[‡]Maizuru City (2021).
[§]Cabinet of Japan (2019a, 2019b).

These direct incentives have some common features. First, although they are for businesses, they may also have indirect positive effects on raising awareness among the general public because they receive visibility through the announcements of awards from both the central and local governments. Another feature is that both types of incentives encourage businesses to obtain government registration or certification with respect to the SDGs since this is usually a precondition to receive SDG-related subsidies and worth additional points on public works bidding.

Corporate Governance Reform and Sustainability

A major corporate governance reform initiative started in 2013 as an integral part of the Japan Revitalization Strategy launched by then prime minister Shinzo Abe. As the first significant milestone, Japan's Stewardship Code was published in 2014, followed by the adoption of Japan's Corporate Governance Code in 2015. The former was based on the British model and the latter was modeled after the OECD Principles of Corporate Governance.[23]

The Stewardship Code provides principles for signatory institutional investors to fulfill their stewardship responsibilities. Becoming a signatory is voluntary, but most prominent institutional investors have accepted the code. As of March 31, 2024, 334 institutional investors were signatories to the code. They are required annually to post on their websites an account of how they implemented the principles. If they did not implement some of them, they must explain why. This is known as the "comply or explain" approach. The original code adopted in 2014 referred to social and environmental issues only in the context of monitoring the risks of investee companies. The references to sustainability, including ESG factors, were strengthened through revisions in 2017 and 2020. The current code requires institutional investors to demonstrate how they integrate considerations of sustainability issues into their strategy to fulfill their stewardship responsibilities and engage with investee companies based on such considerations. The inclusion of the ESG factors in the Stewardship Code turned the financial sector into a driving force to promote the SDGs and ESG principles among companies in Japan.

The Corporate Governance Code provides principles for companies listed on the Tokyo Stock Exchange (TSE) to put effective corporate

23. Milhaupt (2017).

governance in place. Listed companies in the Prime and Standard Markets of the TSE must comply with all the principles of the code, while those in the Growth Market need to comply only with the general principles. In either case, companies that choose not to comply with any of the principles must explain why. The code was revised in 2018 and 2021, and the current code requires listed companies to actively address sustainability issues, including ESG factors, to enhance their medium- to long-term corporate value. It further requires the companies to develop their sustainability policy and disclose their efforts to address sustainability issues.

A question is how these twin codes have effectively encouraged companies to address sustainability issues. One issue is the coverage of the codes: how many institutional investors and companies are subject to them? Among the 334 signatories to the Stewardship Code, 254 have corporate numbers registered in Japan; they represent fewer than 1 percent of the pension funds and about 14 percent of other institutional investors.[24] These numbers may look modest, but most major asset owners and asset managers are signatories to the Stewardship Code, implying that the monetary-based shares of the signatories are significant. As for the Corporate Governance Code, the total number of companies listed in the Prime, Standard, and Growth Markets of the TSE was 3,939 at the end of April 2024. According to the 2021 Economic Census for Business Activity, Japan had roughly 1.78 million companies.[25] This means that only about 0.2 percent of companies are directly influenced by the Corporate Governance Code.

However, far more companies are likely to be influenced indirectly by the Stewardship Code and Corporate Governance Code through engagement with those directly subject to them. According to a survey of five hundred SMEs, 20 percent identified suggestions or requests from their business customers or suppliers as the biggest reason for addressing the SDGs.[26] Again, this implies the potentially extensive impacts of the codes through the supply chains of companies listed on the TSE or through engagement with signatory investors of the Stewardship Code.

---

24. The list of institutional investors that have accepted the Stewardship Code is provided by the Financial Services Agency of Japan and is available at https://www.fsa.go.jp/en/refer/councils/stewardship/20160315.html. As of March 31, 2024, 334 institutions had signed.
25. Statistics Bureau of Japan (2021).
26. Japan Industrial Location Center (2021).

Another issue is how the codes change the perceptions and behaviors of related investors and companies. The TSE periodically studies and publishes the state of implementation of the Corporate Governance Code by its listed companies. The latest report studied 3,293 companies listed on the Prime or Standard Markets.[27] The implementation of sustainability-related principles is reported in table 13.1, and this information indicates that most companies have recognized the importance of addressing sustainability issues for raising their medium- to long-term corporate value and have developed basic policies around sustainability initiatives. However, only two-thirds of them disclose their sustainability initiatives, indicating that some companies have yet to implement sustainability policies. There are no corresponding data for compliance with the Stewardship Code.

We therefore reviewed the policies to address the principles of the code and stewardship reports disclosed by the signatory institutional investors. A list of the access links to these materials is available on the Financial Services Agency website.[28] We found that 71 percent of the stewardship policies referenced ESG principles or sustainability.[29] This may be a good sign that most institutional investors take sustainability seriously. However, many policies provide only a boilerplate statement about sustainability and adherence to ESG principles, merely repeating the phrasing found in the Stewardship Code. Among the ninety-one stewardship reports submitted by a subset of the signatories, 81 percent contained references to ESG principles or sustainability, but the level of detail of the ESG and sustainability engagement varied greatly. Our review suggests that the signatories to the code that have implemented meaningful ESG or sustainability engagement with investee companies are still in the minority.

---

27. Tokyo Stock Exchange (2022).

28. The website for the Financial Services Agency of Japan website is https://www.fsa.go.jp/en/refer/councils/stewardship/20160315.html. The analysis was conducted using the list as of June 30, 2023.

29. In the calculation, duplication was eliminated. When more than one institutional investor referred to the same policy document, it was counted only once. References to ESG principles or sustainability were not counted if they appeared only in the names of positions or divisions. References to "sustainable investment" were counted, but "sustainable growth" was not counted.

Table 13.1. Implementation of Selected Sustainability-Related Principles of Japan's Corporate Governance Code (2021)

Code number	Supplementary principles	Compliance rate (%) Prime	Compliance rate (%) Standard
2.3.1	"The board should recognize that . . . sustainability issues . . . are important management issues that can lead to earning opportunities as well as risk mitigation and should further consider addressing these matters positively and proactively in terms of increasing corporate value over the medium- to long-term."	95.8 (+1.9 pt)	94.0 (+0.7 pt)
3.1.3	"Companies should appropriately disclose their initiatives on sustainability when disclosing their management strategies. . . . In particular, companies listed on the Prime Market should collect and analyze the necessary data on the impact of climate change-related risks and earning opportunities on their business activities and profits and enhance the quality and quantity of disclosure based on the TCFD recommendations . . . or an equivalent framework."	62.5 (−4.2 pt)	59.4 (+0.8 pt)
4.2.2	"The board should develop a basic policy for the company's sustainability initiatives. . . . In addition, . . . the board should effectively supervise the allocation of management resources . . . and the implementation of business portfolio strategies to ensure that they contribute to the sustainable growth of the company."	86.4 (+6.2 pt)	67.2 (+3.5 pt)

Source: Modified from Tokyo Stock Exchange (as of July 14, 2022).

Note: The texts of the supplementary principles are quoted from Japan's Corporate Governance Code (2021). *pt*, percentage point.

Corporate Sustainability Policies in the Context of Regional Development

Corporate governance reform through the two codes, which encourage more corporate and investor efforts to address sustainability issues, primarily targets large companies. Although the codes' influence extends to some smaller companies through large companies' supply chains, the range of influence is still small if one considers the very large number of SMEs. In Japan, SMEs account for 99.7 percent of companies in number, 70 percent of employees, and 53 percent of the value added in the economy.[30] Thus sustainability policies targeting smaller companies are needed.

As a principal example of such policies, the promotion of sustainability initiatives by local companies, including SMEs, has been integrated into the government's policies to revitalize regional economies. The coupling of the SDGs with regional revitalization, which is a central policy agenda in the Japanese context of dwindling regional economies in aging rural communities, is a unique characteristic of the application of SDG policies in Japan. This began when the Japanese government started publishing a strategy document for regional revitalization, *Town, People, Job Creation Comprehensive Strategy*, in 2014; it has been revised six times since.[31] A reference to the SDGs first appeared in the 2016 edition.[32] The latest edition of the strategy (2020) identified the SDGs as a guiding principle and a driving force to implement regional revitalization.[33] The 2020 strategy included initiatives to facilitate the establishment of registration or certification schemes for local companies to address the SDGs and to assist local financial institutions providing SDG- or ESG-related financing for regional revitalization.

The registration or certification schemes are established and operated by local governments. According to the guidelines on local SDG registration or certification schemes commissioned by the Cabinet Office of Japan, there are three types of schemes: registration of declarations, registration of initiatives, and certification of initiatives.[34] The declarations refer to the intention expressed by local companies to address the SDGs. The registration of initiatives registers local companies' initiatives to address the SDGs, including targets, implementation plans, and self-monitoring and evaluation results. Certification occurs when initiatives are reviewed and certified by the local government. As of the end of July 2023, twenty-three prefectures and sixty-four municipalities had established such schemes.[35]

30. The Small and Medium Enterprise Agency (2023).
31. Cabinet of Japan (2014).
32. Cabinet of Japan (2016).
33. Cabinet of Japan (2020).
34. Research and Study Group of SDGs Finance for Regional Revitalization (2020).
35. The Regional Revitalization SDGs Financial Research and Study Group (2021) has published the latest list.

Table 13.2. Results of Corporate Participation in the SDG-Related Registration or Certification Schemes

Category	Feedback from companies on the results of their participation
Internal engagement, and learning	• Better understanding of the SDGs and their linkages with their businesses • Better understanding of their contributions and progress toward fulfilling the SDGs; better understanding of the challenges involved • Enhanced internal uptake of the SDGs
Stakeholder relationships and partnership	• Extended networks with external companies and people • Greater appeal to business partners and prospective employees
Access to finance	• Subsidies awarded for SDG-related initiatives

Source: Compiled by the authors based on feedback information from companies participating in the registration or certification scheme in Tottori and Nagano Prefectures (Tottori Prefecture, n.d.; Act SDGs, 2021).

Only five local governments were running certification schemes as of July 2023. Some local governments run two or three types of registration or certification schemes in parallel. Both the numbers of schemes and the number of companies registered or certified are growing. Examples of the benefits for local companies from participating in such schemes include greater opportunities to receive SDG-related financing from local financial institutions, preferential treatment in public procurement, eligibility for subsidies awarded by local governments, business matching facilitation among companies, opportunities for the exchange of knowledge and experience with peers, and greater corporate visibility and recognition.

As Kanie notes, the governance mechanism of SDGs is based on a voluntary commitment to goals and targets and the monitoring of progress toward them with indicators.[36] The significance of the SDG registration or certification schemes lies in that they bring companies, including SMEs, on board with the SDG governance mechanism. The effectiveness of such schemes, however, is yet to be evaluated. Some anecdotal evidence of their impacts based on feedback from some companies participating in registration or certification schemes in two prefectures is presented in table 13.2.

36. Kanie (2017).

These schemes are designed and operated differently in respective localities, and such diversity could provide many testing laboratories and valuable learning opportunities for devising effective approaches to encouraging companies to address sustainability issues.

Forming Good Corporate Citizens

This chapter has reviewed a range of measures taken in Japan to encourage companies to contribute to the SDGs. These measures can be classified based on the type of motivation they resort to. As Simon Sinek has said, "There are only two ways to influence human behavior: you can manipulate it, or you can inspire it."[37] Manipulations include giving various forms of incentives, imposing formal or informal regulations, or putting pressure on stakeholders. Such manipulations are necessary, particularly to prevent companies from harming human rights and well-being, public safety and order, or the environment. However, we argue that companies need to be inspired if they are to make enduring efforts toward progress on achieving the SDG.

What inspires companies, then? There is no definite answer to that question. The same measure, for example distribution of SDG informational materials or establishing a registration scheme for SDG initiatives, may inspire some but not others. Only manipulative measures can be targeted to specific outcomes. However, the range of awareness-raising and educational activities about the SDGs that have been implemented in Japan to date may have had profound under-the-radar impacts on the current broad social support for the SDGs by inspiring members of society in all walks of life, although such impacts are difficult to evaluate empirically. In addition, a likely ingredient of corporate inspiration is mutual engagement with company stakeholders and between executives, managers, and all employees to discuss how they can progress toward achieving the SDGs as a society and what companies can contribute to that progress. Various SDG platforms are already established in Japan to facilitate engagement, interactions, and knowledge exchange among companies, governments, and civil society organizations.[38] Encouraging more companies to participate in such platforms

---

37. Sinek (2009), 16.
38. See, e.g., Cabinet of Japan (2023), MoE (2023), and the Association for Sustainable Transition's Platform Clover (https://platform-clover.net).

could help participants, including companies, to inspire one another to take actions linked to realizing the SDGs.

However, we cannot expect companies to contribute to the SDGs in isolation. A company's ability to deliver significant progress toward the SDGs will be undermined if its shareholders focus only on maximizing short-term profits, or if its customers demand that the company supply goods and services at the lowest possible price no matter how problematic the production process may be. If we are to fulfill the SDGs as a society, shareholders should request companies to contribute to the SDGs even if this means sacrificing some short-term profits, and customers in turn should expect companies to supply goods and services responsibly even if this leads to higher prices. Of course, this does not mean companies must contribute to achieving the SDGs at any cost. Balance matters. That is why companies need to engage with their shareholders, customers, suppliers, governments, and other stakeholders to discuss what they expect from each other in progressing toward societal realization of the SDGs.

The SDGs are political goals, and achieving them in each society is a political process. Sandel, in giving an account of Aristotle's elaboration of politics, explained that the purpose of politics was to cultivate "distinctive human capacities and virtues—to deliberate about the common good, to acquire practical judgment, to share in self-government, to care for the fate of the community as a whole"—or, in fewer words, to "form good citizens."[39] If we apply this perspective to the SDGs, the purpose of the political process to implement them would not be just achieving these goals but to form good citizens and good companies along the way through collaborative deliberations and interactions within society. The SDGs may change over time if circumstances change or if stakeholders decide to change them. Thus, achieving the current set of SDGs may not in itself be the ultimate purpose. Forming good citizens and companies would have far more enduring positive impacts for ensuring the sustainable progress of society, regardless of what sustainability issues may be most crucial at any given time. In that respect, sustainability education for all (Target 4.7 of the SDGs) deserves more attention in the post-2030 development goals. If lifelong learning about sustainability is institutionalized for all stakeholders in society, the societal transition toward sustainability will be equipped with a steady driving force from good citizens and good companies.

---

39. Sandel (2010), 193.

Companies are essential members of society as corporate citizens, and forming good corporate citizens is of utmost importance to ensure the sustainability of society.[40] Engaging companies in the societal journey toward achieving the goals outlined in the SDGs provides valuable opportunities to form good corporate citizens along the way.

REFERENCES

Act SDGs. 2021. "What Are the Effects of Nagano Prefecture's Company Registration System to Promote SDGs?" *Note* (blog), Act SDGs, June 11.

Board of Education of Koriyama City. 2022. *Koriyama shiritsu gakkou SDGs kyouiku jissen jireishu* [Collection of SDGs education practice cases in public schools in Koriyama City]. https://www.city.koriyama.lg.jp/uploaded/attachment/38250.pdf.

Buchanan, J., D. H. Chai, and S. Deakin. 2019. "Taking a Horse to Water? Prospects for the Japanese Corporate Governance Code." *Zeitschrift für Japanisches Recht* 47:69–108.

Cabinet of Japan. 2023. *Regional Revitalization SDGs Public-Private Partnership Platform*. Tokyo. https://future-city.go.jp/platform/.

———. 2020. *Town, People, Job Creation Comprehensive Strategy: 2020 Revised Edition* [in Japanese]. Cabinet Decision, second term. Tokyo. https://www.chisou.go.jp/sousei/info/pdf/r02-12-21-senryaku2020.pdf.

———. 2019a. *List of Proposals Selected as 'Local Government SDGs Model Project' in 2019* [in Japanese]. Tokyo. https://www.chisou.go.jp/tiiki/kankyo/kaigi/sonota/sdgs_r1model_an.pdf.

———. 2019b. *List of Cities Selected as SDGs Future City in 2019* [in Japanese]. Tokyo. https://www.chisou.go.jp/tiiki/kankyo/teian/2019sdgs_pdf/sdgsfuturecity2019.pdf.

———. 2016. *Town, People, Job Creation Comprehensive Strategy: 2016 Revised Edition* [in Japanese]. Cabinet Decision. Tokyo. https://www.chisou.go.jp/sousei/info/pdf/h28-12-22-sougousenryaku2016hontai.pdf.

———. 2014. *Town, People, Job Creation Comprehensive Strategy* [in Japanese]. Cabinet Decision. Tokyo. https://www.chisou.go.jp/sousei/info/pdf/20141227siryou5.pdf.

———. n.d. *Society 5.0*. Tokyo. https://www8.cao.go.jp/cstp/english/society5_0/index.html.

City of Yokohama. 2024. "Yokohama City SDGs Certification System 'Y-SDGs.'" City of Yokohama Global Offices, last update May 8.

---

40. The term "good corporate citizen" appears in the *Charter of Corporate Behavior of Keidanren*, 5th rev. (Keidanren, 2017).

———. 2022. "Yokohama City's 'Y-SDGs' Certification System for SMEs Receives Award from Minister." City of Yokohama Global Offices, March 21.
Davis, S., S. Suzuki, and H. Sasaki. 2023. "Japan's Approach to the Sustainable Development Goals." In *The Elgar Companion to Corporate Social Responsibility and Sustainable Development*, ed. L. Z. Samuel and O. Idowu, 311–30. London: Edward Elgar.
Dentsu, 2023. "Dentsu Conducts the 6th 'Consumer Survey on SDGs.'" Press release, May 12.
———. 2021. "Dentsu Conducts 4th 'Consumer Survey on SDGs.'" Press release, April 26.
Dooley, B., and H. Ueno. 2022. "Why Is This Colorful Little Wheel Suddenly Everywhere in Japan? It's the Logo of the United Nations' Sustainable Development Goals. And Japan Is All In." *New York Times*, August 25.
Fujita, S. 2023. *Hitode busoku no genjou to kongo no tembou* [Current status and prospects of labor shortage]. Tokyo: Mitsubishi UFJ Research and Consulting.
Gakujo. 2021. *Z sedai no koronaka shukatsu* [Generation Z's job hunting during the COVID-19 catastrophe]. Tokyo.
GPIF (Government Pension Investment Fund). 2023. *For All Generations: 2022 ESG Report*. Tokyo.
Japan Industrial Location Center. 2021. *2020 Survey Report on the State of Recognition and Engagement of SDGs by Small and Medium Enterprises*. Tokyo.
Japanese National Commission for UNESCO. 2021. *Jizoku kanouna kaihatsu notameno kyouiku (ESD) suishin no tebiki* [Manual for promotion of education for sustainable development (ESD)]. Tokyo.
JICA (Japan International Cooperation Agency). 2023. *Annual Report 2023*. Tokyo.
Kanie, N. 2017. "Roles and Functions of Indicators for Governing SDGs." *Haikibutsu Shigen Junkan Gakkaishi* 28 (6): 412–19.
Kanto Bureau of Economy, Trade and Industry and Japan Industrial Location Center. 2018. "Chushou kigyou no SDGs ninchido jittai tou chousa kekka" [Web-based questionnaire survey results regarding the SDG recognition and reality of small and medium enterprises]. https://www.kanto.meti.go.jp/seisaku/sdgs/data/20181213sdgs_chosa_houkoku_syosai.pdf.
Keidanren. 2017. *Charter of Corporate Behavior of Keidanren*, 5th rev. Tokyo, November 8.
Maizuru City. 2021. *Challenge to Realize Maizuru Version of Society 5.0*. Kyoto.
METI (Ministry of Economy, Industry and Trade). 2024. "Introducing Advanced Examples of Small and Medium-Sized Enterprises Working on

SDGs" [in Japanese]. Tokyo. https://www.kanto.meti.go.jp/seisaku/sdgs/sdgs_senshinjirei.html.

Milhaupt, C. J. 2017. "Evaluating Abe's Third Arrow: How Significant Are Japan's Recent Corporate Governance Reforms?" Columbia Law and Economics Working Paper 561. New York: Columbia Law School.

Ministry of Internal Affairs and Communications. 2023. *Economic Census for Business Activity*. Tokyo. https://www.stat.go.jp/english/data/e-census/2021/index.html.

MoE (Ministry of the Environment). 2023. Local SDGs—Circular and Ecological Economy Platform [in Japanese]. Tokyo. http://chiikijunkan.env.go.jp/.

Nikkei BizGate. 2022. "Attitude towards SDGs: 65% Place Importance on Them When Changing Jobs. What Are the Trends in Related Recruitment?" June 15.

Otsuka, A. 2020. "Can the World's Largest Pension Fund, Japan's GPIF, Be a Responsible Steward? Stewardship Responsibility as Asset Owner." *Journal of Governance and Regulation* 9 (1): 44–52.

Regional Revitalization SDGs Financial Research and Study Group. 2023. *Regional Revitalization SDGs: Towards the Promotion of Finance Basic Way of Thinking*. Tokyo. https://www.chisou.go.jp/tiiki/kankyo/pdf/sdgs_kinyu/fundamental2023.pdf.

———. 2021. *List of Local Governments That Have Established the Regional Revitalization SDGs Declaration/Registration/Certification System*. Tokyo. https://www.chisou.go.jp/tiiki/kankyo/pdf/sdgs_kinyu/sengen-toroku-ninsho_list.pdf.

Research and Study Group of SDGs Finance for Regional Revitalization. 2020. *Local Governments' Guidelines on Registration and Certification Schemes of SDGs for Regional Revitalization 2020*. Tokyo. https://www.chisou.go.jp/tiiki/kankyo/kaigi/pdf/sdgs_finance_guideline.pdf.

Sandel, M. J. 2010. *Justice: What's the Right Thing to Do?* New York: Farrar, Straus and Giroux.

SDGs Promotion Headquarters of Japan. 2019. *SDGs Implementation Guiding Principles: Revised Edition*. Tokyo: Ministry of Foreign Affairs. https://www.kantei.go.jp/jp/singi/sdgs/pdf/jisshi_shishin_r011220e.pdf.

Sinek, S. 2009. *Start with Why: How Great Leaders Inspire Everyone to Take Action*. New York: Portfolio.

The Small and Medium Enterprise Agency. 2023. *White Paper on Small and Medium Enterprises 2023*. Tokyo.

Statistics Bureau of Japan. 2021. *2021 Economic Census for Business Activity*. Tokyo.

Teikoku Databank. 2022. *SDGs ni kansuru kigyou no ishiki chousa (2022 nen)* [Awareness survey on corporate SDGs (2022)]. Tokyo. https://www.tdb.co.jp/report/watching/press/pdf/p220811.pdf.

Tokyo Metropolitan Board of Education. 2020. *Jizoku kanouna chikyu wo mezashite—Toukyo to kankyou kyouiku shidou shiryou* [Toward sustainable Earth—Teacher's reference material on environmental education]. Tokyo. https://www.kyoiku.metro.tokyo.lg.jp/school/content/environment/instructional_materials.html.

Tokyo Stock Exchange. 2022. *Response of Listed Companies Regarding Revised Corporate Governance Code* (as of July 14, 2022). https://www.jpx.co.jp/english/equities/listing/cg/tvdivq0000008jdy-att/b5b4pj0000051uty.pdf.

Tottori Prefecture. n.d. *Tottori SDGs Corporate Certification Scheme.* https://www.pref.tottori.lg.jp/301064.htm.

World Economic Forum. 2019. "Global Survey Shows 74% Are Aware of the Sustainable Development Goals." Press release, April 26.

Contributors

ALBERTO ALEMANNO is the Jean Monnet Professor of European Union Law, HEC Paris, and the 2024–2025 Visiting Democracy Fellow at the Ash Center for Democratic Governance and Innovation, Harvard University.

SASJA BESLIK is chief investment strategy officer, SDG Impact Japan.

KEI ENDO is a research fellow, JICA-Ogata Sadako Research Institute for Peace and Development.

EMILY FARNWORTH is director of the Centre for Climate Engagement, Hughes Hall, the University of Cambridge.

ELDRID HERRINGTON is head of academic engagement at the Centre for Climate Engagement, Hughes Hall, the University of Cambridge.

EKHOSUEHI IYAHEN is secretary general of the Insurance Development Forum, a public-private partnership based in London.

HOMI KHARAS is a senior fellow at the Center for Sustainable Development, Global Economy and Development program, Brookings Institution.

KOJI MAKINO is a visiting fellow at and former director general of the JICA-Ogata Sadako Research Institute for Peace and Development, and professor (development specific), Graduate School of Advanced Integrated Studies in Human Survivability, Kyoto University.

WARREN MAROUN is a professor at the University of Witwatersrand School of Accountancy and the University of Leeds. He is a board member of the International Auditing and Assurance Standards Board.

KATSUO MATSUMOTO is a vice president, JICA, and former chief representative of JICA India.

JOHN W. McARTHUR is a senior fellow at and director of the Center for Sustainable Development, Global Economy and Development program, Brookings Institution.

JANE NELSON is the founding director of the Corporate Responsibility Initiative and a senior research fellow at the Mossavar-Rahmani Center for Business and Government at Harvard University's Kennedy School of Government and a nonresident senior fellow in the Center for Sustainable Development, Global Economy and Development program, Brookings Institution.

NDIDI OKONKWO NWUNELI is a serial social entrepreneur who has established organizations in the agribusiness, youth development, leadership, and philanthropic landscapes. She currently serves as president and CEO of the ONE Campaign, a global advocacy organization that fights for a more just world by demanding the investments needed to create economic opportunities and healthier lives in Africa.

PAUL POLMAN is a business leader, campaigner, and co-author of *Net Positive*, London.

LILIANA ROJAS-SUAREZ is director of the Latin America Initiative and a senior fellow with the Center for Global Development, Washington, D.C.

RICHARD SAMANS is senior economic adviser to the World Business Council for Sustainable Development and nonresident senior fellow in the Center for Sustainable Development, Global Economy and Development program, Brookings Institution.

ICHIRO SATO is an executive senior research fellow, JICA-Ogata Sadako Research Institute for Peace and Development.

TOM SEIDENSTEIN is chair of the International Auditing and Assurance Standards Board and co-CEO of the International Foundation for Ethics and Audit.

Index

AA1000AS (AccountAbility), 206
AACE Food Processing & Distribution (Nigeria), 60
Abe, Shinzo, 255
ABP (Netherlands), 125
Access to Medicines Foundation, 102
Access to Nutrition Initiative (ATNI), 102, 240; Spotlight on Lobbying, 232
ACCIÓN Empresas (Chile), 111
accountability. *See* assurance; corporate accountability
AccountAbility, 206, 234, 237
Accountancy Europe, 176, 182
accounting, 209–10; firms' reporting metrics, 12, 175–77; international authorities, 174, 178–82, 187, 194; standards, 10, 15, 21, 85–86, 181, 192. *See also* assurance; auditing; International Financial Reporting Standards (IFRS); reporting; Sustainability Accounting Standards Board (SASB)
Advancing Local Dairy Development in Nigeria (ALDDN), 55
advocacy, 24, 57, 104, 179; positive corporate, 38–39, 47. *See also* corporate accountability; corporate political activities (CPAs); lobbying; net positive mindset; trade associations
Africa, 55, 58, 60, 142, 148, 162–63
African Food Changemakers, 58
African Risk Capacity Limited (ARC Ltd.), 162–63
African Union (AU), 163
Agency for Natural Resources and Energy (Japan), 253
aggregate confusion, 7
agriculture. *See* food and agriculture

AI, 41, 188, 239, 254
Alemanno, Alberto, 24–25, 227–42
alliances, 5, 20, 92–115; evaluation of, 104; Glasgow Financial Alliance for Net Zero (GFANZ), 13, 107–08; Global Alliance for Improved Nutrition (GAIN), 55; Global Energy Alliance for People and Planet, 46, 57; Global Investors for Sustainable Development Alliance, 13; Global Risk Modelling Alliance (GRMA), 161; Kenya Private Sector Alliance, 110; Net-Zero Asset Owner Alliance (NZAOA), 135–36; Net-Zero Insurance Alliance, 108; place-based, 108–12; practice and insights of, 103–12; precompetitive business alliances, 17, 92–93, 95–96, 103–5, 113, 115; Responsible Business Alliance, 103, 175; within value chains, 92; World Benchmarking Alliance (WBA), 12, 43, 91n1, 100–102, 231. *See also* coalitions; collective action; multistakeholder alliances; partnerships
American Chamber of Commerce, 228
American Institute of Certified Public Accountants Accounting Principles Board, 181
Annan, Kofi, 6
antitrust regulations, 20, 86, 108, 113
"antiwokeness," 7–9, 43
Argentina, 150
Aspirational District Programme (India), 222
asset classes, 21, 125, 147, 150–53
Asset Management Advisory Committee (SEC), 178

asset managers, 6, 107, 127, 130, 134, 199–200, 252, 256. *See also* fiduciary obligations
asset owners, 121, 176, 188; challenges to progress and, 128, 130–33; ESG and, 199–200; framework and duties, 122–23; impact measurement and, 132; insurance of, 164, 166; market signals, 127–29; recommendations for, 20–21, 133–36; risk-reward balance, 131–32; sustainable investments debate, 133–34; types, roles, and nuances, 124–27. *See also* insurance; pension funds
assets under management (AUM), 127, 176
assurance, 199–211; adaptability of, 207–08, 210; challenges of, 209; definition of, 201; in the EU, 205, 210; external, 23, 204–06; limited, 208–10; reasonable, 208–10; reliability of, 22–23, 27, 204–06. *See also* International Auditing and Assurance Standards Board (IAASB)
auditing, 201, 204–09; committees, 82; reliability of, 23; SMEs and, 63–64. *See also* accounting; International Auditing and Assurance Standards Board (IAASB); reporting
Australia, 76, 85
Aviva, 126
awards, 25, 223, 248, 251
awareness-raising campaigns, 27, 249–250
AXA, 126

Babcock, Ariel Fromer, 81–82
Bangladesh, 9

banking regulations, 139–53; recommendations for, 143–45, 149–53
banks, 45, 107, 139–53; Bank of England, 73; commercial, 13, 21; State Bank of India, 219
Basel Committee on Banking Supervision (BCBS), 139–40; Basel III, 21, 140–53; Net Stable Funding Ratio (NSFR), 146; recommendations for, 144–45, 152
benchmarking, 104, 194; World Benchmarking Alliance (WBA), 12, 43, 91n1, 100–102, 231
Beslik, Sasja, 20, 121–36
Better Business Better World report (BSDC), 36–37
Beveridge Report (UK), 157
Bezos Earth Fund, 57
Big Four Agenda (Kenya), 110
Bill & Melinda Gates Foundation Trust, 126
biodiversity, 1–2, 39, 74, 100, 189
B Lab Impact Assessment Methodology, 234, 237
Black in Business (Goldman Sachs), 62
blended finance, 106, 130
Bloomberg ESG & Climate Indices, 234, 236
boards of directors, 69–87, 193; changing roles of, 74–75; climate governance guidance for, 77–79; corporate purpose and strategy and, 81–82; directors, non-executive, 19–20, 70–71, 75–79; governance structures of, 84–85; in Japan, 258; large-scale collaborations and, 86–87; material risks and, 79–80; oversight and accountability and, 82–83; recommendations for, 83–87; sustainability competence of, 84–85
Bombay Stock Exchange, 217
bonds, 179; corporate, 143; finance, 146; sustainable, 6–7, 36, 130, 135
Boston Consulting Group (BCG), 104–05
boundaries, planetary, 44, 75, 100
Brazil, 8–9, 140, 209
Brundtland Report (WCED), 72, 93
Building Resilience Against Climate and Environmental Shocks (BRACE) (African Food Changemakers), 58
business actors: benefiting from sustainable practices, 37–48; challenges of, 26, 37–44; recommendations for, 17–20, 193–95. *See also* alliances; boards of directors; CEOs; collective action
Business and Sustainable Development Commission (BSDC), 11, 59, 95; *Better Business Better World* report, 36–37
business associations, 110, 114–15; Keidanren (Japan), 13, 111, 252; lobbying and, 237; SMEs and, 19, 57. *See also* coalitions; industry associations; large companies; public-private partnerships; small and medium-size enterprises (SMEs); trade associations
business parks, 112

C40 Cities consortium, 111
Cabinet Office of Japan, 251, 259
California, 7–8, 10, 177, 185; Public Employees' Retirement Fund (CalPERS), 125

capitalism, 1; refining of, 28; responsible, 23, 202–04; shareholder, 4–5, 7, 15, 70–71; Smith on, 3–4; stakeholder, 4–5, 24, 70–71, 203–04, 224
capital requirements, 141, 146–53; gold-plating of, 21, 142–44. *See also* Basel Committee on Banking Supervision (BCBS); infrastructure; risk
Carbon Border Adjustment Mechanism (EU), 8, 42
Carbon Calculator (SME Climate Hub), 58
Carbon Disclosure Project. *See* CDP
carbon markets, 107
Carbon Pricing Leadership Coalition, 86
carbon reduction. *See* decarbonization
Carney, Mark, 107; "tragedy of the horizon," 19, 73, 127
CDP, 5, 184; Climate Change Scoring Methodology, 234, 237
CDSB. *See* Climate Disclosure Standards Board (CDSB)
CEOs, 76, 174; challenges of, 26, 37–44; International Business Council CEOs (WEF), 190; political influence of, 193, 228n4, 240; supporting ESG legislation, 24, 38–39, 46, 103. *See also* boards of directors; corporate governance; Polman, Paul
Ceres, 73, 84–86
certification schemes in Japan, 259–61
Charter of Corporate Behavior (Keidanren) (Japan), 13, 252
Chile, 111
China, 7–8, 140
CHIPS Act (U.S.), 42

CII National Committee on Corporate Social Responsibility & Community Development (India), 217
cities, 11, 37, 40, 108
city-level coalitions, 111–12, 114
civil society organizations (CSOs), 2, 71, 94–97, 184, 192–93, 261. *See also* public-private partnerships
climate change, 1–2, 41, 187–88; action plans, 109–11; corporate governance and, 73–75, 77–79, 82–83, 85, 228–30, 258; costs to the economy, 39–40; effect on SMEs, 53, 58; investment risks of, 4, 123, 131–32, 134, 136, 166, 199–200; policy responses to, 10, 19–20; risk and resilience, 158–68, 190; US policies, 7–10, 42, 177–78, 185, 227n2. *See also* CDP; decarbonization; net zero; Paris Agreement (2015); planetary boundaries; reporting; Sustainable Development Goals (SDGs); United Nations (UN)
Climate Change Conferences. *See* COP climate negotiations (UN)
Climate Disclosure Standards Board (CDSB), 182, 184, 187
Climate Fit (SME Climate Hub), 58
Climate Governance Initiative, 77–79, 84–85
Climate Vulnerable Forum (V20), 161
coalitions, 38, 94, 100–112; Carbon Pricing Leadership Coalition, 86; city-level, 111–12, 114; Consumer Goods Forum, 103, 175; Fashion Pact, 46; First Movers Coalition (FMC), 46, 105–07; Food and Land Use Coalition, 40; International Council on Mining and

Metals (ICMM), 12, 103, 175; upscaling pathways, 96–97; We Mean Business Coalition, 86, 102. *See also* alliances; collective action; partnerships

collaboration. *See* alliances; coalitions; collective action

collective action, 91–115; categorizing of, 95–98; evaluation of efficacy, 104; financial, 135–36; obstacles to, 108, 112–13; practice and insights, 103–12; priorities of, 98–103; recommendations for, 113–15; risk management and, 161–64

Columbia Climate School, 55

Columbia Law School, 83

Commercial Dairy Ranchers Association of Nigeria (CODARAN), 55

companies. *See* boards of directors; business actors; corporate accountability; corporate actors; large companies; small and medium-size enterprises (SMEs)

Companies Act (UK), 9

Companies Act 2013 amendment (India), 24, 215–18

Confederation of Indian Industry (CII), 217. *See also* CII National Committee on Corporate Social Responsibility & Community Development (India)

Conference on Environment and Development (1992) (UN), 6, 72, 111, 183

Consultative Advisory Group, 201n9

Consumer Goods Forum, 103, 175

Convention on Biological Diversity (CBD) (UN), 10n34

COP climate negotiations (UN), 42; COP15 Agreement on Protecting Biodiversity, 39; COP21, 73; COP26, 105, 107; COP27, 165; COP28, 106, 165, 184; COP29, 74

Cornell College of Agriculture and Life Sciences, 55

corporate accountability, 4–10, 114–15, 174; assurance and, 204–8, 210–11; boards of directors and, 20, 74, 78, 82–83; business leaders supporting, 16, 37–39; grouping of initiatives and standards, 233–42; initiatives and CPAs, 24–25, 43, 228–42; multistakeholder alliances and, 102–03; net positive, 44–47; obstacles to, 15, 43; systems approach to, 99–100; in value chains, 46, 101–03. *See also* assurance; corporate political activities (CPAs); International Standard on Sustainability Assurance (ISSA) 5000 (IAASB); reporting; World Benchmarking Alliance (WBA)

corporate actors, 10–13, 26, 38; corporate boards, 19–20, 69–87; corporate citizens, 25, 261–63; recommendations for, 17–20

Corporate Climate Stocktake (We Mean Business Coalition), 102

Corporate Disclosure Project (CDP), 231

corporate governance, 26; climate change and, 73–75, 77–79, 82–83, 85, 228–30, 258; definition of, 71; evolution of, 72–73; in India, 216, 223; in Japan, 25, 248, 255–63; large-scale collaboration and, 86–87; long-term views, 75–77; mandatory reporting and, 85–86; OECD Principles of Corporate Governance, 255; *Partnerships for Sustainability in Contemporary*

Global Governance (WEF), 113; principles for sustainability, 79–83; recommendations for, 83–87; risk management and, 71, 73–76, 78–80, 82–83; of SMEs, 70; social inequality and, 79–80, 83; sustainability guidance for, 77–79; value creation and, 70–71. *See also* boards of directors
corporate law, 83
corporate political activities (CPAs), 24–25; accountability and, 228–39; accountability initiatives, 233–34; definition of, 230, 237; disclosure of, 229, 235–42; ecosystem, 231–32; failures of, 227–28; mandatory standards for, 239–42; political donations, 238; raters of, 234–37
corporate political responsibility (CPR), 232–33. *See also* corporate political activities (CPAs); corporate social responsibility (CSR); lobbying
corporate social responsibility (CSR), 24, 199n1; background to, 216–17; case studies, 218–20; common aspects of, 220–21; foreign aid agencies and, 223–24; in India, 215–26; investments in, 215–16; lobbying and, 229n8; main issues, 221–22; policy implications of, 224–26; poverty and, 218, 221; responses to challenges, 222–23; target companies and expenditure use, 217–18
Corporate Sustainability Due Diligence Directive (EU), 9, 64
Corporate Sustainability Reporting Directive (CSRD) (EU), 9, 185, 200, 230, 242
Costa Rica, 9
country-level platforms, 109–11, 114

COVID-19 pandemic, 53, 140, 158–59
CPAs. *See* corporate political activities (CPAs)
credit risk mitigation (CRM), 149–50, 153
credit risk weights, 17, 21, 141–45, 147–53
CSR. *See* corporate social responsibility (CSR)
CSRD. *See* Corporate Sustainability Reporting Directive (CSRD) (EU)
C-suite. *See* CEOs

dairy industry, 55, 107
Dalmia Bharat Foundation, 219
Dalmia Cement, 219
Davos Manifesto (WEF), 5n9, 70
decarbonization, 18, 38, 42, 100, 102; of hard-to-abate industries, 93, 106–07; political challenges to, 113, 240
default risk, 17
deforestation, 15, 40, 184n38
Deloitte, 40
devaluation of assets, 123, 132
developing economies. *See* emerging markets and developing economies (EMDEs)
development financing, 26–27, 224
The Development Impact of Risk Analytics (IDF), 160
direct investment signals, 128–29
directors, non-executive. *See* boards of directors
disclosures. *See* assurance; corporate accountability; corporate political activities (CPAs); European Union (EU); International Financial Reporting Standards (IFRS); International Sustainability Standards Board (ISSB); reporting

55–56, 58, 60, 63; subsidies, 40; systems approach to, 99–100, 102
food security, 40, 157, 159, 163
foreign aid agencies, 223–24
Forest and Climate Leaders Partnership, 86
fossil fuels, 42, 108, 123–24, 126, 132
Framework Convention on Climate Change (UN), 10n34, 107, 165
Freeman, R. Edward, 4
Friedman, Milton, 4–5, 70
FSB. *See* Financial Stability Board (FSB)
FTSE4Good, 234, 236

G5 (Group of Five), 182
G20 (Group of Twenty), 150, 178n18; Global Infrastructure Hub (G20), 145, 147, 151; Independent Experts Group, 224; Infrastructure Working Group, 151
Gandhi, Mahatma, 216
gender, 16, 55, 59, 98. *See also* diversity and inclusion (D&I); women's employment
Geneva Association, 159, 166–68
Germany, 157, 161; German Act on Due Diligence in Supply Chains, 64
GHG Protocol Corporate Accounting and Reporting Standard, 192
Glasgow Financial Alliance for Net Zero (GFANZ), 13, 107–08
Global Alliance for Improved Nutrition (GAIN), 55
Global Assessment Report on Disaster Risk Reduction (UN), 160
Global Compact (UN), 6, 11–12, 54, 72, 94
Global Emerging Markets (GEMs) Risk Database, 152
Global Energy Alliance for People and Planet, 46, 57

global financial crisis of 2007–2008, 140
Global Goals. *See* Sustainable Development Goals (SDGs)
Global Impact Investing Network, 132, 134
Global Infrastructure Hub (G20), 145, 147, 151
Global Investors for Sustainable Development Alliance, 13
Global Plastic Treaty, 42
Global Reporting Initiative (GRI), 6, 43, 187, 194, 200, 231, 234, 236
Global Resilience Index Initiative (GRII), 161
Global Risk Modelling Alliance (GRMA), 161
Global Standard on Responsible Climate Lobbying, 232
Global Sustainable Tourism Council, 103
Global System for Mobile Communications Association (GSMA), 12, 103
global warming, 1–2, 123, 131–32. *See also* climate change
Goldman Sachs, 62
gold-plating, 21, 142–44
The Good Lobby Tracker, 24, 232–39
governance, corporate. *See* corporate governance
governance risks, 233
Governmental Accounting Standards Board, 181
government-led pathway, 97
government partnerships, 93–94, 96–97; CSR and, 222–25; with SMEs, 63–64
Government Pension Investment Fund (GPIF) of Japan, 252
green bonds. *See* sustainable bonds
green energy transition, 46

Greenhouse Gas Protocol, 182, 193. *See also* ISAE 3410 (IAASB); Scope 3 GHG emissions
greenhushing, 8
greenwashing, 7, 9, 77, 191, 208
GRI. *See* Global Reporting Initiative (GRI)
Guiding Principles on Business and Human Rights (UN), 187, 216–17

hard-to-abate industries, 93, 106–07
Harvard Management Company, 126
health and well-being, 11, 37, 102, 228
health care, 39, 218–20
health insurance, 22, 60, 157–58
hedge funds, 13
Herrington, Eldrid, 19–20, 69–87
High-Level Political Forum on Sustainable Development (UN), 109
high-net-worth individuals, 20, 126
High Seas Treaty (UN), 39
horizon, tragedy of the, 19, 73, 127
How to Set Up Effective Climate Governance on Corporate Boards (WEF and PwC), 77–78
Human Development Index (HDI) (UN), 157
human rights protections, 38, 45–46, 194, 216
hunger. *See* food security

IAASB. *See* International Auditing and Assurance Standards Board (IAASB)
IASB. *See* International Accounting Standards Board (IASB)
IBM, 37
Iceland, 110

ICGN. *See* International Corporate Governance Network (ICGN) Guidance on Political Lobbying and Donations
ICLEI Local Governments for Sustainability network, 111
ICTI Ethical Toy Program, 103
IDF. *See* Insurance Development Forum (IDF)
IFAC. *See* International Federation of Accountants (IFAC)
IFRS. *See* International Financial Reporting Standards (IFRS)
Ikea, 57
Impact Disclosure Taskforce, 13
Impact Frontiers, 132, 134
impact funds, 135
impact investing, 6, 26
impact measurement, 132, 134
Independent Experts Group (G20), 224
India, 8–9; Aspirational District Programme, 222; Companies Act 2013 amendment, 24, 215–18; Confederation of Indian Industry (CII), 217; Corporate Governance Voluntary Guidelines, 216, 223; CSR in, 24, 215–26; Eleventh Five-Year Plan (2007), 216; infrastructure in, 218–219; Ministry of Corporate Affairs, 216, 220–21, 223; National Guidelines on Responsible Business Conduct, 223; National Voluntary Guidelines on the Social, Environmental and Economic Responsibilities of Businesses, 216–17; Securities and Exchange Board of, 216; State Bank of, 219. *See also* corporate social responsibility (CSR)

indirect investment signals, 127, 129
Indonesia, 8
industrialization, 52
industry alliances, 92–115
industry associations, 114–15; corporate governance and, 86; CPAs and, 229, 237; SMEs and, 54–55, 63–64. *See also* trade associations
Inevitable Policy Response (IPR) consortium, 85
Inflation Reduction Act (U.S.), 42, 227n2
InfluenceMap, 240
informal sector, 51, 59, 61
infrastructure: in Africa, 148; as an asset class, 21, 125, 147, 150–53; in EMDEs, 21, 130, 145–52; G20 Infrastructure Working Group, 151; Global Infrastructure Hub (G20), 145, 147, 151; in India, 218–19; World Bank and, 149–50, 152–53
innovation, 20, 25, 52, 75, 80, 99, 104–05
Institute for Business Value (IBV) (IBM), 37
Institute of Directors (UK) certification programs, 84
insurance, 155–68; asset management of, 155–56; of asset owners, 164, 166; companies, 13, 108, 121, 126; in EMDEs, 22, 158–59; food and agriculture, 159; health, 22, 60, 157–58; history of, 156–57; markets, 22, 167; microinsurance, 22, 162; protection gaps, 17, 22, 159, 164–65; public-private partnerships and, 161–64, 167; recommendations about, 166–68; risk management and, 17, 156, 158

Insurance Development Forum (IDF), 161–62, 166–68; *The Development Impact of Risk Analytics*, 160
integrated thinking, 203–04
internal ratings–based (IRB) approach, 141, 147
international accounting authorities, 174, 178–82, 187, 194
International Accounting Standards Board (IASB), 178, 190
International Auditing and Assurance Standards Board (IAASB): ISAE 3000, 201, 206; ISAE 3410, 201; ISSA 5000, 5, 23, 202–11
International Business Council (IBC) (WEF), 12, 175; CEOs, 190
International Chamber of Commerce, 72
International Corporate Governance Network (ICGN) Guidance on Political Lobbying and Donations, 234, 237
International Council on Mining and Metals (ICMM), 12, 103, 175
International Energy Agency, 39
International Federation of Accountants (IFAC), 176, 201–02, 206n22
International Financial Reporting Standards (IFRS), 17; Accounting Standards, 190; Foundation, 22–23, 182, 190; S1, General Requirements for Disclosure of Sustainability-related Financial Information (ISSB), 182–83; S2, Climate-related Disclosures (ISSB), 182–84, 192
International Institute for Applied Systems Analysis (IIASA), 99
International Labour Organization (ILO), 51

International Organization for Standardization (ISO), 216
International Organization of Securities Commissions (IOSCO), 9, 182–83, 201, 205, 209; Task Force on Sustainable Finance, 178
International Standard on Sustainability Assurance (ISSA) 5000 (IAASB), 5, 23, 202–11
International Sustainability Standards Board (ISSB), 9–10, 17, 42, 179, 190, 194, 201; adoption of standards, 183–87; assurance and, 205; creation of, 22–23, 178, 200; IFRS S1, General Requirements for Disclosure of Sustainability-related Financial Information, 182–83, 234, 236; IFRS S2, Climate-related Disclosures, 182–84, 192
intrapreneurship, 80
investing, 121; climate change risks, 4, 123, 131–32, 134, 136, 166, 199–200; in CSR, 215–16; direct investment signals, 128–29; in EMDEs, 7, 26–27; ESG and, 121–36, 176, 252, 257; impact, 6, 26; indirect investment signals, 127, 129; in infrastructure, 130, 145–52; public, 27; in R&D, 37; reporting and, 132, 134; responsible, 6–7, 128; SDGs and, 122–23, 127–29; stakeholders and, 129, 134; sustainable, 20–21, 121–36, 176; in technology, 38, 41–43, 46, 134. *See also* fiduciary obligations; pension funds; Principles for Responsible Investment (PRI) (UN); sovereign wealth funds (SWFs)
investors, 126–27; CPAs and, 229–32; on nonfinancial reporting, 175–76; reporting and, 176, 179–80; retail, 126; risk management and, 79–80, 84, 123–27, 134–35; value creation for, 202–03. *See also* asset managers; asset owners
IOSCO. *See* International Organization of Securities Commissions (IOSCO)
ISAE 3000 (IAASB), 201, 206
ISAE 3410 (IAASB), 201
ISSA. *See* International Standard on Sustainability Assurance (ISSA) 5000 (IAASB)
ISSB. *See* International Sustainability Standards Board (ISSB)
ISS Quality Score, 234, 236
IWAY initiative (Ikea), 57
Iyahen, Ekhosuehi, 22, 155–68

Jacobson, Mark Z., 41
Japan, 157, 247–63; Agency for Natural Resources and Energy, 253; business awareness of SDGs in, 250–52; Cabinet Office, 251, 259; Corporate Governance code, 25, 248, 255–59; CSR in, 220, 222; Economic Census for Business Activity, 256; education for sustainable development (ESD), 249; ESG in, 251–52, 255–57; Financial Services Agency, 257; Financial Services Authority, 9; Government Pension Investment Fund (GPIF), 252; International Cooperation Agency (JICA), 220–21, 253; Keidanren, 13, 111, 252; large companies in, 25, 247, 258–59; local governments in, 25, 251–55, 258–61; Ministry of Economy, Industry and Trade (METI), 250–51; Ministry of Foreign Affairs, 251; Ministry of the Environment (MoE), 250–51;

NPOs in, 222, 254; public awareness of SDGs in, 249–50; regional development in, 258–61; registration and certification schemes, 259–61; Revitalization Strategy, 255; *SDGs Implementation Guiding Principles*, 249; SDGs Promotion Headquarters, 251; SMEs in, 25, 247, 251–60; Stewardship Code, 177, 248, 255–59; targeted direct incentives for SDGs in, 253–55; *Town, People, Job Creation Comprehensive Strategy*, 259; Yokohoma City, 253–54
Jensen, Michael, 70
Joint Declaration (2020) (G5), 182
just and regenerative mindset. *See* net positive mindset
Just Capital, 43

Keidanren (Japan), 111; Charter of Corporate Behavior, 13, 252
Kenya Private Sector Alliance, 110
key messages, 17
key performance indicators, 176
keystone companies, 101–02
Kharas, Homi, 1–28
KPMG, 14, 91n1
Krupp, Fred, 228n4
Kunming-Montreal Global Biodiversity Framework (2022), 10, 11n34

large companies, 26, 188; COVID-19 effect on, 53; in Japan, 25, 247, 258–59; lack of trust in, 92; partnerships of, 20, 94–95; reporting by, 193–94; risk weights and, 143; SMEs and, 17, 54–59, 63–64. *See also* collective action; corporate actors; small and medium-size enterprises (SMEs)

limited assurance, 208–10
linear solutions, 37–40
liquidity requirements (Basel III), 146, 149
lobbying, 24, 27, 227–42; definition of, 227n1; self-serving, 38–39, 47, 76; watchdogs, 229n11, 230. *See also* corporate political activities (CPAs)
Local Agenda 21 model, 111
local governments, 8, 17, 24; coalitions and, 111–12, 114; in Japan, 25, 251–55, 258–61; SMEs and, 55–56, 58–59, 61, 63–65
local organizations, 17, 19–20, 55–56, 63
London School of Economics and Politics, 83
loss-given-default, 17
loss prevention, 161–62
lower-income countries. *See* emerging markets and developing economies (EMDEs)

Maathai, Wangari, 48
Makino, Koji, 1–28
Malloch-Brown, Mark, 36
mandatory reporting. *See* reporting
market-driven partnerships, 96, 103–04
market failures, 92, 95, 106
market power pathway, 96, 101, 103–04
market signals, 127–29, 131
Maroun, Warren, 23, 199–211
Maruti Suzuki, 219–21
material sustainability risks, 79–80
Matsumoto, Katsuo, 23–24, 215–26
McArthur, John W., 1–28
McKinsey Global Institute, 37
MDBs. *See* multilateral development banks (MDBs); World Bank

metrics, 14–15, 27–28, 43, 195, 250n16; of accounting firms, 12, 175–77; aggregate confusion, 7; boards of directors and, 19, 71, 75; challenges to providing, 191–92; of the IBC, 190; TCFD and, 188–89; value creation and, 81–82, 175. *See also* reporting; Scope 3 GHG emissions
micro firms, 51, 61. *See also* small and medium-size enterprises (SMEs)
microinsurance, 22, 162
Millennium Development Goals (MDGs), 35, 192, 216. *See also* Sustainable Development Goals (SDGs)
minimum capital requirements. *See* capital requirements
mining, 12, 103, 175
Ministers of Finance of the Climate Vulnerable Forum (V20), 161
Ministry of Corporate Affairs (India), 216, 220–21, 223
Ministry of Economy, Industry and Trade (METI) (Japan), 250–51
Ministry of Foreign Affairs (Japan), 251
Ministry of the Environment (MoE) (Japan), 250–51
Moody's, 147–48, 231, 234, 236
MSCI, 231; ESG Ratings, 234, 236
MSMEs. *See* small and medium-size enterprises (SMEs)
Muir, John, 35–36
multilateral development banks (MDBs), 152n29, 153
multisector alliances. *See* multistakeholder alliances
multistakeholder alliances, 12, 20, 37–38, 46, 92–115; aims of, 95, 103–5; challenges of, 112–13; city-level coalitions, 111–12, 114; corporate accountability and, 102–03; High Level Panel of Eminent Persons, 11, 35; World Benchmarking Alliance (WBA), 12, 43, 91n1, 100–102, 231. *See also* alliances; coalitions; collective action

National Guidelines on Responsible Business Conduct (India), 223
National Health Insurance Scheme (Nigeria), 158
National Health Service (NHS) (UK), 157
national-level action, 109–11, 114
Nationally Determined Contributions (NDCs), 109–10
National Voluntary Guidelines on the Social, Environmental and Economic Responsibilities of Businesses (India), 216–17
natural catastrophes, 22, 161–62
nature-related financial disclosures, 42
near-zero emissions, 106. *See also* net zero
negative externalities. *See* externalities
Nelson, Jane, 1–28, 91–115
Netherlands, 125
Net Positive (Polman and Winston), 45
net positive mindset, 44–47, 76
Net Stable Funding Ratio (NSFR) (BCBS), 146, 149–50
Network for Greening the Financial System, 178
net zero, 16, 40, 121, 164; Glasgow Financial Alliance for Net Zero (GFANZ), 13, 107–08; Net-Zero Asset Owner Alliance (NZAOA), 135–36; Net-Zero Insurance Alliance, 108; Race to Zero campaign (UNFCCC), 107

New Zealand Superannuation Fund, 125
NFRD. *See* Non-Financial Reporting Directive (NFRD) (EU)
NGOs. *See* nongovernmental organizations (NGOs)
Nigeria, 9, 158; AACE Food Processing & Distribution, 60; Advancing Local Dairy Development in Nigeria (ALDDN), 55; Commercial Dairy Ranchers Association of Nigeria (CODARAN), 55
1992 "Earth Summit" (Rio de Janeiro), 6, 72, 111, 183
Non-Financial Reporting Directive (NFRD) (EU), 177, 185, 230
nongovernmental organizations (NGOs), 63, 95
nonprofit organizations (NPOs), 24, 74, 102, 218, 220–24, 254
Nordic Green Bank (Nefco), 136
Norges Bank Investment Management (NBIM)—Government Pension Fund Global (Norwegian Oil Fund), 125
Norway, 125
NSFR. *See* Net Stable Funding Ratio (NSFR) (BCBS)
Nwuneli, Ndidi Okonkwo, 19, 51–65

Oceans and Biodiversity treaties, 42
One Million Black Women: Black in Business (Goldman Sachs), 62
Open-es (Eni), 57
operational risk, 4
Organization for Economic Cooperation and Development (OECD), 52, 159n29, 229, 231; Principles for Transparency and Integrity in Lobbying, 234, 236;
Principles of Corporate Governance, 255
Our Common Future (WCED), 72, 93
output floor (Basel III), 147, 149

Paris Agreement (2015) (UN), 1–2, 10n34, 73, 91–92, 109–10. *See also* COP climate negotiations (UN); Sustainable Development Goals (SDGs); United Nations (UN)
Partnership for Global Infrastructure and Investment, 86
partnerships, 113; categorizing of, 94–97; financial, 135–36; obstacles of, 97–98; project-level financing and implementation, 95. *See also* alliances; coalitions; collective action; public-private partnerships
Partnerships for Sustainability in Contemporary Global Governance (WEF), 113
pathways, upscaling, 96–103
pension funds, 8, 13, 121, 124, 131–32; ABP (Netherlands), 125; California Public Employees' Retirement Fund (CalPERS), 125; First Swedish National Pension Fund (AP1), 125; Government Pension Investment Fund (GPIF) of Japan, 252; insurance gaps, 159; New Zealand Superannuation Fund, 125; PGGM (Netherlands), 125; in the UK, 158; in the U.S., 7. *See also* asset owners; fiduciary obligations
PGGM (Netherlands), 125
philanthropic spending, 46, 62–64, 94–95, 110, 216, 221, 229
Philippines, 9, 142, 184
place-based alliances, 108–12
planetary boundaries, 44, 75, 100

policies: about SMEs, 55, 64; coalitions and, 104–05; corporate governance and, 85–86; financial, 135–36; gaps in, 15, 97–98; implications of CSR, 224–25
policymakers: questions for, 27–28; recommendations for, 17, 22–25, 143–44, 167
policy signals, 128–29
political donations, 238
pollution, 46, 189
Polman, Paul, 18, 35–48, 75–76; *Net Positive*, 45
Positive Compass, 234, 237
Post-2015 Development Agenda, 11
post-2030 goals, 26–28, 183, 192–95. *See also* Sustainable Development Goals (SDGs)
poverty, 14, 35–36, 40, 52, 139, 158; CSR and, 218, 221; energy, 46, 57
precompetitive business alliances, 17, 92–93, 95–96, 103–05, 113, 115
Principles for Responsible Investment (PRI) (UN), 6, 85, 176, 231, 237, 252; guidance on SDGs, 13, 73; Investor Expectations on Corporate Climate Lobbying, 234, 236
Principles for Transparency and Integrity in Lobbying (OECD), 234, 236
Principles of Corporate Governance (OECD), 255
private equity, 13, 61, 125
Proceedings of the National Academy of Sciences, 99
profit, definition of, 2–3
Project Gigaton (Walmart), 57
Public Interest Oversight Board, 201n9
public investment, 27
public policy integration pathway, 96

public-private partnerships, 94, 105–06, 130, 136; capital requirements and, 150; insurance and, 161–64, 167; in Japan, 254. *See also* alliances; coalitions; collective action; partnerships
PwC, 78

Race to Zero campaign (UNFCCC), 107
racial bias, 98
rating systems, 6–7, 141, 147, 230–42
RE100, 219
reasonable assurance, 208–10
recommendations: for asset owners, 20–21, 133–36; for banking regulations, 143–45, 149–53; for the BCBS, 144–45, 152; for boards of directors, 83–87; for business actors, 17–20, 193–95; for business leaders, 193–94; chapter summaries and, 17; for collective action, 113–115; for corporate governance, 83–87; for financial actors, 17, 20–22; about insurance, 166–68; for policymakers, 17, 22–25, 143–44, 167; for regulators, 17, 22–25, 167; for shareholders, 262; of the TCFD, 200
Refinitiv ESG scores, 234, 236
regenerative agriculture, 44–45, 63
regenerative mindset. *See* net positive mindset
registration schemes in Japan, 259–61
regulations, 27; antitrust, 20, 86, 108, 113; coalitions and, 105; corporate governance and, 85–86; gaps in, 15
regulators: ESG disclosure and, 177–78; questions for, 27–28; recommendations for, 17, 22–25, 167; reporting and, 181

renewable energy, 38–39, 41, 63, 134–35, 219
reporting, 9–10, 12–13, 43, 91n1, 115, 175–92, 194, 199–200; boards of directors and, 83; business leaders supporting, 16, 175; coalitions and, 103–04; corporate governance and, 85–86; guidance from European Commission, 180–81, 185–87; international accounting authorities and, 178–82; investments and, 132, 134; investors and, 176, 179–80; on natural ecosystems impact, 39; necessity of, 203; obstacles to, 22–23, 179–81, 183–92; reliability of, 23, 204–08; requirements, 81–83, 177–79, 187–90; risk management and, 174–175, 203, 206; signals and, 129; templates, 22; voluntary, 91–92, 173–74, 181, 194, 200, 203. *See also* auditing; corporate accountability; corporate political activities (CPAs); Corporate Sustainability Due Diligence Directive (EU); Corporate Sustainability Reporting Directive (CSRD) (EU); European Financial Reporting Advisory Group (EFRAG); European Sustainability Reporting Standards (ESRS); GHG Protocol Corporate Accounting and Reporting Standard; Global Reporting Initiative (GRI); International Financial Reporting Standards (IFRS); International Standard on Sustainability Assurance (ISSA) 5000 (IAASB); International Sustainability Standards Board (ISSB); Non-Financial Reporting Directive (NFRD) (EU); recommendations; Securities and Exchange Commission (SEC) (U.S.)

Reporting Exchange (WBCSD), 179–80

RepRisk, 231, 234, 236

reputational risk, 4, 77, 229–30, 238

research and development (R&D), 15, 24, 37, 104–05

resilience, 155–56, 158, 160–68, 188

Resilient Cities Network, 111

Resilient Planet Data Hub, 161

Responsible Business Alliance, 103, 175

responsible capitalism, 23, 202–04

Responsible Lobbying Framework, 234, 237

Responsible Minerals, Labor and Factory Initiatives, 103

retail investors, 126

Revitalization Strategy (Japan), 255

Rio de Janeiro 1992 "Earth Summit," 6, 72, 111, 183

risk: assessment, 80–81, 134, 152–53, 206; climate change investment, 4, 123, 131–32, 134, 136, 166, 199–200; CPAs and, 233; default, 17; environmental, 4, 43, 233; financial, 4; Global Emerging Markets (GEMs) Risk Database, 152; Global Risk Modelling Alliance (GRMA), 161; governance, 233; insight, 160–61; material, 79–80; mitigation, 79, 125, 144, 156, 161–66, 258; operational, 4; reputational, 4, 77, 229–30, 238; risk-reward balance, 131–32; in SDG targets, 22, 156; sharing, 130, 158; social, 4, 43, 233; value chains and, 79; weights, 17, 21, 141–45, 147–53

risk management, 4, 6, 11, 22, 26–27; in Africa, 162–63; capabilities, 160–61; climate change and,

160–63, 190; collective action and, 161–64; corporate governance and, 71, 73–76, 78–80, 82–83; of governments, 167; innovation and, 80; insurance and, 17, 156, 158; investors and, 79–80, 84, 123–27, 134–35; reporting and, 174–75, 203, 206; for SMEs, 61
"Roadmap to Infrastructure as an Asset Class" (Argentina), 150
Rockefeller Brothers Fund, 126
Rockefeller Foundation, 57
Rojas-Suarez, Liliana, 21, 139–53

Sabin Center for Climate Change Law, 83
Sahel Consulting, 55
Samans, Richard, 22–23, 173–95
Samhita, 223
SASB. *See* Sustainability Accounting Standards Board (SASB)
Sato, Ichiro, 25, 247–63
Schwab, Klaus, 4, 70
Scope 3 GHG emissions, 3, 52, 182, 191–92
SDG2000 (WBA), 101
SDG Partnership Platform (Kenya), 110
SDGs. *See* Sustainable Development Goals (SDGs)
SDGs Implementation Guiding Principles (Japan), 249
SDGs Promotion Headquarters (Japan), 251
Securities and Exchange Board of India, 216
Securities and Exchange Commission (SEC) (U.S.), 7, 10, 181, 200; Asset Management Advisory Committee, 178; Nature-Related Financial Disclosures, 42
securities markets, 178

Seidenstein, Tom, 23, 199–211
seven systems transformations (WBA), 100–102
shared sustainability officer, 64
shared value, 4–6, 194
shareholder capitalism, 4–5, 7, 15, 70–71
shareholders, 4–5, 7; corporate responsibilities toward, 70–71, 81–82; CPAs and, 230n15; in family-owned businesses, 77; non-executive directors and, 19; recommendations for, 262
Silicon Valley Bank, 140n4
Sinek, Simon, 261
Singapore, 9, 184–85; Stock Exchange Group, 84
single materiality, 80
skill gaps, 60, 63–64
Sloan Management Review (MIT), 58
Small and Medium Enterprise Agency (Japan), 251
small and medium-size enterprises (SMEs), 8, 51–65, 92, 94, 114; auditing and, 63–64; Basel III and, 140–45; business associations and, 19, 57; business parks and, 112; capacity building of, 193; challenges of, 53–54; climate change effects on, 53, 58; corporate governance of, 70; ecosystem approach, 54–56, 64; in EMDEs, 21, 51, 61–62, 64–65; ESG standards and, 53, 56–57; financing access of, 56, 61–63, 140–45; food and agriculture in, 55–56, 58, 60, 63; government partnerships with, 63–64; industry associations and, 54–55, 63–64; adoption of ISSB standards, 191; in Japan, 25, 247, 251–60; large companies and,

Index 287

17, 54–59, 63–64; local governments and, 55–56, 58–59, 61, 63–65; policies about, 55, 64; priorities for, 63–65; reporting requirements for, 185–86; risk management for, 61; Small and Medium Enterprise Agency (Japan), 251; SME Climate Hub, 54, 58, 94; supply chains and, 52, 56–57, 59, 64–65; support for, 17, 19, 54–65; sustainability goals of, 54–55; talent and workforce capabilities, 59–60; value chains and, 19, 52, 55–57, 64; World Bank on, 51
smallholder farms, 56
Smith, Adam, 3–4
Social Academy of Learning (India), 223
Social LobbyMap, 240
social risk, 4, 43, 233
Society 5.0, 111, 252, 254
solar energy, 38–39, 63, 135
South Africa, 5, 53
South America, 70, 142, 148, 206
sovereign wealth funds (SWFs), 121, 125
S&P, 231; 100, 227n2; Global Corporate Sustainability Assessment, 234, 236
Spotlight on Lobbying (ATNI), 232
stakeholder capitalism, 4–5, 24, 70–71, 203–04, 224
stakeholders, 4–5, 203–05, 210, 261–62; corporate responsibilities toward, 70–71, 76, 81, 84; CPAs and, 229; engagement of, 26, 74; investment and, 129, 134
standards: corporate accountability and, 233–42; for CPAs, 239–42; SMEs and, 53, 56–57, 63–65. *See also* accounting; assurance; International Financial Reporting Standards (IFRS); metrics; reporting
standard setting, 42, 114, 189–90, 192–95, 200–201; of coalitions, 103–05; for reporting, 177, 181–82
Stanford University, 96
State Bank of India, 219
state-owned enterprise (SOE), 70
Status Report of the Task Force on Climate-Related Financial Disclosures, 188
Stern, Nicholas, 73
Stewardship Code (Japan), 177, 248, 255–59
stock exchanges, 177; Bombay Stock Exchange, 217; listing requirements, 84; Singapore Stock Exchange Group, 84; Tokyo Stock Exchange (TSE), 255–58; UK FTSE 100, 76
Stockholm Resilience Centre, 44, 75
stock market crash of 1929, 10
Strong, Maurice, 6
subsidies, 40
Sullivan principles, 5
supply chains, 25–26; coalitions within, 94, 103–04; German Act on Due Diligence in Supply Chains, 64; human rights protections in, 38; large companies and, 56–57, 59, 101; SMEs and, 52, 56–57, 59, 64–65. *See also* value chains
sustainability. *See* ESG (environmental, social, and governance); Sustainable Development Goals (SDGs)
Sustainability Accounting Standards Board (SASB), 175, 187–88
Sustainability Council (Iceland), 110
sustainable bonds, 6–7, 26, 130, 135

sustainable development concept origin, 72, 93–94
Sustainable Development Goals (SDGs), ix, 1–3, 10–15; banking systems and, 139–41; cost of achieving, 40; country-level action on, 109–11; CPAs and, 227–28; CSR and, 24; Goal 1 (no poverty), 14; Goal 2 (zero hunger), 14; Goal 3 (good health and well-being), 11, 37, 102, 228; Goal 4 (quality education), 14; Goal 5 (gender equality): *see* gender; women's employment; Goal 6 (clean water and sanitation): *see* water consumption; Goal 7 (affordable and clean energy), 14; Goal 8 (decent work and economic growth), 14, 52, 60, 140–41, 145–52; Goal 9 (industry, innovation, and infrastructure), 14, 52; Goal 10 (reduced inequalities), 140–45; Goal 11 (sustainable cities and communities), 11; Goal 12 (responsible consumption and production), 11, 14, 40; Goal 13 (climate action), 10n34, 14, 40, 228; Goal 14 (life below water), 10n34, 14; Goal 15 (life on land), 10n34, 14; Goal 16 (peace, justice, and strong institutions), 14, 228; Goal 17 (partnerships for the goals), 14, 35–36, 86, 94; in India, 222–23, 225–26; insurance and, 156–59; investing and, 122–23, 127–29; motivation for action, 79, 81; not meeting deadlines, 39; obstacles to achieving, 92; origins of, 10–11, 35–36, 72, 121n1; reporting on progress, 91–92, 175, 190; SDG washing, 38; targets, 22, 36, 156, 262; unique indicators, 156. *See also* cities; energy and materials; food and agriculture; food security; health and well-being; infrastructure; innovation; partnerships; poverty; reporting; United Nations (UN)
Sustainable Development Investments Asset Owners Platform, 13
Sustainable Finance Disclosure Regulation (EU), 9
Sustainable Iceland, 110
Sustainalytics, 231, 236
Sweden, 125
Swiss Re Institute, 159, 161
systems approach, 20, 99–103; collective action and, 113–14; obstacles to, 97–98

Task Force on Climate-Related Financial Disclosures (TCFD), 73, 77, 80, 177–78, 182, 234, 236, 258; compliance with, 187–90; recommendations of, 200; Status Report, 188
Taskforce on Nature-Related Financial Disclosures (TNFD), 73–74, 80, 189
Task Force on Sustainable Finance (IOSCO), 178
Task Forces on Climate, 42
Tata, 218–19
Taxonomy (EU), 42
TCFD. *See* Task Force on Climate-Related Financial Disclosures (TCFD)
technology, 106–07; decarbonization and, 18, 41; investments in, 38, 41–43, 46, 134; in Japan, 25, 254; SMEs and, 53, 63
10,000 Women Initiative (Goldman Sachs), 62
Thailand, 12, 13n43

Theory of Moral Sentiments (Smith), 3
think tanks, 24, 227, 237
third-party assurance. *See* assurance
tipping points, 44, 131
TNFD. *See* Taskforce on Nature-Related Financial Disclosures (TNFD)
Tokyo Stock Exchange (TSE), 255–58
Town, People, Job Creation Comprehensive Strategy (Japan), 259
Toyota Kirloskar Motor, 223
trade associations, 24, 38–39, 86, 114–15. *See also* business associations; corporate political activities (CPAs); industry associations; lobbying
"tragedy of the horizon" (Carney), 19, 73, 127
transformation pathways, 99–103
transparency. *See* assurance; corporate accountability; reporting
trust. *See* assurance
trusteeship, 216
Turkey, 9, 140, 184, 209
2030 Agenda, 100, 262; obstacles to achieving, 1–2, 13–16, 39–44, 183–84; post-, 26–28, 62–65, 84–87, 113–15, 183–84, 192–95; voluntary national reviews (VNRs), 109–11

UK FTSE 100, 76
Uncertain Times, Unsettled Lives (UN), 157
Underwriters Laboratory, 157
United Arab Emirates (UAE), 106
United Kingdom (UK), 76, 157, 247; 2016 reporting regulations, 177; Beveridge Report, 157n11; Companies Act, 9; Institute of Directors certification programs, 84

United Nations (UN), 5–6, 38; Conference on Environment and Development "Earth Summit" 1992, 6, 72, 111, 183; Convention on Biological Diversity (CBD), 10n34; COP climate negotiations, 39, 73–74, 105–07, 165, 184; deputy secretary-general, 36; Environment Programme, 6; Food and Agriculture Organization (FAO), 55; Framework Convention on Climate Change (UNFCCC), 10n34, 107, 165; *Global Assessment Report on Disaster Risk Reduction*, 160; Global Compact, 6, 11–12, 54, 72, 94; Guiding Principles on Business and Human Rights, 187, 216–17; High-Level Political Forum on Sustainable Development, 109; High Seas Treaty, 39; Human Development Index (HDI), 157; Principles for Responsible Investment (PRI), 6, 13, 73, 85, 176, 231, 234, 237, 252; Secretary-General High Level Panel of Eminent Persons, 6, 11, 35; *Uncertain Times, Unsettled Lives*, 157
United States (U.S.), 157; American Chamber of Commerce, 228; American Institute of Certified Public Accountants Accounting Principles Board, 181; CHIPS Act, 42; climate legislation in, 7–10, 42, 177–78, 185, 227n2; companies in, 81–82; CPAs in, 231, 237, 238n29; disclosure requirements in, 85; ESG debates in, 7–8, 113; Inflation Reduction Act, 42, 227n2; minimum capital requirements in, 142; Securities and Exchange

Commission (SEC), 7, 10; SMEs in, 53; S&P 500, 76
University of Cambridge, 70
upscaling pathways, 96–97

value chains, 15, 101–02; alliances within, 92; corporate responsibility in, 46–47; partnerships within, 95, 97; risk and, 79; SMEs and, 19, 52, 55–57, 64. *See also* supply chains
value creation, 11, 26–27, 194; corporate governance and, 70–71; double materiality and, 4–5; long-term, 71, 74, 76, 81–82; reporting of, 175–76; responsible capitalism and, 202–03
Value Reporting Foundation, 182
venture capital, 61–62, 107
Vision 2050 (WBCSD), 15
Voluntary Business Report for Sustainable Development (Chile), 111
voluntary national reviews (VNRs), 109–11
Vulnerable Twenty (V20) Group, 161

Walmart, 57
waste production, 57, 63
water consumption, 16, 45, 63, 107, 114
WBA. *See* World Benchmarking Alliance (WBA)
WBCSD. *See* World Business Council for Sustainable Development (WBCSD)
WCED. *See* World Commission on Environment and Development (WCED)

The Wealth of Nations (Smith), 3
WEF. *See* World Economic Forum (WEF)
We Mean Business Coalition, 86; Corporate Climate Stocktake, 102
Who Cares Wins (UN Global Compact), 6
wholesale funding, 146, 149
"wokeness," 7–9, 43
women's employment, 55, 61–62
World Bank, 51, 149–50, 152–53, 216, 224
World Benchmarking Alliance (WBA), 12, 43, 91n1, 100–102, 231; Social Transformation Framework, 234, 236
World Business Council for Sustainable Development (WBCSD), 6, 72, 97, 99–100; guidance for SDGs, 11–12; Reporting Exchange, 179–80; Vision 2050, 15
World Commission on Environment and Development (WCED), 72, 93
World Economic Forum (WEF): Davos Manifesto, 70; First Movers Coalition (FMC), 46, 105–07; *How to Set Up Effective Climate Governance on Corporate Boards*, 77–78; International Business Council (IBC), 12, 175, 190; Measuring Stakeholder Capitalism, 234, 237; SDG survey, 247
World Resources Institute, 96

Yokohama City, Japan, 253–54
youth employment, 55, 59–60, 62

Zurich Insurance, 126

www.ingramcontent.com/pod-product-compliance
Ingram Content Group UK Ltd.
Pitfield, Milton Keynes, MK11 3LW, UK
UKHW020646260426
470352UK00007B/76